THE BACKBENCHER AND PARLIAMENT

The Backbencher and Parliament

A Reader

Edited by

DICK LEONARD
MP for Romford

and

VALENTINE HERMAN
University of Essex

**MACMILLAN
ST. MARTIN'S PRESS**

Selection and
 Editorial matter © Dick Leonard and Valentine Herman 1972
 PART I Chapter 1 © Dick Leonard 1968
 Chapter 2 © Richard Rose and Dennis Kavanagh 1966
 Chapter 3 © Anthony Barker and Michael Rush 1970
 Chapter 4 © R. E. Dowse 1963
 Chapter 5 © Anthony King 1971
 Chapter 6 © Norman Hunt and Lord Redmayne 1963
 Chapter 7 © Anthony King 1968, 1972

 PART II Chapter 1 © John Rose 1972
 Chapter 2 © Valentine Herman 1972
 Chapter 3 © Dick Leonard 1970, 1971, 1972
 Chapter 4 © Valentine Herman 1972
 Chapter 5 © Arthur Palmer 1970
 Chapter 6 © Keith Ovenden 1972

 PART III Chapter 1 © David Menhennet and John Palmer 1968
 Chapter 2 © Times Newspapers Ltd, 1966
 Chapter 3 © George Cunningham 1970
 Chapter 4 © G. R. Strauss 1965
 Chapter 5 © Richard Hornby 1965
 Chapter 6 © Julian Critchley 1972
 Chapter 7 © John P. Mackintosh 1970

All rights reserved. No part of this publication
may be reproduced or transmitted, in any form
or by any means, without permission.

First published 1972 by

THE MACMILLAN PRESS LTD

London and Basingstoke
Associated companies in New York Toronto
Dublin Melbourne Johannesburg and Madras

Library of Congress catalog card no. 78-185906

SBN 33 12811 7

Printed in Great Britain by
RICHARD CLAY (THE CHAUCER PRESS) LTD
Bungay, Suffolk

To Irène and Carol

Contents

The Editors *page* xi

The Contributors xii

Introduction xiii

PART I: THE BACKBENCHER, HIS CONSTITUENCY AND HIS PARTY

1. How Candidates are Chosen   3
   by DICK LEONARD

2. Campaigning for Parliament   21
   by RICHARD ROSE and DENNIS KAVANAGH

3. Members' Postbags   29
   by ANTHONY BARKER and MICHAEL RUSH

4. The MP and his Surgery   46
   by R. E. DOWSE

5. The Case of Flora Ginetio   61
   A BBC investigation by ANTHONY KING

6. Whips and Backbenchers   74
   MARTIN REDMAYNE interviewed by NORMAN HUNT

7. The Chief Whip's Clothes   80
   by ANTHONY KING

PART II: THE BACKBENCHER AND THE WORK OF THE HOUSE

1. Questions in the House   89
   by JOHN ROSE

2. Adjournment Debates in the House of Commons   108
   by VALENTINE HERMAN

3. Private Members' Bills since 1959   126
   by DICK LEONARD

4. Backbench and Opposition Amendments to Government Legislation   141
   by VALENTINE HERMAN

5. The Select Committee on Science and Technology   156
   by ARTHUR PALMER

6. Policy and Self-perception: Some Aspects of Parliamentary Behaviour   171
   by KEITH OVENDEN

PART III: VIEWS FROM THE BACK BENCHES

1. A Day in the Life of an MP   195
   by DAVID MENHENNET and JOHN PALMER

2. New MPs have kept their Zeal for Reform   207
   from THE TIMES

3. Sanctuary of Conservatism   212
   by GEORGE CUNNINGHAM

4. The Influence of the Backbencher: a Labour View   218
   by GEORGE STRAUSS

5. The Influence of the Backbencher: a Tory View   228
     by RICHARD HORNBY

6. Returning to the House   238
     by JULIAN CRITCHLEY

7. Parliament Now and a Hundred Years Ago   244
     by JOHN P. MACKINTOSH

   Bibliography   259
   Index   263

The Editors

DICK LEONARD has been Labour MP for Romford since 1970 and is Parliamentary Private Secretary to Anthony Crosland. He held a Social Science Research Council Senior Research Fellowship at the University of Essex, 1968–70. Was formerly a teacher, journalist and broadcaster. Deputy General Secretary of Fabian Society, 1955–60. Author of *Guide to the General Election* (Pan Books, 1964), *Elections in Britain* (Van Nostrand, 1968). Contributor to *Guardian, Sunday Times, New Society*, etc.

VALENTINE HERMAN is a lecturer in the Department of Government at the University of Essex. He is co-author, with Professor Jean Blondel, of *A Workbook in Comparative Government* (to be published by Weidenfeld & Nicolson, 1972), and has contributed articles on comparative and British politics to the *American Political Science Review, Parliamentary Affairs*, and other social science journals.

The Contributors

Anthony Barker is Chairman of the Department of Government at the University of Essex.
Julian Critchley is Conservative MP for Aldershot.
George Cunningham is Labour MP for Islington South-West.
R. E. Dowse is Reader in Politics at the University of Exeter.
Richard Hornby is Conservative MP for Tonbridge.
Norman Hunt is a Fellow of Exeter College, Oxford.
Dennis Kavanagh is Lecturer in Government at the University of Manchester.
Anthony King is Professor of Government at the University of Essex.
David Menhennet is Deputy Librarian of the House of Commons.
John P. Mackintosh, Labour MP for Berwick and East Lothian, was formerly Professor of Politics at the University of Strathclyde.
Keith Ovenden is Lecturer in Government at the University of Essex.
Arthur Palmer, Labour MP for Bristol Central, was Chairman of the Select Committee on Science and Technology from 1966 to 1970.
John Palmer is Deputy Assistant Librarian of the House of Commons.
Lord Redmayne was Government Chief Whip in the Commons from 1959 to 1964.
John Rose is a Senior Clerk in the Table Office of the House of Commons.
Richard Rose is Professor of Politics at the University of Strathclyde
Michael Rush is Lecturer in Politics at the University of Exeter.
George Strauss, Labour MP for Lambeth, Vauxhall, is a former Minister of Supply.

Introduction

THIS volume differs from other books on Parliament in that its focus is on the work of the backbencher. With the exception of Peter Richards's *Honourable Members*[1] and, to some extent, Ronald Butt's *The Power of Parliament*,[2] previous works on Parliament place little or no emphasis on either the role or the work of the backbencher. Richards's study first appeared in 1959, and since that date there has been no systematic examination of the backbencher which has taken into account the considerable changes in both Parliamentary procedure and British politics of the 1960s.

One explanation for the neglect of backbenchers in most works on Parliament could be that this represents a realistic assessment of their unimportance in the scheme of things. Certainly, there are not lacking those who argue that backbench MPs, and even Parliament itself, play only a peripheral role in the British political system. Part of the object of this volume is to enable a more informed judgement to be made of the validity of this assessment.

Backbench MPs perform many different functions, but few, if any, are specific to them. No precise tabulation of the various roles of Members of Parliament appears to have been attempted – the nearest approach being a rather light-hearted listing by Richard Rose:

> While the number of recognisable roles is limited, the disparity between them is great. Law-making is a role of little importance to MPs, for the task of drafting complex legislation is left to specialist barristers outside the House, and major

---

[1] Peter G. Richards, *Honourable Members* (London: Faber, 1959).
[2] Ronald Butt, *The Power of Parliament* (London: Constable, 2nd ed., 1969).

policy decisions concerning legislation are confined to a small number of Cabinet ministers. MPs can take explicitly political roles, such as front-bench statesman or aspirant; spokesman for constituency interests; spokesman for pressure group interests; ideologue; party loyalist; party intriguer; advocate of cross-party ideas, e.g. homosexual law reform, or eccentric ideas, e.g. a revolving toothbrush. Many recognisable roles consistent with membership in the Commons have little direct bearing upon politics: barrister or aspiring High Court judge; company director; free-lance journalist; servant of the House, e.g. chairman of the Kitchen Committee; House jester; social climber; gentleman of leisure; trade union pensioner, or parliamentary bore.[3]

If Rose's classification is incomplete, the two most conspicuous omissions are the functions, however imperfectly performed, of probing government administration and of acting as a quasi-Ombudsman on behalf of individual constituents. A graphic indication of the multiplicity of MPs' roles and of the fragmented character of their working day is conveyed by David Menhennet and John Palmer in their chapter on 'A Day in the Life of an MP' in Part III of this book.

There is no lack of information about who gets elected to Parliament – the biographical details of Members are readily available and have been much analysed.[4] Less is known of the personality of backbenchers – no research, for instance, has yet been attempted to test the hypothesis of Harold Laswell[5] that politicians tend to suffer from marked feelings of personal inadequacy or inferiority and seek out political opportunities to compensate for these feelings! Nor has anyone presumed to specify with any precision the character traits which are most desirable in backbench Members of Parliament – perhaps because it would be difficult to improve on Max Weber's dictum

---

[3] Richard Rose, *People in Politics* (London: Faber, 1970), p. 102.

[4] Most recently in David Butler and Michael Pinto-Duschinsky, *The British General Election of 1970* (London: Macmillan, 1971), pp. 292–304.

[5] See Harold Laswell, *Power and Personality* (New York: Viking, 1962). This hypothesis, among others, was tested in a brilliant study of the motivations of members of the Connecticut House of Representatives. See James David Barber, *The Lawmakers* (New Haven: Yale University Press, 1965).

of fifty years ago that 'three qualities are decisive for the politician: passion, a feeling of responsibility and a sense of proportion'.[6] This volume cannot claim to advance the frontiers of knowledge to a major extent in this connection, though the editors believe that many incidental shafts of light are thrown by several of the contributors.

There was a time when Members of Parliament could conveniently be divided up between 'amateurs' and 'professionals'. Indeed, a fairly recent study of the career patterns of MPs incorporated these terms in its title.[7] But, with each succeeding general election, the number of true 'amateurs' is inexorably reduced, and the trend is strongly towards a House predominantly made up of 'full-timers' with an increasingly professional attitude to their Parliamentary work.[8] It is reassuring that, in the view of most observers, an improvement in the general quality of MPs is proceeding step by step with this progression. Mr Speaker King told the Select Committee on Procedure in 1966 that 'the quality of Members of Parliament [is] higher on average than ever before in our history', a view endorsed by Ronald Butt, who qualifies it by saying that 'where contemporary Parliaments may fall below those of the nineteenth century is in the men of exceptional ability among MPs'.[9]

If the general level of competence of MPs has increased, there is no denying that their status has declined. A hundred years ago Trollope could write, without a trace of irony:

> It is something to have sat in the House of Commons though it has been but for one session.... To die and not to have done so is to die and not to have achieved that which it most becomes an Englishman to have achieved.... It is the

[6] Max Weber, 'Politics as a Vocation', in H. H. Gerth and C. Wright Mills, *From Max Weber: Essays in Sociology* (London: Kegan Paul, 1948), p. 115. Weber's father had been a 'backbench' member of the Prussian diet and of the Imperial German Reichstag.

[7] P. W. Buck, *Amateurs and Professionals in British Politics 1918–59* (Chicago: University Press, 1963).

[8] See Rudolf Klein, 'What MPs think of their Jobs', *The Observer*, 27 March 1963, reprinted as Appendix B in Bernard Crick, *The Reform of Parliament* (London: Weidenfeld & Nicolson, 2nd ed., 1968).

[9] *The Power of Parliament*, p. 468.

highest and most legitimate pride of an Englishman to have the letters of MP written after his name.[10]

Modern novelists have a less elevated view of the House of Commons, and that is no bad thing, but there is little doubt that one of the reasons for the apparent fall in public esteem of Members of Parliament[11] is that they are denied the facilities which would enable them to achieve the higher standards of competence of which they are capable and to which increasing numbers of them aspire. The paucity of MPs' facilities (and their salaries!), which is discussed exhaustively by Bernard Crick,[12] was highlighted in 1969 by John Smith, then Conservative MP for the cities of London and Westminster, who announced that he was giving up his seat because 'the working arrangements for members – greatly to the detriment of the country – will remain inadequate for many years to come'.[13] Since 1969 there has been some improvement, but the House of Commons remains one of the worst equipped of democratic legislatures.

These shortcomings are not the principal limitation on the power of backbenchers within the political system, but they do inhibit the ability of MPs to exercise, to the fullest potential, that degree of power which is open to them. As Members gradually achieve better conditions the pressure on government to extend the scope of Parliament's authority will increase further, and the prospect is that the trend towards more Parliamentary control over the executive, which produced the modest Crossman reforms[14] in 1966–68, will continue, however fitfully.

[10] Anthony Trollope, *Can You Forgive Her?*, cited in Henry Fairlie, *The Life of Politics* (London: Methuen, 1968), p. 13.

[11] Although this decline is taken for granted by many political commentators it is based on no empirical evidence. Indeed, a contrary view is advanced by Anthony Barker, who argues, in a note to the Editors of this book, that the Nineteenth Century 'public' consisted of 'a very limited "political class" and narrow electorate, while today we have a wider and much more varied "political class" and a universal electorate – with mass media to boot. My own guess is that MPs have a very high public status out of respect, at least, for their office and that this could, in aggregate, be higher than 50 years ago.'

[12] *The Reform of Parliament*, pp. 56–72. See also the Boyle Report on Ministers' and Members' salaries (Cmnd 4836. December 1971).

[13] *The Times*, 25 June 1969.

[14] These are discussed in detail in Crick, pp. 209–34.

INTRODUCTION xvii

How much power do backbenchers possess? On this point, opinions are profuse but firm evidence hard to come by. In a vivid passage Aneurin Bevan gave strong support to the argument that MPs are impotent:

> When I was quite a young boy my father took me down the street and showed me one or two portly and complacent looking gentlemen standing at the shop doors, and, pointing to one, he said, 'Very important man. That's Councillor Jackson. He's a very important man in this town.' I said, 'What's the Council?' 'Oh, that's the place that governs the affairs of this town,' said my father. 'Very important place indeed, and they are very powerful men.' When I got older I said to myself, 'The place to get to is the council. That's where the power is.' So I worked very hard, and, in association with my fellows, when I was about 20 years of age, I got on the council. I discovered when I got there that the power had been there, but it had just gone. So I made some inquiries, being an earnest student of social affairs, and I learned that the power had slipped down to the county council. So I worked very hard again, and I got there – and it had gone from there too. Then I found out it had come up here [the House of Commons]. So I followed it, and sure enough I found it had been here, but I just saw its coat tails round the corner.[15]

By contrast, the MPs interviewed by Keith Ovenden, in his study published in Part II of this volume, showed a fairly high belief in their own efficacy, which in several cases he was able to corroborate from objective evidence. If rather little is known of the actual influence of backbenchers on government it is only partly because of the paucity of research in this field. If it is true, as Lord Redmayne suggests, that governments operate by a kind of law of anticipated reactions – seeking to avoid trouble with their backbenchers by modifying in advance their proposed policies – at best only an incomplete assessment of the influence of backbenchers can be gained by adding up the relatively rare occasions when governments *publicly* change course in response to backbench pressure. Perhaps the greater part of

---

[15] Hansard, 15 December 1943, col. 1617.

backbenchers' influence, whether it be large or small in total, is not susceptible to measurement but only to judgement.

John P. Mackintosh, in the final contribution to this book, makes a notable attempt to exercise such a judgement by comparing the influence of backbenchers in the Parliamentary sessions of 1967–68 and 1968–69 with those of 1857–59 – 110 years earlier. It seems probable, as he argues, that the short-term influence of backbenchers reached its modern apogee during those two sessions, and in more normal circumstances it would amount to less. But perhaps the most significant impact made by the backbenches is more long-term and indirect than this. Unlike in many other democratic countries – particularly those with federal structures such as the United States and Germany – there is effectively only one route to high political office in Britain, and that lies through membership of the House of Commons. With rare exceptions, ministerial office is preceded by a lengthy apprenticeship on the back benches, and the moulding effect which this has on future ministers, intangible though it is, may represent the most puissant example of back-bench influence. Not every MP may carry a Prime Minister's baton in his brief-case, but it's a comforting thought during the long watches of an all-night sitting.

* * *

This reader differs from other similar volumes in that only a minority of its contents have been written by academic political scientists. In fact about half the book has been contributed by Members of Parliament and by Officers of the House of Commons. The editors hope that this 'inside view', juxtaposed to assessments by outside scholars, will contribute to a more balanced understanding of the Parliamentary process and will help to convey a genuine feel of the life of the House of Commons.

It also differs from other readers in not being restricted to the re-publication of articles already in print. About a quarter of the book consists of original contributions, and others are reprinted from sources not readily available either to students or to the general reader. The volume was planned from the outset as an organic whole, to cover what seemed to the editors to be the most important and relevant topics, and where significant gaps existed original work was commissioned.

The readings presented here fall into three distinct parts, each of which illustrates different roles that the backbencher plays. The first of these, 'The Backbencher, His Constituency and His Party', examines the way backbenchers are selected as candidates, how they campaign for Parliament, how, when elected, they deal with various constituency matters, and their relationships with their Parliamentary parties. The second part, the majority of which is based on original research, is entitled 'The Backbencher and the Work of the House'. It focuses on the Parliamentary behaviour of backbenchers, and considers the role which they play in a number of aspects of the legislative process. The final part, 'Views from the Backbenches', presents evaluations from a number of different standpoints of the parts that the backbencher and Parliament play in the governing of Britain.

Part I

THE BACKBENCHER, HIS CONSTITUENCY AND HIS PARTY

1. How Candidates are Chosen

By DICK LEONARD

An essential prerequisite for all but a handful of Members of Parliament is to achieve selection as candidate by one of the major political parties. In this extract* the selection procedures are described, and the point is made that in both parties the influence of the national party organisation is very limited and that the effective choice is made by the local party activists in each constituency. It has, in fact, been plausibly argued that the selection of Parliamentary candidates is the only important political function still performed by local party organisations.

The procedures of the three main political parties for selecting candidates differ in a number of important details, but are basically similar. In each case the selection is the responsibility of the local constituency party and the influence of the party headquarters is relatively minor.

A pamphlet published by the Conservative Central Office for the guidance of local associations states: 'Subject to certain simple party rules each association has complete freedom to select the man or woman of its choice.' There are well-established procedures within the Conservative Party which limit, however, the degree of local variation in methods of selection.

The executive council of a Conservative association wishing to select a new candidate appoints a selection committee, usually of about six members, who would be among the most influential and senior members of the association. The chairman of the association is invariably included unless, which is not infrequently the case, he has ambitions to be selected himself. The purpose of the selection committee is to consider all the

---

* Reprinted from R. L. Leonard, *Elections in Britain* (London, D. Van Nostrand, 1968), pp. 67–81, with the permission of the publisher and the author.

possible aspirants for the candidature and reduce them to a small number from which the executive council may make its choice.

The constituency chairman is expected to obtain from the Central Office a list of names of suitable people, together with biographical details. One of the vice-chairmen of the National Union, assisted by the standing advisory committee on candidates, is responsible for maintaining an official list of approved potential candidates from among whom a number of names would be sent. Any member of the Conservative Party may apply to be included on the official list, and he is then interviewed by the vice-chairman or by members of the standing advisory committee, and, if approved, his name is added to the list.

Together with the names obtained from Central Office, the selection committee considers any members of the constituency association who have expressed an interest in the candidature and also the names of Conservatives who may have written asking to be considered. If it is a safe Conservative seat there may be a large number of those and it is not uncommon for a selection committee to have over a hundred names from which to choose.

The selection committee quickly whittles this number down to about seven or eight, and in the case of a safe seat few of the applicants would have much chance of surviving to this stage unless they were nationally known figures, were obviously extremely well qualified or were personally known to a member of the selection committee.

The seven or eight people chosen are invited to attend to be interviewed by the selection committee which then chooses normally two or three names from whom the executive council may make its final choice. Occasionally however, when the selection committee decides, in the words of the Central Office pamphlet, that 'a candidate is available whose record is so distinguished and whose qualifications are so outstanding that his adoption is practically a foregone conclusion' only one name is put forward to the executive council.

Before this stage is reached the names of any of the surviving nominees who are not included on the approved Central Office list are submitted to the standing advisory committee for endorsement. If endorsement is refused and the constituency proceeds to select a nominee in spite of this, he is not regarded as an official party candidate at the ensuing election. Cases of an association selecting a candidate who has not been previously approved, are however extremely rare.

The nominees put forward by the selection committee attend a selection conference of the executive council. Each makes a short speech (normally limited to a period varying between ten and thirty minutes) and answers questions put to him from the floor. A secret ballot is then held to choose who will be the candidate. There is no provision in the party rules as to the conduct of this ballot. It is possible for the nominee leading on the first ballot to be chosen forthwith, even though only a minority may have voted for him. It is far more usual however for an exhaustive ballot to be held, with the bottom candidate falling out if no overall majority is obtained on the first ballot.

The executive council's choice is submitted for approval to a general meeting of the whole association. This is normally a formality, but there have been occasions in which the executive council's choice has been challenged at this stage and another name substituted.

Money nowadays plays no significant part in the selection of Conservative candidates. This has not always been so. Up till 1948 it was very common for Conservative candidates to defray the whole of their election expenses and in addition to pay a large annual subscription to the constituency association. Consequently wealth was a prerequisite for potential Conservative Members, with very few exceptions.

The shock of defeat in 1945, however, led to a comprehensive reappraisal of the organisation of the Conservative Party following the report of a committee presided over by Sir David Maxwell Fyfe (who later became Lord Kilmuir). Its recommendations, which were accepted by the party, have fundamentally altered the financial relationship between Conservative MPs and candidates and their constituency associations. Under the new rules a Conservative candidate is precluded from making any contribution whatever towards the election expenses, other than his personal expenses. The maximum contribution which he may make to his association is £25 a year as a candidate, and £50 a year as an MP. In no circumstances, state the party rules, may the payment of a subscription be made a condition of adoption.

There can be no doubt that the new rules are substantially adhered to, and the result has been that a large number of Conservative candidates without private means have been selected in the period since 1948. While wealth is no handicap in the Conservative Party and rich men are often selected as candidates, money no longer plays a direct part in their selection.

The Labour Party's selection procedure is laid down in more detail in the party rules, and it is complicated by the existence of two classes of membership, individual and affiliated (principally trade unions). When a constituency party decides to select a candidate, its executive committee first consults with the regional organiser of the party to agree a time-table for the selection. The regional organiser is the representative of Transport House and it is his responsibility to ensure that the selection takes place according to the party rules. When the time-table has been approved by the general management committee of the constituency party, the secretary writes to each local or ward party or affiliated organisation inviting them to make a nomination before a certain date, normally a minimum period of one month being allowed for this.

No person may be considered for selection unless he or she has been nominated by a local party or affiliated organisation. There is no provision in the Labour Party for members to nominate themselves, though if a member has good personal contact with organisations with the right to nominate it is often not difficult for him to obtain a nomination.

Like the Conservative Central Office, Transport House maintains a list of possible Parliamentary candidates. It is in two parts: List A contains the names of individuals nominated by trade unions and in respect of whom the appropriate trade union is prepared to assume financial responsibility for the candidature. List B consists of persons nominated by constituency Labour parties and for whom no financial responsibility has been assumed.

The executive committee of a constituency party may ask for copies of either list for its own reference or to circulate to affiliated organisations, but there is no compulsion on them to do so, and frequently, particularly in the case of safe Labour seats, they make no effort to obtain the lists. There is little point in local parties in safe Conservative areas consulting list A, as trade unions are rarely willing to sponsor candidates who have no prospect of being elected. The more hopeless the seat, however, the more likely is a party to make use of list B and to write to perhaps a large number of the people included, asking them to accept nomination.

The number of nominations made varies enormously. In a 'hopeless' rural constituency many miles from a large centre of population there may be as few as two or three. In a safe Labour-held seat in a borough, with many affiliated organisations, there is likely to be anything from ten to twenty-five nominations, and even the latter figure is often exceeded. Trade union branches in safe Labour seats, particularly those of the larger unions, are likely to be approached by their union headquarters and asked to nominate a member of the union's parliamentary panel. These nominations must be accompanied by a letter from the general secretary of the union confirming that it will assume financial responsibility for the candidature. Trade union branches are also able to nominate unsponsored members of their unions whose standing is the same as that of nominees of ward or local Labour parties.

When the period for nomination has passed it is the responsibility of the executive committee (which itself has the right to make one nomination) to consider all the nominations received and to draw up a short list. If there are fewer than half a dozen nominations this is normally unnecessary, but this is a rare event except in strong Tory areas. The executive committee may decide to interview all the nominees before drawing up a short list, or it may send them questionnaires to fill in. Often however it does neither.

The executive committee usually recommends a short list with from four to six names and this is reported to the General Management Committee for its approval. It is open to any member of the GMC to move the addition, substitution or deletion of names and this occurs with considerable frequency, though more often than not amendments are voted down.

People on the approved short list are then invited to a selection conference of the GMC whose procedure is not unlike that of the executive council of a Conservative association, though an exhaustive ballot is prescribed in the party rules. The choice of the GMC does not have to be confirmed by a general meeting of members, as in the case of the Conservative Party, but his candidature must be endorsed by the national executive committee of the party.

It is paradoxical that financial considerations now play a greater part in the selection of Labour candidates than of Conservatives. The restrictions on individuals are similar – no Labour candidate may subscribe more than £50 a year to his constituency party, and this rule is seldom transgressed. In fact the average Labour candidate or MP undoubtedly subscribes less to his constituency party than his Conservative counterpart.

The monetary element in the Labour Party is represented by the system of trade union sponsorship of candidates, which goes back to the early days of the party when there was no individual membership and every candidature had to be sponsored by an official organisation. Under the so-called Hastings Agreement, dating from the Labour Party conference at Hastings in 1933, a trade union is permitted to contribute up to 80 per cent of the election expenses incurred on behalf of its nominee and a maximum of £420 a year, or 60 per cent of the agent's salary, to the constituency party.

There is thus a strong temptation for hard-up constituency parties to choose a sponsored candidate, and this applies especially in safe Labour seats in industrial areas. Many constituency parties take a pride in choosing the best nominee available irrespective of financial considerations and many sponsored nominees are able and public-spirited men. There have, however, certainly been cases where more competent nominees have been passed over in favour of a mediocrity whose principal recommendation has been the income which his selection would ensure.

Under the party rules no mention of financial matters may be made at a selection conference and the regional organiser, who attends on behalf of Transport House, strictly enforces this rule. The significance of the distinction between trade union and local party nominees is likely however to be appreciated by at least the most alert of GMC members. But it is at the short-listing stage that sponsorship carries the greatest weight. For the executive committee of a constituency party is acutely aware of the difference that a sponsored candidate can make and, composed as it is of the dozen or so people with the greatest responsibility for the party's affairs, financial worries are likely to be very much on its mind. If an executive committee is determined to have a sponsored candidate it will recommend a short list made up entirely of those with financial backing, and there are fairly frequent examples of this occurring in safe Labour seats.

It is a difficult problem, as it is probably only the sponsorship system which enables a fair number of people from manual occupations to go straight from the workbench to the House of Commons and thus enable Parliament to contain a reasonable cross-section of the nation. If the system were abandoned it might result in the long run in the House being composed merely of people of the professional and middle classes, with a solid block of miners remaining as the only representative of manual workers. It is to be hoped however that one day the Labour Party will devise some method of supplanting the sponsorship system without losing what has always been one of its most attractive features – the very wide range of background and occupation from which its candidates are drawn.

The Liberal Party's selection procedure is virtually identical to the Conservatives': the principal difference in practice is that there are nearly always far fewer nominees, and in many cases a Liberal association has the claims of only one contender to consider. In the relatively small number of cases where a candidate has to be found for a Liberal-held seat or one where there is a good chance of a Liberal victory, the competition is far stronger and the method of selection is very similar to that of the Conservative Party.

Unlike in the Conservative and Labour parties, there is no limit to the amount of money which Liberal candidates or MPs are allowed to contribute to their election expenses or donate to their constituency party. It is unlikely that more than a handful contribute more than the maximum imposed by both the Conservative and Labour parties.

The methods of selection of minor parties differ considerably from that of the major parties, principally because they have so few members. Decisions, normally taken in the larger parties by constituency associations, are more likely to be taken by the national committees of the smaller parties. Selection conferences of the type described above are the exception rather than the rule.

A few general points may be made about selection procedures of all parties. One is the small number of people involved in making the choice. The drawing up of the short list – a vital stage – is the responsibility in the Conservative Party of less than a dozen people and in the Labour Party of less than twenty. The final selection is seldom made by more than 200 people and most often by between 50 and 150. In the Liberal Party the numbers involved are even smaller.

The Selection Conference

The actual selection conference is the most dramatic stage in the selection process, and it is one that imposes considerable strain on the would-be candidates, as the author knows only too well from personal experience. It has been described by a former Tory MP, Nigel Nicolson, as 'a gala occasion for the selectors; slow torture for the candidate'.[1]

The nominees are asked to attend a conference lasting anything up to three or four hours, though most of the time they are cooped up in an ante-room with the other contenders while procedural matters are being discussed or one of their number is making his speech. There is a certain tactical advantage in being the last to speak (the order is normally decided by lot), but this is often offset by the tension of waiting until all your rivals have spoken. All one can hear of the proceedings are occasional muffled sounds of applause from which one imagines that one's rivals are making an extremely good impression. In fact the audience normally goes out of its way to encourage the nominees whose ordeal they can imagine, and are very free with their applause.

At last it is your turn. You are ushered into the conference, which as often as not is housed in a bleak Nonconformist church hall or school, but may occasionally be in the more regal surroundings of the council chamber of the town hall. Before you

[1] Nigel Nicolson, *People and Parliament* (London: Weidenfeld & Nicolson, 1958), p. 40.

are perhaps eighty people, predominantly middle-aged, and you search eagerly for the encouragement of a familiar face, probably in vain.

You reach your seat on the platform, shake hands with the chairman, who announces that you are Mr X, whose biographical details have been circulated to all the delegates. You have fifteen minutes to speak and another fifteen minutes for questions. After fourteen minutes the chairman will sound a warning bell and after fifteen you will be stopped – if necessary in mid-sentence.

You stand up, try to show a confidence which you do not feel and launch into a well-prepared speech, which has been carefully timed in front of your bedroom mirror to last fourteen and a half minutes. In the event, you have either sat down after nine and a half minutes or are rudely cut short after fifteen minutes – less than a third of the way through your oration. You then deal rather better than you had expected with three or four questions and are surprised to hear that another fifteen minutes have gone by.

Back to the ante-room and the interminable wait while a succession of ballots is taken. At last after two or three false alarms the regional organiser of the party will come into the room, look at you straight in the eye and announce that Mr Y has been selected. You shake hands with Mr Y and utter a few modest words of congratulation. Meanwhile that blithering idiot Mr Z is slapping Mr Y on the back and saying he had always known that Y would be chosen.

Back to the conference chamber with the other nominees. Deafening applause. The chairman says that all the nominees were absolutely first class (even if this was patently not the case). They would have liked to have chosen all of them, nevertheless they had to make a choice, however difficult, and the mantle had fallen on Mr Y. He was quite sure that such excellent people as Messrs W, X and Z would have no difficulty in being chosen soon by another constituency, and the members of his constituency would follow their future careers with interest. Then votes of thanks all round, a few words from the selected candidate and a final rousing call from the chairman to rally round and ensure that Mr Y becomes the next Member for the constituency.

It is not easy for nominees to decide what to talk about in their set speeches. Should they talk about party policy or their personal records of work for the party? There is no set formula for success. The speech which would be an utter failure in constituency A may turn out an unqualified success in constituency B. All the nominee has to go on is his experience and the degree of his knowledge of local feeling. His main consolation is that all his rivals are confronted by the same dilemma.

Who is chosen?

Looking at it from the other side, what are the members of the selection conference looking for in their candidate? This varies with the nature of the constituency, and especially according to the prospect of electoral success. If it is a marginal constituency the delegates are most likely to be impressed by the vote-winning prospects of their candidate and a pleasing personality would be the number one qualification. In a safe seat delegates are conscious of choosing the future Member rather than a candidate and are more concerned to choose a man with the requisite knowledge and experience to perform what they conceive to be the functions of an MP. In a hopeless constituency energy and enthusiasm count a great deal and younger candidates are much more likely to be chosen.

Policy differences are relatively unimportant. It is commonly anticipated that left-wing constituency Labour parties are certain to select left-wing candidates and that right-wing Conservative associations similarly will pick extremist candidates. In fact this happens much less frequently than is imagined. Selection conferences of all parties are more likely to pick the man or woman who 'looks the part' rather than to insist on the nominee whose political views most exactly coincide with their own.

Local interests undoubtedly often play a part. If one is nominated for a farming constituency it is prudent to show some knowledge of and interest in agriculture, similarly with industrial areas where one industry is predominant. But in mixed industrial areas and especially in suburban constituencies there is likely to be more interest in national than in purely local issues.

Age may play an important part in deciding between nominees, though this again will vary very much. There are a few parties which would regard a man of fifty as a 'young stripling', while others would regard a forty-year-old as a has-been. In general, the optimum age range is from thirty-five to forty-five, with a certain preference for younger candidates in hopeless and marginal seats and for older ones in safe constituencies.

Unlike in the United States and certain other countries, it is not customary for a candidate to be resident in the area which he seeks to represent. In fact the great majority of candidates in British Parliamentary elections are 'carpet baggers' with no personal stake in the community they seek to represent. At some selection conferences it is a major advantage to be a local man, but equally often it can be a handicap. To come in from outside with no previous connections with local factions, can in many cases be a strong recommendation.

Regional prejudices seldom come into the picture in England, though in Scotland and Wales it is rare for a non-Scotsman or non-Welshman respectively to be chosen. Religion is not an important factor outside Northern Ireland, though Jews encounter strong prejudices in some local Conservative associations. In a few constituencies on Merseyside and in Glasgow Labour nominees who are Roman Catholics start with a distinct advantage.

A certain prejudice undoubtedly exists against women candidates, which is stronger in the Conservative Party than in the Labour Party and in rural areas than in towns. Many fewer women than men are selected and they tend to be chosen for the less hopeful seats.

In 1966 there were twenty-one Conservative women candidates out of 629, but of elected Conservative Members there were seven out of 253. At the same election Labour fielded thirty women candidates out of 621 and nineteen Labour women MPs were returned out of 363. There are undoubtedly many fewer women than men with Parliamentary ambitions but those who wish to be considered as candidates encounter stronger resistance than men. This apparently comes most often from their fellow women who are usually in a majority at Conservative selection conferences. A large number of these seem convinced that voters would be less likely to vote for a woman candidate than for a man.

The evidence for this belief is scanty. A Gallup poll taken in July 1952 revealed that 16 per cent of the voters thought that they would be less inclined to vote for a woman candidate, but this was partially offset by the 10 per cent who said they would be more inclined, 67 per cent saying that it would make no difference and 7 per cent expressing no opinion. On the basis of this poll it might be concluded that women candidates encountered a handicap of 6 per cent.

In practice it proves much less than this. The present author has made an exhaustive analysis of the results of the 1955 and 1959 elections, recording every constituency where a woman candidate in the 1955 election was replaced by a man of the same party in 1959 and vice versa, and comparing the results in these constituencies with the national trend.

The result of this analysis was that when a Conservative woman candidate had replaced a man, the pro-Conservative swing had averaged 0·4 per cent against a national average of 1·2 per cent. Where a Conservative man had replaced a woman candidate, the pro-Conservative swing was 1·6 per cent. This means that in the average constituency a woman Conservative candidate might expect to receive about 300 votes less than a man. The same analysis revealed no difference at all in the case of Labour candidates, while for Liberals and minor party candidates and independents the numbers involved were too small to point to any reliable conclusion. The analysis does suggest that there is a small minority of normally Conservative voters who will not vote for a woman candidate.[2]

It is not only women candidates who encounter difficulties in the Conservative Party. Despite frequent appeals from Central Office, culminating in a recommendation in the Selwyn Lloyd report of June 1963 that each selection conference should include one woman and one trade unionist among the nominees from which it makes its choice, it has proved virtually impossible to

[2] A similar analysis covering the 1964 and 1966 elections again showed that Conservative women candidates did worse than men. It also suggested that, in these later elections, Labour women candidates did slightly better than men. See *Daily Telegraph – Gallup Analysis of the Election '66* (London: *Daily Telegraph*, 1966), p. 27.

persuade Conservative constituency associations to select working-class candidates. Only two Conservative MPs in the 1966 Parliament were working trade unionists when selected. Immediately after the 1966 election the then chairman of the Conservative Party, Edward du Cann, announced a tightening up of selection procedures in order to achieve a better and more representative choice of candidates. It remains to be seen whether this new initiative will prove more successful than others taken in the past.

The occupational backgrounds of candidates and elected members in the 1966 election are shown in Table 1:

TABLE 1
Occupational Backgrounds of Candidates, 1966

	Conservative		Labour		Liberal	
	Elected	Defeated	Elected	Defeated	Elected	Defeated
	%	%	%	%	%	%
Professions	47	48	43	50	50	48
Business	29	38	9	17	25	30
Miscellaneous	23	12	18	24	25	20
Workers	1	2	30	9	0	2

In the professions category the law, particularly the bar, is dominant in the Conservative and Liberal parties, and is very well represented in the Labour Party. There are a number of reasons for this. Traditionally the bar and politics have been associated professions. By virtue of their training and professional practice barristers are skilled at arguing a case and it may be expected that they would face a selection conference with more confidence than most. Barristers and solicitors also undoubtedly find it easier than most to organise their time in such a way that they can combine their profession with their Parliamentary work.

There is a fair sprinkling from the other professions among the candidates of all parties, but it is only teaching – at both school and university level – which comes near to challenging the predominance of the law. In fact, teachers form by far the largest occupational group among Labour candidates, nearly a quarter of whom in the 1966 general election were teachers, either at university, adult education or school level. In the Liberal Party too, large numbers of candidates come from the teaching profession. Only a handful of Conservative candidates however are teachers – and those normally in unpromising constituencies.

It will come as a surprise to nobody to discover that business is largely represented in the Conservative Party and makes a good showing in the Liberal Party. The smaller number of Labour candidates with a business background is not really comparable, as a majority of these are small businessmen or employees of larger companies, often in junior positions, whereas a majority of the Conservatives in this category are company directors.

The largest groups in the miscellaneous category are farmers on the Conservative side and journalists in the Labour Party. Journalists and especially public relations and advertising men are well represented in the Conservative and Liberal parties too. Among the workers, the largest group are the miners, who have practically a monopoly of Labour representation in coal-mining areas. Out of thirty-five miners who stood for Labour in 1966, no less than thirty-two were successful. A good proportion of the 'workers' who stood in 1966 were full-time trade union officials, but the majority were working at their trades when first elected, and each general election brings to the Labour benches of the House of Commons reinforcements of members straight from the workbench. Most of these are sponsored candidates.

Only a derisory number of workers have at any time been selected as Conservative or Liberal candidates, and fewer still have been elected. In the Labour Party a majority of candidates would have been classified as workers in the period up to 1945 and a third of Labour MPs still fall in this category. But since that date the proportion of professional men (especially teachers) has greatly increased, and this has been largely at the expense of 'workers'. In very many cases the new aspirants have come from working-class families, but unlike their parents have enjoyed the benefits of a grammar school and/or university education. Ironically, workers stand a much better chance of being chosen to fight safe Labour seats rather than hopeless or marginal ones. This is because of the system of trade union sponsorship described on page 8 above. In 1966, 30 per cent of successful Labour candidates were workers, but only 9 per cent of unsuccessful ones.

TABLE 2
Background of MPs 1951 and 1966

	Conservative MPs 1951 %	Conservative MPs 1966 %	Labour MPs 1951 %	Labour MPs 1966 %
Occupation				
Professions	41	46	35	43
Business	37	29	9	9
Miscellaneous	22	23	19	18
Workers	—	—	37	30
Education				
Elementary	1	1	26	22
Secondary	24	18	50	60
Public School	75	80	20	18
(Eton)	(24)	(21)	(1)	(1)
Oxford and Cambridge	52	56	19	23
Other Universities	10	10	22	28

Table 2, reprinted from *The British General Election of 1966*, reveals how the composition of the House of Commons has altered over a fifteen-year period. The authors, David Butler and Anthony King, comment: 'It seems that the Conservatives have gone on choosing the same sort of people, in social and economic terms at least. The Labour Party has changed its emphasis more; the result is an intellectually livelier Parliament but not necessarily a more representative one.'[3]

In all parties there is a recognised route which the majority of would-be MPs are expected to follow. They must first fight a hopeless seat and, fortified by this salutary experience, they may then proceed to a marginal constituency and later perhaps to a safe one. A fair number of aspirants in both major parties however succeed in by-passing this route and secure election to the House of Commons at their first attempt.

How much influence have the party headquarters on the choice of candidates? It is clear that no HQ can force an individual on an unwilling constituency party. The most they can do is to try to persuade the constituency, through the regional organiser or agent, to include someone whom Transport House or the Central Office would like accommodated on the short list. Very often a constituency party is quite willing to accede to

[3] D. E. Butler and Anthony King, *The British General Election of 1966* (London: Macmillan, 1966), p. 211.

this, but it frequently happens that the constituency party executive committee will have other ideas about whom to include on the short list, and it is their view which prevails. Even when someone recommended from headquarters is included it is by no means always an advantage for this fact to be known. Once an officially recommended nominee is on the short list he takes his chance with everyone else.

The negative powers which the party headquarters possess to refuse endorsement to selected candidates are sparingly used. In the Labour Party, except in the rare case of someone who is clearly unsuited for personal reasons (such as the nominee for a Midlands constituency some years ago who, it later transpired, had recently been cashiered from the RAF for embezzling mess funds) it is in practice only used to exclude those with strong Communist or Trotskyist connections. In the Conservative and Liberal parties it is even rarer for selected candidates to be blackballed for political heterodoxy.[4]

How much security do prospective candidates enjoy? Not very much. Their relationship to their constituency parties is a delicate one. Disenchantment easily sets in on either side. This is not perhaps surprising, as candidate and constituency party have usually had only the most fleeting view of each other prior to selection.

Opportunities for disagreement abound. Parties and candidates often differ on how much work the candidate is expected to put in. It frequently happens that a prospective candidate visits the constituency less often than his party would like; less commonly parties may decide that they see altogether too much of their candidate. Changes in the personal position of the candidate may also occur. He may be offered a better job, or his

[4] An exhaustive account of the procedures for selecting Parliamentary candidates is given in Austin Ranney, *Pathways to Parliament* (Madison: University of Wisconsin Press; and London: Macmillan, 1965). His view is that 'the national organisations' actual influence over candidate selection is substantially weaker than their formal supervisory powers allow'. He concludes: 'while British national party organisations play distinctly more active roles than their American counterparts in the selection of candidates for national offices, the great majority of the choices have been made in "law" and in fact by the constituency organisations.' See also Michael Rush, *The Selection of Parliamentary Candidates* (London: Nelson, 1969).

employers may prove unexpectedly difficult about allowing time off. His health may suffer, or that of his family. He may take on other commitments which leave him less time for his candidature. Or he may wish to be considered for another, more promising constituency; so, for one reason or another, a sizeable number of prospective candidates withdraw 'for personal reasons' long before polling day, and the procedure for selecting a new candidate has to be gone through all over again.

On the other hand, once a candidate has been elected as a Member he normally has no difficulty in retaining the support of his own party, and unless his seat is a marginal one, he normally continues to represent it, if he wishes, until the end of his working life. It is extremely difficult for a constituency party to rid itself of an unwanted Member, the required procedure for doing this in both the Conservative and Labour parties being weighted heavily on the side of the Member. Surprisingly, in view of the fact that political differences are usually stronger in the Labour Party, it is constituency Conservative associations who more frequently attempt to unseat a Member with whom they disagree. Such efforts, however, are normally unsuccessful and it is rare for more than one or two Members to be forced out by their constituencies during the course of a Parliament.

An exception was the aftermath of the Suez operation, when feelings were running extremely high and four Conservatives and one Labour Member lost the support of their constituency parties. Two of these resigned their seats forthwith, the others were replaced by more orthodox party candidates at the subsequent general election.[5]

Many members of constituency parties would like their Members to behave as delegates of the party rather than as representatives of the constituency, but they have little opportunity to enforce their will. Each of the three major parties sets its face firmly against such a conception of a Member's responsibilities, the Labour and Liberal parties implicitly, the Conservative Party explicitly. The Central Office pamphlet *Notes on Procedure for the Adoption of Conservative Candidates in England and Wales* quotes Burke with approval: 'Your representative owes you not his industry only, but his judgement; and he betrays instead

[5] See also L. D. Epstein, 'British MPs and their Local Parties: The Suez Case', *American Political Science Review*, Vol. 54, No. 2, June 1960.

of serving you if he sacrifices it to your opinion . . . authoritative instructions, which the Member is bound blindly and implicitly to obey, though contrary to the dearest convictions of his judgement and conscience, are utterly unknown to the laws of the land, and against the tenor of our constitution.'

In practice, few Members encounter serious difficulties with their constituency parties over policy matters, though disagreements are frequent. It is rare for a Member who deviates towards an extreme position on the outside edge, as it were, of his party, to run into trouble with his constituency party. This is because constituency parties are normally more extreme than the party leadership. Members who deviate towards the centre may however find themselves in difficulty. It is not surprising that none of the Suez rebels on the right of the Conservative Party found themselves out of step with their constituency association, though four out of the five Conservative Members who most strongly opposed the original attack on Egypt were disowned by their associations. Conversely, in the Labour Party right-wing deviants are much more likely than left-wingers to meet trouble in their constituency parties. In general however the vast majority of constituency parties accept, however reluctantly, that they are unable to dictate the political line of their Members. It is in most cases a more serious matter for a Member to be out of step with his party leadership in the House of Commons than to be in disagreement with the members of his constituency party.

2. Campaigning for Parliament
By RICHARD ROSE and
DENNIS KAVANAGH

How do candidates behave during an election campaign? This study* of campaigners in the 1966 general election by Richard Rose and Dennis Kavanagh shows that many candidates derive enjoyment from campaigns regardless of the result. Their account, 'shows how false it is to assume that politicians have electoral victory as their sole or necessarily primary goal'. In addition, the authors pay particular attention to the difficulties that campaigners face in keeping in touch with electors, the relatively high importance placed on canvassing and conversation and the relatively low importance placed on opinion polls and the local press during an election. Rose and Kavanagh also illustrate the low level of attention paid to party leaders: to candidates, 'politics is still about issues of national importance rather than personalities'.

The activities of candidates during an election campaign present a puzzle. Substantial evidence has been accumulated in the Nuffield election studies to suggest that in the great majority of constituencies a candidate can have no influence on the result. Thus, one might expect candidates and MPs to treat a campaign as a three-week holiday from their normal work. But there is also evidence that candidates do not treat campaigning with the scepticism of a psephologist; many commit their energies and emotions in ways suggesting the belief that their personal efforts can make all the difference to their own result.

During the 1964 general election we approached this puzzle by an intensive time-and-motion study in a reasonably safe Labour constituency in the north. The most striking finding was that both candidates played it cool, spending an average of about four hours a day on campaign activities in the weeks

---

* Reprinted from *New Society*, 28 July 1966, pp. 122-4, with the permission of *New Society* and the authors.

immediately before the poll. The question then arose – is this behaviour now typical? Have most candidates adjusted to their electoral unimportance, save in the special spotlight of an important by-election or a marginal seat? If not, why do they persist in exhausting themselves, their supporters and sometimes their families? Perhaps winning an election is not the sole or prime motive force for candidates.

The day after the 1966 election, we posted questionnaires concerning activities and attitudes to a representative sample of 420 MPs and candidates in 165 English constituencies. Ministers of Cabinet rank and five key Conservative strategists were excluded from the sample, on the grounds that their constituency relationships would be unusual because of responsibilities in London. Wales and Scotland were omitted because of the importance of minor parties in both areas, and the peculiar difficulties of campaigning in the Welsh hills and in the Highlands. A total of 83·6 per cent of campaigners (i.e. candidates and sitting MPs) returned valid replies; only 2·9 per cent wrote refusing to answer. Judging by the swift response and the carefulness with which the majority replied, many appeared to welcome the opportunity of unburdening themselves of judgements accumulated from their election experiences.

The study was designed to explore, within the limits of a three-page set of open-ended questions, a wide range of relationships of very different types. A campaigner is after all not only trying to influence voters, but also a key figure in a sometimes sectarian party organisation, a potential advocate of public policies, a representative or a bystander in a centralised, national campaign and, not least, a person with ordinary human hopes, frustrations and reactions to events.

Before adoption as a parliamentary candidate, the ties of many campaigners with their constituency were weak or non-existent. Of MPs fighting for re-election, 51 per cent had no previous ties; 39 per cent of Conservative and Labour candidates and 32 per cent of Liberal candidates were similarly strangers to their constituencies. Moreover, 43 per cent of all campaigners, including half the MPs, were fighting their campaign without the benefit of a home or weekend retreat in or near their constituency.

The ability of an MP to keep free from involvement in his

constituency permits British parliamentarians to devote far more attention to central government concerns than is true, say, in America. But it also places a higher premium on the need for information about distant and possibly unfamiliar constituents. In a constituency with about 55,000 voters, especially one carved amorphously from a large metropolitan area, even a local man may have difficulty keeping in touch with his electors. Campaigners were asked to rate nine different sources of information about constituents' views. The great majority showed confident reliance in a multiplicity of channels for sampling opinion. The median campaigner ranked three sources of information as 'good', and only 14 per cent said they had none or only one good source of information.

Of all the sources of information, canvassing was rated good by two-thirds of respondents, and talking with ordinary constituents ranked second. Conversations with the party agent and with local party workers came next in the opinion of campaigners. Only a fifth regarded opinion polls as a good source of information about voters, and the local press was held in even less esteem. It should be remembered however that just because campaigners talk with voters, it does not necessarily follow that they listen intently to the comments that voters make to them. This caution is suggested by the emphasis that some respondents explicitly gave to the importance of intuition as a source of information. Moreover, canvassing that has as its aim maximising the amount of 'flesh-pressing' that a candidate does, allows no time for oral communication with voters.

During the campaign, 88 per cent of respondents said that they spent a lot of time daily in canvassing, and 71 per cent said they spent a lot of time addressing meetings. These activities are not only expected by local party workers, but also approved by the campaigners. When expressing views about desirable changes in campaign behaviour, virtually all who referred to the eighteenth-century institution of canvassing wanted it increased, and only 14 per cent thought there should be fewer public meetings. The importance of routine organisation work is heightened by the fact that two-thirds of the respondents said that nothing had happened locally during the campaign to affect their activities.

In terms of impact on voters, campaigners seem reasonably

satisfied with their efforts. A total of 79 per cent rated the campaign as good in getting out regular supporters. With turn-out declining at two successive elections, this task may well become increasingly important in marginal constituencies. In addition 44 per cent rated their work good for attracting don't knows, but only 16 per cent rated it good for changing voters' minds.

In the great majority of seats, the relations between the campaigner and his constituency association are more important than contact with local voters; the result is a foregone conclusion, as the evenness of the national swing in 1966 again demonstrated. In a safe constituency a campaigner need only maintain the confidence of his local constituency association in order to be assured of a long tenure in Parliament. In a hopeless seat, creating a good impression with local workers may assist a candidate in gaining adoption for a safe seat elsewhere.

Campaigners regard the month-long electoral contest as an important and beneficial stimulus to constituency activity; 86 per cent specifically referred to the morale-building value of campaigning. In addition, 21 per cent praised the campaign as a means of mobilising additional members, voluntary helpers and money. Since the majority of associations will suffer defeat at the polls, it is specially noteworthy that 79 per cent of respondents made no reference to the impact of the result on constituency association morale. Of those making reference, satisfaction rather than dissatisfaction was stressed by a ratio of almost two to one.

Surprisingly, the majority of MPs seem satisfied with their local party organisations, and only 12 per cent of MPs said that they had to spend much time on organisation work. By comparison, one-third of Conservative, Labour and Liberal candidates had to spend substantial time doing their own organisation work, and they were more likely to desire greater provision of full-time paid agents. Many understaffed Labour and Liberal campaigners may be uncomplaining because they are resigned to doing without professional help locally. In addition, the amount of attention given to central party communiqués, especially by Liberal candidates, suggests that professional assistance from Smith Square may be more highly valued because less easily provided at the local level.

In their role as formulator and advocate of policies, MPs and candidates speak to local audiences, but they usually speak about national problems. A total of 93 per cent of campaigners gave great emphasis to national issues, whereas local issues were given major emphasis by only 21 per cent; 14 per cent stressed regional issues. Interestingly 44 per cent of Liberal candidates said they gave little or no attention to local issues, and 49 per cent said they gave little or no attention to regional issues. If the survey had included Scottish and Welsh candidates, one would expect more attention to constituency problems, but perhaps even there many campaigners might have approached seemingly local problems as specific symptoms of nationwide difficulties.

The relations between MPs, candidates and the party leaders are complex. The leader not only symbolises the party during the campaign, but also distracts attention from the local worthy, whether a first-time candidate or a long-serving back-bench MP. In return, many campaigners ignore their leaders. A total of 43 per cent of Labour MPs and 44 per cent of candidates said they gave little or no attention to Harold Wilson; similarly, 51 per cent of Conservative MPs and 50 per cent of candidates gave little or no attention to Edward Heath.

While often ignoring leaders, most campaigners gave regular attention to the press reports of their party chiefs. Some did so with little resentment; in the words of one Labour MP from a safe constituency, 'It serves to remind us where ultimate power lies.' But many expressed sharp resentment, recommending less press and TV coverage of party leaders during the campaign and more publicity for constituency campaigns. Public opinion polls did not attract resentment of the depth and scale roused by the media's collaboration with headquarters in 'presidential-style' campaigning. It was termed 'a serious threat to democracy' by one veteran backbencher, and 'a reduction in the status of parliamentary candidates to that of mere puppets of the party' by another.

Resentments may be fed by the fact that campaigners regard their efforts as personally important. The average MP reported campaigning approximately 10 hours a day, the major party candidates about $9\frac{1}{2}$ hours daily, and the Liberals, 8 hours. The shorter time devoted by Liberals reflects the fact that more than one-quarter had to devote some attention to their normal job, even as polling day approached. In the narrowest of egoistic senses, the time spent might be justified on the grounds that 85 per cent rated campaigning as a good way to make themselves known personally; this was thus the most frequently mentioned of all the many functions of campaigning.

The desire of campaigners to publicise themselves should not be regarded as a calculated device to win votes undertaken dispassionately by calm technocrats. One of the most striking findings of the survey was that 66 per cent of respondents nowhere made any reference to the result. Among those referring to the result, favourable comments outnumbered unfavourable reactions, even among the ranks of Liberal candidates. Reactions took very different forms. An elderly Liberal frankly wrote, 'Success at my time of life would have been a personal disaster.' By contrast, a Conservative correspondent had once believed sufficiently in the efficacy of local campaigning to conclude, after his third defeat: 'I feel that I have literally wasted eight years of my life nursing constituencies. I would have done as well by never appearing at all.'

The survey provides great evidence for the simple but often overlooked point that many politicians maintain their emotional equilibrium by deriving enjoyment from playing the game without regard to victory. In all, 64 per cent expressed substantial pleasure with the campaigning. One Liberal candidate in a permanently Conservative seat wrote, 'The only thing really worth doing in life.' A Labour candidate facing a five-figure Conservative majority wrote, 'I look forward eagerly to the next time.' Even among the 22 per cent who referred to physical exhaustion, a majority quickly added that they none the less were happily exhausted.

Only one-sixth of the campaigners expressed the view that their efforts were a waste of time. Most of these respondents were resigned to the need to keep going through the motions of trying to influence voters, if only, as one defeated MP wrote, 'to prevent one seeming bloody and idle'. Two per cent of campaigners indicated strong hostility to their gruelling and sometimes unsuccessful experience.

Taken in conjunction with other research, this study emphasises how false it is to assume that politicians have election victory as their sole or necessarily primary goal. Candidates (especially Liberals) and party workers are voluntary workers with little hope of material rewards from politics. It is hardly surprising that they attach so much importance to pleasure in being seen by people and talking with them. The lack of consistent and compulsive concern with winning elections also implies that it is unrealistic to expect elected officials to make policy decisions simply in accord with changing whims of voters, or changing figures in opinion polls. The reliance of MPs and candidates upon face-to-face contacts for information about the electorate further reinforces this conclusion, since it is relatively easy for a politician to interpret casual conversations in terms consistent with already established predispositions.

The campaigners' replies also indicate that for them, at least, politics is still about issues of national importance, rather than about personalities. Half the campaigners thought their efforts good for explaining national problems to their constituents and 39 per cent rated campaigning good for increasing acceptance of national party policy. In addition, 37 per cent rated campaigning good as a means of calling attention to local problems.

While the attitudes of individual MPs and candidates often differ in detail and in nuance, it is possible to generalise about the chief *political* role of campaigners. The carpet-bagger candidate, arriving with no ties with his constituency and leaving with little information at the end of his campaign, is a rarity. The Westminster-oriented candidate regarding time spent canvassing as a waste of time, is also in the minority. Another rarity is the 'isolated flagwaver', carrying the party banner but completely out of touch with party headquarters.

The chief role of campaigners seems to be that of branch representative of a nationwide concern. The candidate's job is to travel around the constituency on behalf of party headquarters, providing personal knowledge and personal contact concerning matters of local detail that cannot be provided from the centre. The majority of campaigners, like any good executive stationed away from headquarters, make a point of keeping in touch with affairs at the centre. From half to two-thirds said that they spent a lot of time reading the national press, the opinion polls, the speeches of party leaders and headquarters communiqués.

The average MP or would-be Member is thus in the classic position of the man in the middle, a link between the party leadership and the rank-and-file voter, relaying communications from the centre to the periphery and back again. The pattern of responses suggests that campaigners regard the task of telling their constituents about central government problems as more important than that of telling the central government about their constituents' concerns.

Emotionally, some campaigners happily accept their intermediary role, relishing the reflected glory that comes from association with the leaders of the nation. As one Labour candidate wrote: 'Campaigning is enormously enjoyable as long as you accept yourself as a front man for the national campaign.' But a larger number, perhaps sensing that the limelight and authority of the front bench will never be for them, show resentment of the domination of the campaign by national party leaders; they urge the reform of campaigning in order to give attention to all of the candidates in a general election, rather than just a few.

3. Members' Postbags

By ANTHONY BARKER and MICHAEL RUSH

MEMBERS of Parliament are clearly seen between elections as public figures, although on polling day they are close to being mere partisan cyphers. As MPs they are 'both insiders and outsiders' (Ronald Butt's phrase) because they have access to the Government without being part of it. Their postbags are often seen as their main personal link with the public in general and their constituents in particular, but it is important to see the Member's postbag in the context of the information network which he inhabits. This network includes the mass media and (on constituency matters) his local party's prominent members, his constituency's local press and his own local social contacts – as well as any letters he may receive. By no means all people are equally likely to write a letter to their MP, some preferring to speak with him. Letters are therefore functionally indistinguishable from 'surgery' visiting (the subject of the next study). This* extract is drawn from the first full-length study of MPs and their House to be based on a sample survey of Members' behaviour and attitudes.

The postbag from the constituency

According to the Almond and Verba survey of 1963, the British people often do feel competent to raise their views on a problem or issue, and have a preference for doing so with an elected representative such as a councillor or MP. How they do

---

* This extract is drawn from *The Member of Parliament and his Information* by A. Barker and M. Rush (Allen & Unwin for PEP and The Study of Parliament Group; University of Toronto Press) 1970. The random, structured sample of 177 MPs on which the book is based was of the 531 non-ministerial MPs serving on 1 January 1967. Sixty-three per cent (111 Members) were interviewed (according to a pre-tested interview guide incorporating many open-ended questions) for an average period of about one hour. Full details appear in the book.

this may well depend on their normal habits and customs, some writing a letter while others try to speak to the representative and explain matters personally. The letters received by an MP from his constituents are obviously likely to prove a principal source of his information on both the views and affairs of his constituents and perhaps, by inference, on those of people all over the country.

We sought to establish first the volume of post which each interviewed Member estimated he received from his constituency in normal circumstances, during an average week. We then asked how much of his parliamentary time was taken in dealing with all his post, including non-constituency letters (we could not, unfortunately, establish the time spent by Members on only their constituency post). We then asked: 'What do you think about spending this amount of your parliamentary time in this way?' The answers to this open-ended question almost entirely revolved around the idea of the modern Member being seen by the public as a 'welfare officer' or 'case worker' to whom they can take their problems or complaints concerning public authorities of all kinds, or, sometimes, concerning private firms or bodies, their neighbours, or their own family.[1]

'First, on the post you receive as an MP. . . . How many letters do you receive from constituency sources (i.e. individual constituents, firms and organisations in the constituency) in an average week?'

Looking first at the total figures for all parties, only about one Member in ten among our respondents claimed to receive either less than 25 or more than 100 letters per average week from his constituency. Just over 80 per cent said they received less than 75, and over half said they got less than 50. There are some differences between the parties; approximately the same proportion receive less than 50 constituency letters per week but more Labour MPs receive between 50 and 74, while more Conservatives get 75 or more. These differences are not great, and may be attributable to factors other than party label.

One such factor is the differing sizes of Members' electorates. As is to be expected the size of an MP's electorate does affect the

[1] This question is developed in the original book text.

volume of his constituency postbag. All four Members with electorates of fewer than 40,000 received less than fifty letters per week, whereas those with much larger electorates were rather more likely to appear in the higher bracket. But other factors were involved: the urban Members claimed to receive fewer letters than those representing rural seats, despite the fact that the electoral system has deliberately made rural constituencies less populous.

We then turned to two other possible factors: the size of their majority and their length of service in the House. Both these scales showed a wide dispersion among Members in the same postbag brackets for both majority size and length of service. Neither showed any clear correlation with the Members' estimates on constituency postbags. This may seem rather surprising, since it is widely thought that newer MPs try to 'dig themselves in' to a seat, especially when their majority is precarious. Whether Members do appear to think in these terms we shall consider below, when seeking a pattern in these findings on constituency postbags in the context of the 'welfare officer' role of Members of Parliament.

In our examination of the actual letters etc. in some twenty-four Members' postbags,[2] we noticed that every one of a very varied group of constituencies produced more letters raising personal cases and problems than offered opinions on local or national issues. These personal case letters also exceeded in each instance the number of letters of all kinds received by the Member from outside his constituency. The most common personal cases were about social security and housing, especially in mainly working-class constituencies. Where housing conditions and overcrowding were particularly bad there was no greater flow of letters, and people who were apparently experiencing such conditions did not figure prominently, let alone proportionately, in the Member's postbag. Almost all the letters we saw were very articulate and some complaints did not involve personal deprivation such as overcrowding but rather the delay in fitting a telephone or the refusal of planning permission on land owned by the constituent. From what we saw it would

[2] Each examination lasted four weeks and included data on which of the printed items the MPs tended to discard unread. This project was not exact enough for numerical presentation.

seem that working-class people write only under grave provocation, preferring if possible to visit the Member's surgery.

We may ask whether one reason why urban Members, as a group, claim to get somewhat less constituency post than rural Members is the greater frequency with which urban Members offer themselves at surgeries. Labour Members, as a group, also do this more often than the Conservatives, and nearly all Labour Members sit for urban seats (forty-four out of fifty-two among our respondents). A further small influence in this direction may be the fact that the urban constituents of London seats can and do telephone their Member at the House without great expense, or go and seek him out there, rather than write a letter.

The constituency postbag is a topic, like many others in our survey, which we are looking at through only the Member's eyes; we have no figures on what kinds of constituent write most or least letters to their MP, since we lacked the resources to interview a representative sample of constituents. We were offered a few informal impressions by Members, such as the view that working-class country people are less ready to write to their MP than similar people in towns. Several Members sitting for constituencies which are, in whole or part, deeply rural, mentioned 'rural illiteracy', by which they mean that village and farm folk are in their experience particularly reluctant to take up the pen and thus particularly glad to tell their Members their troubles at his surgery or at some less formal moment when they meet. At the same time we have some reason, based on our impressions when analysing actual postbags, to believe that the rural or semi-rural 'middle classes' (that is, in modern usage, everyone except the working class) are so comparatively prone to write to their MP that their efforts rather more than make up for the rural working class and place rural Members under a generally rather heavier burden than urban Members. There are quite a few rural seats with a traditional attraction for retired middle-class people who may be the source of some of this effect. The 'literate retired' are not confined to rural areas of course: several Conservatives sitting for resort and spa towns and prosperous city suburbs particularly mentioned this element while giving us rather high estimates of constituency postbag figures. 'I have a highly literate constituency' . . .

'nothing much else to do but write letters' . . . 'mine is a very good quality constituency', were among the comments we had. Civil service, colonial and military pensions, plus the 'animal lobby' were said to be prominent features of this kind of correspondence.

A second question deserving some thought is the lack of a common pattern of constituency post among marginal, safe, new and established Members respectively, and we may ask whether 1964 and 1966 entrants particularly, were not 'digging themselves in' during the early summer of 1967 when we spoke to them, by the traditional means of serving both constituents and constituency, and getting publicity credit for it in the local newspaper. This does of course go on. One 1964 Labour entrant was willing to describe his careful plans for relating his Westminster activity to his constituency's newspaper's deadline.

It is not only marginal new Members who feel a need to establish themselves in their seats: younger Members of both parties (more often Conservatives) who hold safe seats told us privately that they would like to build up a good credit balance of personal and constituency service to draw on when they disagree with elements in their local party on a bitter national issue. The memory of Nigel Nicolson, pushed out of a safe Conservative seat after opposing capital punishment and the Suez invasion, lives on. As one younger Conservative in a safe seat put it: 'My taking a firm stand against the warble fly may help me to take a similar attitude to Ian Smith.'

Whether a Member trying to become known and accepted is in a marginal or a safe seat, his main device is personal contact with people when he can show interest and concern in their lives and problems. The idea of a Member deliberately building up his constituency postbag must imply that he can generate letters from constituents if he wants to, or, alternatively, by inference discourage them. Getting about in the constituency (with the local Press photographer following) and writing in, or being written about in, the local paper, are the obvious ways. Publicly inviting letters and surgery visits, is of course an even stronger course. One new Member displayed a poster in his constituency: 'In trouble? Ring or Write to X', and at about the same time, when making a regional broadcast on a certain topic, invited listeners (not just his constituents) to write to him if they had a problem in that field. Between them, these two actions led to a fivefold increase in his mail which went well outside the topic specified in the broadcast and lasted for a considerable time. Normally, the Member does not deliberately generate extra letters but does what he is asked as best he can, in the knowledge that his letters to constituents may pass from hand to hand and the news of his helpfulness may spread through family, neighbours, local pub and factory canteen, until dozens of other people know something of it.

Liberal Members receive extra post, including the personal case work, from Liberal supporters throughout the country; those we spoke to agreed it formed an extra burden, although a useful source of knowledge on affairs and problems in parts of the country which lack a Liberal representative. Another small group who attract a national correspondence on personal problems are the 'public figures' among MPs – the television stars, newspaper columnists and journalists, and ex-Ministers. We did not meet enough of these either in our interviews or during our postbag analyses, to gather how they reacted to this aspect of fame. It is possible they distinguish in their minds between getting letters of opinion (which indicate their effectiveness as communicators even if their correspondents do not always agree with them) and personal case letters which ought strictly to be directed to the writer's own Member. We mention these few 'star' MPs as they are good examples of the only explanation of the pattern of Members' constituency post that offers itself – that it is Members' individual personalities and the conduct which flows from them, which determine the level of their constituency post. We have seen that party, size of electorate, urban or rural character have only partial influence with a widespread fluctuation between individuals in each case; we found marginality and length of service similarly unhelpful. It is plainly possible both to build up and to minimise constituency correspondence compared with any existing base. A Member can develop his surgery work in addition to receiving letters, or try to keep both written and oral communications from his constituents down to the minimum level possible, given his constituency's social characteristics.

It is important to note that there is no logical difference between constituents with problems of various kinds first approaching their Member by letter or telephone on the one hand, and by turning up at his surgery on the other. It may be true that better educated constituents will tend to write a letter while people who prefer to explain their problems orally (perhaps from a lack of self-confidence in their letter-writing) will tend to come to the surgery, but there must be many cases where the choice of approach to the Member is random as between these two courses. Quite often, Members receive either a brief note from a constituent saying he has a case to raise and asking to meet him, or a long, but none too clear, letter setting out the story as seen by the constituent, and asking for the Member's help. In either case, the Member will ask the person to attend during or just after normal surgery hours to hear the story and to try to unravel it if necessary. It would be easy to understand why the Member often tries to question a constituent for himself in as systematic a way as possible to sort out the facts of a case presented to him in the style of this imaginary, but fairly typical, example of a letter to a Labour Member which concerns a dispute or misunderstanding between a private landlord and his statutory tenant:

Dear Sir,
    I hope you will allow me to write to you as a lifelong resident of the town and who has been in the union and dyed-in-the-wool Labour all my life and so are my children too because this new landlord is enough to make a saint swear and my wife gets so worried every time they send this chap round to find fault and it upsets her so she worries about the doctor telling her to take it easy as well as the thing about the house and the rent.
    The rent tribunal told us in 1948 and we went to them again about six year ago that we were in the right about them putting in a larder but now he says it's an extra 2/6d a week for the bath although we said years back we would take on the decorating side if they'd put us in the bathroom.
    And now this new chap he's a bit more civil than the other one was says it's all to do with a letter we got last Christmas from a solicitor but we never did and we've got no dog to eat the letters up before we get to them. So please help me tell this new company what I told the other landlord about this

because if it goes on like this my wife can't stand it and I don't know what'll happen.

The postbag on national affairs

There are national 'public opinions' on British relations with Nepal, Manchester taking water from Ullswater, the farm-gate price of milk and the supply of engineering apprentices. MPs receive some letters and much printed material offering opinion and information on hundreds of issues which count as national, however small or sectionally-based that issue may seem to be. They are national issues – albeit of a minor kind – because the people who care about them may live anywhere in Britain and because the promotion of their particular cause lies with the Government, in part at least: that is why they give their views to MPs.

Concentrating first on individual letters which appear at least to be directed specifically to an individual MP, we asked our respondents to say, if they could, how many such letters they received from outside their own constituencies.

Two-fifths of the Members answering this question could not offer any average estimate because variation is too great. Of the others, about two-fifths said they received fewer than ten.

There is some evidence here that Labour MPs receive more individual letters from outside their constituencies than do Conservatives, which may indicate the tendency for some people and organisations to write to government supporters in the hope of their more readily influencing Ministers. Another speculation, based on our study of Members' actual postbags, is that Labour Members receive more 'ideological' letters, possibly from party supporters who wish to discuss national issues or express enthusiasm or disappointment at what they see as the Labour Government's policies. Further analysis shows a trend for these letters to increase with a Member's years of service. It is possible that the longer an MP serves the greater chance he has of being identified by the public with particular issues, or types of issues, based on his record of activity in previous years.

Letters on national affairs are clearly not a major item for most Members. Very many Members said of their own accord that this flow is small unless a Member becomes involved in some issue which attracts publicity or unless there is a national campaign on, such as the battle over the Abortion Act, 1967. Two Members (one in each main party) told us they received very few of these letters because they were silent in the House. The inference of this statement is that publicity, and thus letters, would flow to them if they simply spoke more often in the House, but that would in fact depend upon whether the mass media chose to report their remarks. One Opposition front-bench spokesman said that although his appearances on radio and TV generated letters, this was not true of his speeches in the House. A back-bench Labour Member on the other hand recounted how she had received so much national correspondence after raising a very 'popular', although controversial, matter in the House that she had been deterred from doing so again, preferring instead to try to press her case with Ministers in personal conversations. The difference in the apparent role of speeches or Questions in the House is plain: this front-bench spokesman happens to speak for the Conservatives on a subject which is even further away from everyday life than is political debate on matters such as housing and health, while the lady Member had raised an issue on which probably every person feels qualified to pass an opinion. The popular and general news media ignore the one topic and splash the other. The House is a news source and not (except for Hansard whose readership is not what it was) a mass medium for news; Members are totally dependent on the editorial decisions of the media on which of their activities will interest the public, and only a continuous (or nearly so) radio or television broadcast of parliamentary proceedings direct to the country would allow the House to escape these editorial judgements.

Members therefore attract letters from the country as a whole by being active on an issue which the media think worth covering. The effect of such activity can last a long time once the association is made in the mind of people who make up the public opinion on that issue. Any MP whose Private Member's Bill gets at least a second reading may expect to receive some letters from people affected by that branch of the law for years afterwards – often people whose own personal concern for the topic may post-date the Bill but who have been studying the subject's history and background because they now find themselves involved. For the most part, however, the reaction to a Member taking a position on an issue and gaining publicity by so doing is fairly quick and short-lived after the Member ceases his activities, or ceases to get publicity for them.

An example of the major generation of letters by public activity is Duncan Sandys' national campaign to restore hanging in certain cases of murder. During the winter of 1967–68, Mr Sandys send a long standard letter together with a memorandum to every weekly newspaper in England, Scotland and Wales and saw it published widely. It described his petition to Parliament for the restoration of capital punishment and offered general and statistical arguments in its support. He wrote that he had received 'a vast number of letters expressing agreement, many of them enclosing cheques or postal orders' and concluded, 'those who wish to help should write to me at the House of Commons'.

Mr Sandys' exercise was, of course, purely political, in aid of his legislative aim: the only 'information' he could draw from it was the simple number and opinions of his correspondents on the subject as people could hardly tell him of murders they had known about which official statistics did not cover. Normally however the Member does stimulate letters in the hope that they will reveal not only the existence of citizens who agree with him but also new facts and examples which he will use as ammunition. There are frequent examples in Hansard of Members' claiming that their postbag reveals public concern on an issue along the lines similar to the Member's own concern.

Although a very large number of Members mentioned to us that their appearance on TV or a story about them in a national daily newspaper or (for a different or narrower milieu of potential correspondents) a letter by them in *The Times* would always produce a certain number of letters from different parts of the country, the main factor in the fluctuation which characterises this kind of post is the rise and fall of national campaigns on certain issues. We were very fortunate to survey backbenchers during the climax of the 1966–67 campaigns on abortion. As David Wood of *The Times* described it (27 January 1967):

The voice of the people has been coming through to Westminster very stridently for six months, with all the signs of energetic organisation by Roman Catholic guilds and groups and by the Society for the Protection of Unborn Children on one side, and the Abortion Law Reform Association in the forefront on the other.

The 'quality' of abortion letters varied from the very closely argued to the very stereotyped, some of which bore signs of being copied out under the guidance of an opinion leader. These stereotyped letters are one degree of individuality above the 'printed postcard' campaign (where people merely add their name and address to a printed and paid message card and send it to Members) which in turn is itself only a little different form of the traditional, but still quite popular, parliamentary petition.

Members are, we believe, very much influenced in their view of a campaign by the size of any 'quality' element it may have. Reported comments on abortion show how often Members distinguish between the original, or, at least, reasoned, letter and the simple, rather stereotyped assertion of opinion. There are dangers in dismissing uneducated letter-writers or balancing them off in a ratio of five or ten to one against a closely reasoned and reasonable letter on the other side of the issue. We formed the impression during our interviews that many Members were doing this when assessing their post on the abortion issue. To some degree it is a natural and reasonable reaction, but a Member's attitude may be based simply on his boredom with repetitive and unoriginal messages. It is as well to remember that an ill-educated constituent is just as capable as an articulate one of withholding his vote at the next general election. This comparison between the two individuals is not affected by the general reality that few British voters do seem, in fact, to apply such personal sanctions, preferring usually to vote for the Government they want rather than reviewing their MP's record on non-partisan issues. Because the petition, group letter or printed postcard is the rather public or collective approach usually adopted by most people, it does not follow that they feel less strongly than the person who sits down at home to write a reasoned, individual letter.

One kind of letter-writing campaign on national issues is in a class by itself. Occasionally, all or some MPs receive handwritten letters from a single person; they are understandably fairly uncommon but during our analysis of Members' postbags we saw a handwritten card and a similarly-produced letter appearing in the postbags of several Members simultaneously. The postcard called for 'England for the English' and denounced Celtic hegemony, as finally revealed by the moving of the Mint to South Wales, while the letter offered a message from God warning that the Yellow Peril would overwhelm Britain if she failed to mend her ways.

The letter-writing campaign to Members merges gradually with the more impersonal material they receive. The pure stereotyped letter, following an identical form, or an obviously organised variation of wording, is next in a scale of 'quality' to the printed postcards we have mentioned. One Member told us he had entirely discounted the signing and posting of printed and paid postcards protesting against the breathalyser tests by customers in some of his constituency's pubs who had picked them up from the counter, on the grounds that 'they came from the licensed victuallers, not from my constituents' – a course which may, as we have noted, have its dangers.

Beyond the printed postcard campaign lie the many kinds of obviously impersonal material on many aspects of national affairs.

We asked Members their 'general opinion of the printed and published material you get sent from organisations, firms, embassies, etc.'. Members gave the hostile answers we expected, but with an undercurrent of acceptance or even welcome for those items which any particular Member finds interesting. Three-quarters of our 107 respondents thought the sending of these circulars and printed items to them was largely or completely a waste of both the organisation's money and the Member's time. But one-third of the Members agreed that they found some of these items useful sources of knowledge in their own special fields of interest. About one-fifth of the Members were solidly against the whole business and little more than one-eighth were in favour of it, offering a general welcome to circulars on any subject.

Party differences on this matter while not sharp, are interesting: a few more Conservatives than Labour Members are really hostile to this flow of material but more Labour Members gave a critical tone to their overall attitude by declaring that circulars are largely but not wholly a waste of time and by being less likely than Conservatives to say they welcome them generally. It is important to note that in spite of Labour Members' objecting to circulars as largely a waste of time, notably more of them said they found them useful in their special fields: a possible confirmation of Labour MPs being more 'specialist-minded'. Only a couple of Conservatives said flatly that they had no view because their secretaries dealt with all routine post but their position was in effect shared by a limited group of Members (mainly, but certainly not entirely Conservatives) who clearly did not now bother with this post but who perhaps remembered the days when, lacking a secretary, they had been obliged to do so and thus offered us an opinion on it. It may well be that the rather more favourable attitude to circulars among Conservatives is due to their seeing only those in their special fields which they have told their secretaries to retain, without having to bother with the rest. On the other hand, many Members told us in passing that it is little trouble to throw away the 95 per cent they do not want since they recognise the wrappers of the unwanted regular items and discard them unopened.

Apart from the differences between parties, we also found some differences in respect of parliamentary service. Longer-serving Members generally were more likely to say that circulars are a complete waste of time and money, this being the view of more than a quarter of our respondents with nine or more years of service in the House. Looking at education, the diversity of views among graduate MPs is aptly illustrated by their great hostility compared with non-graduates to the indiscriminate nature of much of the material which MPs receive: they are more likely as a group to feel that the organisations concerned should become more selective among Members. Yet more graduates than non-graduates said that they welcomed circulars generally.

Two-fifths of our respondents thought that the circulars which fell within their special interests were excellent or well-presented and a similar proportion felt that the quality varied considerably. Less than an eighth regarded such material as being generally poorly presented. MPs' views can be summed up by saying that they are really rather hostile to the aggregate flow of printed and duplicated material which a large number of organisations of many different kinds believe it worth while to post to them. This general irritation is however significantly neutralised by Members' welcome for a mere handful of the stuff they get which they do find useful.

Although 'lack of selectivity' and of 'a personal touch' was probably the most common complaint among our respondents, there was also a general feeling that these printed circulars and brochures did not offer what we have earlier called 'facts about situations' so much as information about the organisation's opinion of that situation. There is very little 'pure' information to be had in politics and it is not surprising that the messages sent to MPs by organised interests at some trouble and expense should contain those interests' views as well as basic facts about the situation in question. It is, of course, the essential doctrine of good public relations that arguments should not be thrust at the person to be influenced, nor blatantly selected facts disguised as the objective truth.

There is clearly a need felt by Members for some of the material sent them by organised interest groups. Most of this flow is wasted but a little of it is read and perhaps kept at least for a time. If it comes at the right time it can be turned to by some Members with particular gratitude to help them form a judgement. The major Private Members' Bills often present MPs with decisions which they feel they should take but which they have not thought much about in the past. One such matter current during our interviews was the so-called 'social clause' of the Abortion Bill which the House had to consider and decide upon on the Bill's report stage, after its long period in the standing committee. The clause provided that a woman could legally claim an abortion if two doctors certified that the extra child's presence in the family would prejudice her ability to cope with her existing children and generally damage their family environment: no specific medical or mental risk to the safe delivery of the unborn child was necessary to this decision. Several Members we spoke to wanted information on the social background to this proposal unadorned with the general philosophical or religious arguments on abortion with which they were by this stage of the Bill thoroughly familiar. They seemed to be unsatisfied with the material they received from the main abortion protagonists and the main latecomers on the scene, the organised gynaecologists. These Members' difficulty points towards the House of Commons Library as a potentially better source of impartial advice on how a fair judgement of the 'social clause' of that Bill may have been made – assuming, of course, that the 'relevant social facts' of such a morally taxing question are available which on this matter was hardly the case. Where facts are limited the exchange of opposing opinions tends to increase to take their place.

Although the 'rationality' and 'efficiency' of the modern processes of trying to influence the thinking and perceptions of Members of Parliament leave a great deal to be desired, there is of course no question of people and organised groups being free to send their material as often and in whatever form they like. Members, for their part, are free to ignore it but they may conceivably run into political trouble if they do. Judging from our interviews, we would expect all Members to accept that they should be open to information and influence from anybody – provided they do not have to reply in a way which would reveal whether or not they have studied what they were sent. The contrast with the letter allegedly sent to Anthony Henley in 1727 is almost complete:

Gentlemen:

I received yours and am surprised by your insolence in troubling me about the Excise.

You know what I very well know, that I Bought you. And I know, what perhaps you think I don't know, you are now selling yourselves to somebody Else. And I know what you don't know, that I am buying another Borough.

May God's curse light on you all. May your houses be as open and common to all Excise Officers as your Wifes and Daughters were to me when I stood for your Scoundrell Corporation.

Yours,

Anthony Henley.

A modern Member's letter can be different:

> House of Commons
> London
> S.W.1.

Thank you so much for your kind letter. It was nice of you to write.

I am very glad to know that you agree with the line I have been taking. I have been much encouraged by the many letters of support which I have received from all over Britain and from overseas.

Please forgive me for not answering sooner. But I have been extremely busy just lately, and have had to make one or two journeys abroad.

> With best wishes,
> Yours sincerely,

(Text of a stock, all-purpose reply letter sent by one current MP to people who write giving their support to his political views on any of a number of issues.)

Clearly, the extension of the franchise and the elimination of corrupt electoral practices since 1727 have improved politicians' civility rather than their prose style.

MPs talk about printed circulars and brochures

'I ignore some, such as South African material, but find others, such as from tenants' associations, valuable.' (Labour)

'It's not really worth their sending it because they're not read: they should be selective among Members and send a précis on the front.' (Liberal)

'The things I'm interested in, such as Vietnam, are very valuable, but printed material rarely alters an experienced man's mind when he's held a general view on an issue for years. MPs therefore tend to pick out the things they can use to support their views.' (Labour)

'Most is blatant propaganda and is thrown out, e.g. Chinese and Spanish diplomatic stuff.' (Conservative)

'I'm a strong believer in anybody's right to express themselves to MPs. Nearly all this bumph is open, plain and honest. MPs can tell disguised or dishonest stuff easily.' (Conservative)

'I rate the diplomatic flow of stuff very low although foreign affairs is an interest of mine.' (Conservative)
'The French embassy material is very useful to a foreign affairs specialist like myself.' (Conservative)
'I have a low opinion in particular of the very extravagant stuff. Too much money is spent, for example, on glossy PR for BBC and ITV programmes which an MP is most unlikely to be able to see.' (Conservative)
'We're lumbered with stuff: it's terrible, the waste.' (Labour)
'There's no other way for them to do it. If 5 per cent of MPs are interested in something, it's probably worthwhile to send it.' (Labour)
'Even from the most prominent bodies, such as CBI and the Iron & Steel Federation, the quality can be low and its arrival too late. The Federation should have had a man with us in the standing committee on steel re-nationalisation for instant briefing.' (Conservative)
'It is good that we read what outsiders are saying: it wouldn't do if all or much of MPs reading was specially designed for us.' (Conservative)
'All commercial sources are untrustworthy except the bank reviews, especially Barclays.' (Labour)
'If they could all agree on some standard format, like a Minister's papers, they would get more attention.' (Conservative)
'I always skim the stuff to keep informed: that way I don't have to read books.' (Conservative)
'Receiving this flood of stuff certainly has a psychological impact on MPs and makes them feel important.' (Conservative)
'It's fabulous; stupendous' (Member describing the flow of this material. Pressed for an estimate, he reckoned four to six items per day)
'The large waste paper baskets they give us here are the most important tool of our trade.' (Labour)

4. The MP and his Surgery

By R. E. DOWSE

MUCH of what an MP does is visible to the public. Controversial speeches made in the Commons, for example, are usually widely reported by the Press. In the following article* R. E. Dowse shifts attention from backbenchers' well-documented and frequently reported legislative activities to their constituency activities which are much less evident. Although these rarely attract much attention, Dowse suggests that they are both regularly performed and important in adding a human element to the anonymity of government. In performing services for constituents the MP acts as a link between the people and the government. In his constituency role the MP is, in the words of the author, '... a strategically placed intermediary between people and the executive ... a kind of minor and part-time ombudsman ... (and a) watchdog of liberties and people's welfare'.

Perhaps one of the more abiding and widespread myths of the British constitution is that MPs are, or should be, legislators or the critics of legislators – that is, men and women who either orate on the floor of the House of Commons or else fail in their chosen task. The MP who does not speak regularly is, according to the myth, only half a representative, a fine brute vote, but little else. The Demosthenes complex is used by television and the newspapers to demonstrate that some MPs – those who never or rarely speak – are mute and inglorious failures. A popular television programme singles out thirteen MPs who have held their peace, and *The Guardian* complains that Parliament is 'inefficient' because 'Hundreds of members are kept hanging around the House for large parts of the day, with little or no

---

* Reprinted from *Political Studies*, Vol. 11, 1963, pp. 333-41, with the permission of the Clarendon Press and the author.

THE MP AND HIS SURGERY

chance of being heard in debate'.[1] MPs themselves often speak and write as though legislation and debate were their most important functions. 'Our first task is to legislate, approve the Budget, and generally get through the necessary business. . . . The second main function of the House of Commons is to be the great council – or debating chamber – of the realm.'[2] If this is the case, then clearly the MP who in fact speaks infrequently is neglecting his job! However, it may be that the concept of the MP as a fledgling Draco only waiting an opportunity to legislate and orate, no longer fits the facts. Certainly, it is only a small minority of MPs who speak regularly in the Commons, and among them the predominance of Privy Councillors is evident. At present most MPs are not public legislators in any but the loosest sense, i.e. they quiz and criticise those who are, or, as Professor Harrison has put it, 'Parliament does not so much legislate or administer as ventilate'.[3]

While few commentators would dispute the proposition that most MPs are neither legislators nor frequent orators, it is curious just how little attention is paid to their activities outside the House.[4] It is significant that most textbooks discuss at considerable length the problems of whether an MP is a delegate or

[1] 'That Was The Week That Was', 19 January 1963; *The Guardian*, 13 March 1959.

[2] Philip Goodhart, MP, 'What's Really Wrong with the Commons', *Crossbow*, Vol. 4, No. 10. See also B. Crick, *Reform of the House of Commons* (1959 Fabian Tract), p. 13, 'It is rather depressing to find most MPs view the whole topic of parliamentary reform as simply meaning suggestions as to how to find more time for more members to speak more often on the floor of the House'.

[3] W. Harrison, *Government in Britain* (London: Hutchinson, 3rd ed., 1955) p. 54. See also the volume of *Parliaments* (London: Cassell, 1962) published by the Inter-Parliamentary Union, p. 298, 'The old notion that the "legislature" was the same as Parliament would appear to have gone by the board, for the legislative function is no longer the preserve of Parliament.' If they are debaters and legislators, it is quite probable that the majority are so in the specialised party committees and in the meetings of the PLP and the 1922 Committee; that is, where they are more likely to be effective.

[4] See, for example, H. M. Stout, *British Government* (Oxford U.P., 1953) a book of 400 pages in which two sentences on MPs' visits to their constituencies is all that is needed to cover the subject. Lord Morrison of Lambeth, *Government and Parliament* (Oxford U.P., 2nd ed., 1959) touches briefly on the subject in an epilogue and elsewhere remarks that the Commons is in danger of becoming 'monastic'.

a representative; that is, they discuss those occasions when matters of policy, legislation, and potential conflict are involved and when the MP can be seen in his dramatic role as legislator and critic. This may reflect a preoccupation with the constitution of the late nineteenth and early twentieth centuries when issues of deep principle were held to divide the parties. Today, when differences – in office at least – are frequently of a highly technical nature and speeches about principles are less relevant, it is more appropriate for an MP to devote his attention to *detail* and the *actual* effect of government on people's lives. Not only is this so, but the development of party discipline and the activities of pressure groups has cut away the area in which public debate is desired or is necessary.[5] Further, the development of the welfare state involves the Government far more in the day-to-day life of the country, a circumstance which ensures that the MP will be in constant demand as an intermediary.[6]

Although no attempt will be made to correlate the 'decline' in the oratorical role of the MP with the development of the surgery – with which this paper is concerned – it is not unlikely that there is a connection. My concern is essentially not historical: to describe the extent, nature and implications of the MP's surgery in 1963. The discussion will be based upon a questionnaire which I sent to a random sample of 100 MPs requesting information concerning their surgery activities. Sixty-nine MPs replied as follows:[7]

[5] See Robert E. Dowse and Trevor Smith, 'Party Discipline in the House – A Comment', *Parliamentary Affairs*, Vol. 16, 1962–63, pp. 159–64.

[6] P. G. Richards, *Honourable Members* (London: Faber & Faber, 1959), p. 168. See also W. Crane, 'The Errand Running Function of Austrian Legislators', *Parliamentary Affairs*, Vol. 15, 1961–62. 'Deprived of some of their traditional functions, legislators may devote more to administrative functions which are normally regarded as executive prerogatives.'

[7] Three Conservative MPs wrote declining to answer – they are not included in the 35. For the rest of the paper, I ignore the one Liberal reply. When MPs did not answer a question I have excluded them from the tables. The percentage response was high for a mail questionnaire; however, anything short of a 100 per cent response may indicate an element of bias. In the results, prima facie, the non-respondents do not seem to fall into any particular group, e.g. Front Benchers, rural constituencies, etc., and it seems reasonable to assume that what bias may exist does not seriously vitiate the conclusions. Although not the most ideal method of investigation – it is not foolproof or watertight – the mail questionnaire is nevertheless useful in this

TABLE 1

	Conservative	Labour	Liberal	Total
Sample	54	45	1	100
Response	35	33	1	69
Percentages	64·8	73·3	100	69

The MPs were also asked whether they held a surgery, and their replies are summarised in the following table.

TABLE 2

	Conservative	Labour
Yes	29	28
No[8]	6	5
Total	35	33
Percentage who do not	20·7	17·9

The MPs were asked how constituents raised matters with them; they were given four methods and asked to rank these in order of importance. The methods were as follows: (*a*) by letter; (*b*) through the local party organisation; (*c*) by arranging individual appointments; (*d*) by surgery. As might have been expected the majority in both parties regarded (*a*) as the most important – 31 of 35 Conservatives and 18 of 33 Labour MPs.[9] Only those replies where (*a*) was put first were analysed for second choice: 58 per cent of the Labour and just under 26 per cent of Conservative MPs put (*d*) as their second choice. Of the remainder who did not put (*a*) as their first choice, 10 of the 15 Labour chose (*d*) and 1 of the 4 Conservative MPs chose (*d*). Thus of the 35 Conservatives (just under 26 per cent) ranked (*d*) as first or second choice and 64 per cent Labour did the same.

---

type of research. The 100 were selected as a systematic random sample from the alphabetical list of MPs in Dod's *Parliamentary Companion* (1962).

[8] Two of the six Conservative and one of the Labour MPs who do not hold surgeries used to do so, but discontinued them since they were badly attended.

[9] See Sir Ivor Jennings, *Parliament* (Cambridge U.P., 2nd ed., 1957), p. 27. The larger percentage of letters to Conservative MPs is probably to be accounted for by the higher educational level and literacy of Conservative voters. One Conservative MP remarked that 'those who attend [surgery] are mainly ill-educated'.

That Labour MPs as a group are consulted more by their constituents in surgery than are Conservative MPs probably arises from the greater difficulty that the average Labour voter must have in writing letters.[10] This difference between the parties' attitude to surgeries was reflected in some of the comments and experiences offered by their respective MPs. On the whole, of those MPs who did hold surgery, Labour MPs were more likely to write positively of their value. One Labour MP wrote that 'after seventeen years as an MP I am fully convinced of the value of "surgery"' and many others echoed this sentiment, but a more typical Conservative response was 'Don't overstress its importance'.

Since criticism has been directed at MPs for holding their surgeries in party offices, the questionnaire asked them where they were held.[11] They replied as follows:

TABLE 3

	Conservative No.	Per cent	Labour No.	Per cent
At MP's home	2	5·1	3	8·3
In local party office	29	74·4	23	63·9
In local government premises	8	20·5	10	27·8
Total	39	100	36	100

Quite clearly the overwhelming number of surgeries are held in party offices with local government premises coming a poor second. Although it would be perhaps asking a great deal for MPs to disassociate themselves completely from the party when helping constituents, it would probably encourage more people to use the MPs' surgery.[12]

The replies to the questionnaire indicated no positive correlation between the holding of surgery and the MPs' majority or

[10] The assumption that Labour MPs are consulted mostly by Labour voters is borne out in Table 5.
[11] Where more than one venue was indicated I have counted each as one, hence, there are more venues than respondents who actually hold a surgery. 'Neutral' premises, such as House of Commons or WVS offices have been included under the heading 'local government premises'.
[12] Thus one MP wrote that he was consulted more by people who voted for him because he held his surgery in the party political club.

THE MP AND HIS SURGERY

the distance of his constituency from London. Fifty per cent of Labour MPs were in unsafe seats – those with a majority of less than 5,000 in 1959 – but less than 15 per cent of all Labour MPs did not hold surgeries. Twenty-two per cent of Conservative MPs were in unsafe seats, but only 17 per cent of all Conservative MPs did not hold surgeries. Clearly MPs were not simply vote-hunting. It was plain that MPs hold them if there was felt to be a demand. By far the most frequently mentioned figure was once a fortnight and for as long as necessary – usually available for about two to three hours. This was true both of Conservative and Labour MPs. Hence the somewhat cynical explanation for constituency nursing suggested by Sir Ivor Jennings, that a 'few hundred votes' may be important is by no means the most appropriate.[13] In order to 'test' such a viewpoint the MPs were asked whether they thought that surgery work won them votes.[14] They replied:

TABLE 4

	Conservative		Labour	
	No.	Per cent	No.	Per cent
Yes	9	29·0	8	26·7
A few	1	3·2	2	6·7
No	13	41·9	14	46·6
Don't know	8	25·9	6	20·0
Total	32	100	30	100

One of the interesting aspects about the replies to this question was the evident embarrassment felt by MPs of both parties in answering it – (Conservatives) 'not concerned', 'electors like to think an MP is available', 'This is not the purpose of surgery', 'I regard this work as genuine "social" work'; (Labour) 'in-

[13] *Parliament* (2nd ed., 1957), pp. 26–7. He later hints, p. 28, that such activities have more to do with satisfying the 'political views, personal needs and ambitions' of 'the active party members'. Richards, op. cit., pp. 164–5 remarks 'it is quite wrong to suggest that members bestir themselves to deal with the problems of electors out of a shrewd calculation of advantage; willingness to give service to others is a traditional feature of the public life of this country'.
[14] It will be noticed that MPs in each party who *did not* hold surgeries expressed opinions on their value as 'vote catchers'.

directly', 'at least it holds your support', 'elections are decided on other issues', 'possibly I lose some from people I am unable to agree with or help'. It was quite clear that the main motive was the genuine desire of MPs to win public esteem and to be of service to their constituents. Further evidence that this was so came in response to a question 'Do you think you are consulted more by people who voted for you than voted against you?'[15] Their answers are tabulated in the following table:

TABLE 5

	Conservative		Labour	
	No.	Per cent	No.	Per cent
Yes	9	29·0	19	63·3
No	4	12·9	3	10·0
Don't know	18	58·1	8	26·7
Total	31	100	30	100

MPs of both parties were clear that they would never ask attendants how they voted: (Conservative) 'I never ask them about their political opinions', 'Have no idea', 'Difficult to say'. (Labour) 'Not known', 'The political point is seldom raised', 'No means of knowing'. However, the startling difference between the Labour and Conservative answers to this question, despite their virtual agreement on whether or not surgery wins votes, suggests prima facie that Conservative MPs either take more of a 'constituency' view than a 'party' view of attendants than do Labour MPs and that they are more committed to the 'one nation' theory than are their Labour colleagues, or that class is not such a sure indication of propensity to vote Conservative as it is for a Labour voter. A Conservative MP would be much less sure that a working-class attendant voted Labour than would a Labour MP that the same person voted Labour. The rough breakdown of working-class votes – 30 per cent Conservative, 70 per cent Labour – would add a distinct element of uncertainty to a Conservative MP's assessment.[16] Yet the possibility must be emphasised that Labour

[15] Some MPs who did not hold surgeries took this question to mean any type of consultation – their answers have been included.
[16] See Mark Abrams' table in *The Future of the Welfare State* (Conservative Political Centre, 1958).

MPs might interpret any dissatisfaction felt by surgery attendants with present arrangements as an indication of a pro-Labour voter. However, a certain amount of evidence suggests the plausibility of assuming a Conservative bias towards the 'one nation' thesis.

MPs were asked to name the two most frequent matters about which they were consulted; the results were as follows:[17]

TABLE 6

	Conservative		Labour	
	No.	Per cent	No.	Per cent
Agriculture	2	3·4	—	—
Housing	27	46·6	28	51·8
Pensions	16	27·6	19	35·2
Education	1	1·7	—	—
Planning	3	5·2	2	3·7
Personal	5	8·6	5	9·3
Local Government	4	6·9	—	—
Total	58	100	54	100

Clearly the two items Housing and Pensions are by far the most important problems, and, probably the table underemphasises their significance in that Planning and Local Government might well include items covered by Housing. It is not unlikely that a considerable majority of the attendants bringing Housing and Pensions problems to their MPs are, in fact, working-class, since such problems are mainly concerned with the working class.[18] The suspicion that this 'blindness' actually springs from intellectual presuppositions concerning one nation – the end of the class struggle signalised by the 1959 general election – is also suggested by the answers given to the question 'Do you think that more of your surgery attendants are middle or working class?' They replied:

[17] Although asked to name only two problems many MPs gave more, and in that case only the first two given have been used. A few MPs simply wrote 'varies' – these have not been included.

[18] See W. Crane, op. cit., who mentions that 40 per cent of the Austrian Socialist Party respondents placed health and welfare as constituents' problems compared with 23 per cent Peoples Party (roughly Conservatives). Their major problems were health and housing.

TABLE 7

	Conservative No.	Per cent	Labour No.	Per cent
Middle class	5	17·2	—	—
Working class	14	48·3	25	89·3
Don't know	1	3·4	1	3·6
Equally	9	31·0	2	7·1
Total	29	100	28	100

The Conservative MPs are, perhaps, consulted by an unusually high proportion of middle-class people with pension and housing problems or they are more 'class blind' than their Labour counterparts. However, the explanation of the higher percentage for Labour MPs in Table 7 could be that they are apt to assess a wider variety of people as working class than are Conservative MPs.

It is extremely likely that some of the difference in assessment of class arises from the objective fact that Conservative constituencies are on the whole more middle class than Labour constituencies and on that basis alone one might have expected a larger middle-class attendance at surgery. And, of course, the reverse is true. Yet it is not impossible that a bias in the figures of attendants results from the consideration that middle-class Conservative voters in Labour seats might prefer to take their housing problems to Conservatives on the local council. Equally, it is not impossible that working-class Labour voters in Conservative-held seats take their housing problems to Labour councillors. However, the same can hardly be true of pensions – a concern of the central government – where there is equally close inter-party agreement. That Conservative MPs are more prone to dismiss class considerations is suggested by some of the remarks made in answering the question. 'I find it very hard to define class', 'It is impossible to make hard and fast distinctions between the middle and working classes', 'I am not sure who is middle or working class', 'One simply hasn't time to be bothered with such distinctions'.[19]

Since the MP is concerned with the state of public opinion, the problems of his constituents and no doubt wishes to have an intimate knowledge of the effect that legislation has on people's

[19] A few Labour MPs also dismissed the question.

lives, it was felt that the surgery would be one method of keeping a finger on the public pulse. In order to test whether MPs saw their surgery from this point of view, they were asked whether their surgery work helped them to get 'the "feel" of the electorate'. They replied as follows:

TABLE 8

	Conservative		Labour	
	No.	Per cent	No.	Per cent
Yes	17	58·6	19	65·6
No	8	27·6	5	17·2
Don't know or doubtful	4	13·8	5	17·2
Total	29	100	29	100

Again no substantial difference of emphasis between the parties emerged from this question, but the affirmative answers of the Labour MPs were couched a little more strongly than were those of their Conservative colleagues. Many Conservatives replied in such terms as 'only a little', while Labour respondents were more likely to answer 'definitely', or 'it shows where the shoe pinches'. The only difference of any substance to emerge concerns the greater percentage of Conservatives who considered that surgery gave them no insight into the electorate and its problems. It is quite possible that this would arise from the fact that, as the governing party, they might consider problems of housing and pensions as atypical of the electorate. This was perhaps what was in the mind of one Conservative MP who wrote that 'those who come cannot be regarded as representative of the electorate' and probably of another who replied 'Emphatically *not*, they are unusual'. Quite possibly, as members of the Opposition, Labour MPs are liable to regard people with such problems as pensions and housing as *typical* of the electorate.

Such a consideration might have led to the expectation that Labour MPs would regard their surgeries as a potential source of irritating questions rather than as focus of problems which can best be solved behind the scenes! It was in order to test such an assumption that MPs were asked 'How many times in the previous two years has a matter brought to your attention in surgery led to a question in the House of Commons?' If Labour

MPs, that is *Opposition* MPs, were motivated mainly by a desire to criticise the Government, they would probably attack it in public more frequently – on the basis of cases coming up in surgery – than would Conservatives.[20]

TABLE 9

	Conservative No.	Per cent	Labour No.	Per cent
1 Never	13	44·9	4	14·3
2 Rarely (1–10)	12	41·4	16	57·1
3 Frequently (more than 10)	3	10·3	6	21·4
4 Don't know	1	3·4	2	7·1
Total	29	100	28	100

Clearly there is a difference in the attitude of Labour and Conservative MPs to asking public questions in the House, but the difference may be between Opposition MPs and Government MPs (or Front-Benchers). What does emerge from the answers of MPs and more particularly Conservative MPs is that in general they regard a question as the desperate last possibility rather than the first resort. Many of the MPs who gave extended answers to this question pointed out that a letter to the appropriate Minister was the most effective way of obtaining redress or help with problems. It was quite evident that, as one respondent put it 'I do not put down a question unless the correspondence [with the Minister] has failed to satisfy me'. The position was, indeed, admirably summed up by the Conservative MP who wrote 'When I became a Member, I was told by an experienced Member that if I wanted my name in the papers, I should ask a question, but if I wanted something done, I should write to the appropriate Minister'. It surely says a very great deal for the average MP that he obviously attaches far more importance to obtaining redress or help for his constituents than to personal advantage or scoring party points.

[20] There was difficulty in tabulating the answers to this question since MPs sometimes wrote 'several', 'infrequently' or 'rarely'. Where they used such 'weak' expressions I have included them under 'rarely (1–10)'. Where they used 'stronger' adjectives such as 'often' or 'frequently' I have put them in column 3 – 'Frequently (more than 10)'.

Since the MP does observe a decent reticence and does genuinely attempt to help his constituents by writing letters to the appropriate Minister, it is clearly a 'good thing' that Lord Morrison's view, that 'It [is] not reasonable to regard correspondence with Ministers as a proceeding in Parliament',[21] was rejected on 30 July 1958 by the Home Secretary. Today, as a consequence of the Home Secretary's assurance, letters of MPs to Ministers are protected by 'qualified privilege'.[22] It might be suggested that absolute privilege be extended at least to the MP's covering or explanatory letter and that the constituent's letter or case be granted qualified privilege. This would at least completely protect all MPs equally and remove the cause of Lord Attlee's suspicion that juries were too ready 'without any evidence, to find malice in the action of a Labour MP.'[23] Another obvious advantage of such a reform is that it would foster and protect a part of political life which is of such importance to those sections of the community who need an MP's assistance.[24] Moreover, as Lord Morrison himself suggested, it is often possible for an MP to phrase a constituent's grievance in non-libellous terms;[25] but there is no obvious reason why the MP should be liable at all.

That MPs as a whole do attach considerable importance to redress of grievance and constituency welfare work is evident from the amount of time spent on surgery. Asked how often they held surgery, the answers were as follows:

---

[21] Morrison, op. cit., p. 360 for a discussion of the 'Strauss Case'.

[22] See Richards, op. cit., pp. 265–6 for an excellent and concise account of the doctrine of qualified privilege. Very briefly, the present position is that qualified privilege is vitiated as a legal defence if malice can be proved. K. C. Wheare in *The Listener*, 12 March 1959, argued 'it seems to me better to err on the side of more immunity rather than of less. It will be difficult, if not impossible for an MP to take up grievances or allegations brought to his notice by constituents, if his immunity from proceedings in the court is to be narrowly interpreted', p. 443.

[23] *Fabian Journal*, November 1958.

[24] This is true both of Conservative MPs who deal mostly with letters and correspondence and of Labour MPs who attach more importance to personal contact. Further, if it is true that, as many MPs pointed out, a letter to the Minister via the MP is the best way of getting things done, it is surely absurd to make the forwarding of a letter hazardous?

[25] Op. cit., p. 361.

TABLE 10

	Conservative	Labour
Once a week	3	5
Once a fortnight	7	7
Every three weeks	3	1
Once a month	8	7
As necessary (rarely, etc.)	6	7
Total	27	27

Once again, the major point that emerges from the survey is the relatively unimportant difference between Conservative MPs who do hold a surgery and Labour MPs who do the same. The motives of MPs in holding surgery and engaging in constituency welfare work have already been briefly touched upon, but the role of the MP *vis-à-vis* the attendants at surgery has not been mentioned. Richards, while rightly stressing the formal aspects – that an MP cannot win preferential treatment for a case, but he can ensure that the decision taken was intended – neglects the more personal dimension of the relationship.[26] No doubt the visitors to surgery are mainly the 'hard cases', those whose problems cannot easily be 'solved', yet surgery is not merely a one-way communication–visitor–MP–Department. In surgery the person who is rarely heard in public, who is a spokesman for nobody but himself, is heard and hears: as one Labour MP put it 'Surgery provides an insight into people's lives and problems', and even if nothing can be done 'people find it helpful to know *why* nothing can be done and how governmental machinery works'. This aspect of surgery, the exchange of information, was emphasised by another MP who spoke of it 'as an essential link in democratic self-government'.

Whether or not the choice for the British public is between MPs as 'welfare workers or senators' is a matter of opinion.[27] What is hardly open to serious dispute is that the present chaotic 'system' leaves the MP with the worst of both choices: he can hardly be a serious 'senator' lacking, as he does, the most elementary research assistance and accommodation. Yet, he cannot be a 'welfare worker' without some sort of trained

[26] Op. cit., p. 169.
[27] Miss Joan Quennell, MP, cited in the *Observer*, 17 March 1963.

assistance and, possibly more important, the scrapping of the Demosthenes complex. That the British MP is now, albeit for different reasons, almost as assiduous a 'fence-mender' as the American Representative is plain and should be recognised.[28] Arguments such as those of Earl Attlee that the present 'system whereby many MPs spend the bulk of their weekends dealing with constituency cases is a bad one', are simply irrelevant.[29] The facts are that they do so and will continue to do so: also, the 'present' system is ludicrously chaotic. Further the bulk of informed opinion does not lie behind Earl Attlee, and the condemnation of a relatively new development in the function of MPs smacks of the social-democratic conservatism remarked upon by Dr Hanson.[30] The question is not one of end or mend, since surgery and intervention spring from much deeper causes than Attlee recognises, but rather one of bringing about a measure of coherence and order.[31]

At present an MP if he or she is lucky, has some secretarial assistance in the constituency and this enables a preliminary sorting out of problems, but it is clear that a great deal more is required. It is, for instance, obvious that if an MP is not to be completely immersed in 'social' work, a trained social worker is needed to help with the problems brought to him.[32] Equally clearly, many of the surgery attendants bring problems which are within the ambit of local government – housing – and for such cases it is probably best that a local councillor be present. As the system operates at the moment it is entirely within the discretion of the MP whether a councillor attends or not, but,

[28] For a sociological discussion of the American system see Edward Shils 'The Legislator and His Environment', *University of Chicago Law Review*, Vol. 18, No. 2.

[29] *Fabian Journal*, November 1958.

[30] See, for example, Nigel Nicolson in *Crossbow*, Vol. 4, No. 10, 'He [Attlee] would not find many present members to agree with him'. Crick, op. cit., argues 'Everything is so geared towards the business of carrying on central government that the public is actually reprimanded for wasting the time of MPs.' For A. H. Hanson's views, see his cyclostyled address to the 1963 Political Studies Conference, p. 1.

[31] That some sort of reform is needed is evident from a comment by one MP who wrote that 'I can no longer spare the time to do real justice to this very important semi-welfare work'.

[32] Mr Richard Marsh, MP, has recently suggested that a social worker should be attached to small groups of MPs.

while it cannot be made compulsory that a councillor be present it is plain and in the interest of both MP and council that they work in closer liaison.[33]

The one conclusion that it is abundantly suggested above all others in this paper is that MPs do not put party considerations first when dealing with grievances and it would, surely, be wise to bring the institutional arrangements for surgery into line with the 'constituency' nature of surgery?

Possibly the best way of doing this would be to make it obligatory for the local council to provide a room within which the MP could hold his surgery. It is, surely, incredible that MPs are actually *refused* such facilities by local councils.[34] Finally, and perhaps most important of all, it is time that both public and MPs recognised the facts of the parliamentary situation. The average MP cannot be regarded and judged solely by the number of speeches he makes or questions he asks: for better or worse the average MP has assumed the role of strategically placed intermediary between people and executive. He is, in a sense, a kind of minor and part-time ombudsman and should be helped to become efficient in this task. Such a reform would have the obvious advantage already stressed, but there is another. If the MP has become relatively weak *vis-à-vis* the executive and if, as has frequently been suggested, the House of Commons cannot be regarded either as a source of policy or as a legislature pure and simple, then the MP's role as the watchdog of liberties and people's welfare would be enhanced by making him an efficient intermediary.

[33] In discussing the 'errand boy' role of local government councillors, Mr Trevor Smith points out that 'overwhelmingly housing' is the main problem brought to their attention. Clearly if the authority studied is typical, the case for a closer association between the local housing Committee and the MP's surgery is strengthened. I am grateful to Mr Smith for allowing me to quote from his forthcoming study of Town Councillors for the Action Society Trust.

[34] One MP stated he had been refused a room by the local council.

5. The Case of Flora Ginetio

A BBC investigation* by ANTHONY KING

'THE Case of Flora Ginetio' was first broadcast on BBC Radio 4 during the Easter recess in 1971 in a series called 'Talking Politics'. As far as the authors of this volume are aware, it is the only really full account in existence of the handling of a typical constituency 'case'. Anthony King interviews the various participants in the case from the moment when a constituent came to see her MP at his surgery to the time when, in the words of the MP, 'a little bit of bureaucracy . . . was destroyed'. The case presented here suggests that, although MPs may not be able to influence the content of decisions that Civil Servants and Ministers finally take, they can have a decisive impact in bringing cases like this to their attention because they have more knowledge than the average citizen of the workings of Westminster and Whitehall. In other words, MPs do not directly influence the substance of decisions, but they are able to influence the process by which decisions are taken in a way that may have substantial consequences.

King: I suspect that most of us, when we think of politics, think instinctively of party politics – of sharp differences of opinion, slanging matches, point-scoring, and so on. Most of us, too, when we hear about Members of Parliament probably think of the House of Commons itself and the debates that go on there. But a great deal of politics doesn't involve the parties at all, and a lot of the work of an MP doesn't really have much to do with standing up and making speeches in the House; it goes on whether Parliament is in recess or not. These are important facts about the system of government we have in Britain, and to illustrate them we are going to spend the whole of our time this

---

* Reproduced with the permission of Anthony King. The original radio programme was conceived and produced by Mrs Anne Duncan-Jones.

morning telling a story. A simple story in itself, an interesting one, and we think an important one. Our story involves a Birmingham housewife, a girl from Italy, a Member of Parliament, two Ministers, and three Civil Servants. It is a true story, and of course it has a happy ending.

It all began last autumn. Every fortnight Roy Hattersley, the MP for the Sparkbrook division of Birmingham, holds two surgeries in different parts of his constituency. That is, he does the same as most MPs: he makes himself available at a particular time, and people are free to come along to him with their problems. His visitor one September morning was Mrs Iris Whitehouse, the wife of an inspector in a Birmingham car factory. What was the problem she put to him?

Whitehouse: That we had an Italian girl living with us who had been coming for a number of years, and she wanted to stay in this country, and she'd got to find employment, which she did do. And that she was told that, if she could find employment, she would be given a work-permit to stay in the country. She got the employment. We applied for the work-permit, and it was refused.

King: So you were asking Roy Hattersley to find some means whereby she could be allowed to stay in the country.

Whitehouse: Yes.

King: The girl's name was Flora Ginetio. She was twenty years old. She had no real family in Italy, she had lived most of her life in children's homes of one sort and another, and long before last autumn she had come to think of the Whitehouses' modest semi-detached home in Acocks Green, Birmingham, as her only home. And Mr and Mrs Whitehouse, who already had a daughter of their own, also thought of Flora as a real member of the family. How had all this happened?

Whitehouse: Well, quite a number of years ago, at the school my daughter was attending, the headmistress asked one day if any family would be prepared to give a summer holiday to deprived children in foreign countries. We said we would, and Flora was the child who came to us from Italy. And from that time she came yearly for a summer holiday when possible. When she was seventeen, she was allowed to stay for nine months. Then she had to leave the country because she wasn't allowed to take up employment. She finally returned to us last year, in

July, hoping to stay and take up employment. And that is when the trouble started.

King: In Italy Flora had worked for a time helping to look after mentally retarded children. She liked the work and wanted if possible to do the same kind of thing in Britain. And she was lucky, or so she thought. She was offered a position caring for children at the Warwick House Short-Stay Unit, run by the Birmingham Public Health Department. But then, as Mrs Whitehouse says, the Department of Employment would not give her a work-permit. Why not? We asked Bill Winter, the Department's Midlands Regional Controller.

Winter: She had been allowed originally into the country as a visitor and, when she made the application, my headquarters found that it was a non-residential job and, as things were, they rejected the application on those grounds.

King: So there it was. The Warwick House job was not a living-in job. Therefore, no work-permit. And worse was to follow. Mrs Whitehouse went to see Roy Hattersley in the first place because Flora had been given a fortnight to leave the country.

Whitehouse: That's right, yes. We received a letter from the Home Office in which they said that, as the Department of Employment and Productivity cannot agree to your employment with the City of Birmingham Public Health Department, you should either forward to this department an alternative offer of employment or make arrangements to leave the United Kingdom.

King: What did Mrs Whitehouse think her Member of Parliament could do for her when she went to see him?

Whitehouse: Well, we were sure that somehow he would be able to help us and that, if he couldn't help us, no one could.

King: Why did you go and see your MP? After all, you might have written a letter to the local paper; you might have got in touch with the Home Office yourself.

Whitehouse: Well, it was an instinctive reaction in the family, I think, that we should go to our local MP, who we thought could help.

King: Roy Hattersley thought he *could* help, mainly because he and other MPs have to deal with cases like this all the time. But what about *this* one? When Mrs Whitehouse first told him about Flora, did he think this was a particularly striking case or was it fairly routine?

Hattersley: Well, in one sense all cases are fairly routine in that one has twenty or thirty every week. Indeed one is sitting there four times a month waiting for cases. But in another sense it was more than routine. There was an orphan girl who wanted to do some very important social work in Britain, who had the chance of living with a British family and being, one hopes, happy for the next fifteen, twenty or thirty years, and one little bit of bureaucracy was stopping that from happening. And it seemed rather important to destroy that bit of bureaucracy.

King: Roy Hattersley's first move was to write to the Foreign Office to get an extension on Flora's permission to stay in the country. Within a day or two his letter was on the desk of one of the Foreign Office Ministers, Anthony Royle, the Parliamentary Under-Secretary. And it was Anthony Royle who replied. We asked him how many letters of this sort he got from MPs about constituents' complaints.

Royle: Well, I get quite a number. I knew you were going to ask me this question. I've done some investigation and I discover that over the last four and a half months I've had somewhere in the region of a hundred and twenty. It varies of course from month to month and week to week.

King: The draft answers to the letters Ministers get from MPs are prepared by Civil Servants. But how often does someone like Anthony Royle look at a letter and think 'No, I don't think that's quite right' and send it back to have changes made?

Royle: Oh, quite, quite often. The original drafts are produced by officials in the office and submitted to me, and with the draft comes the file with all the background information on which this draft is based, and I read this extremely carefully. Most of the people one is writing back to are colleagues in the House of Commons whom I know personally, as for instance I know Roy Hattersley personally, and I believe that it is not only courteous but very important that Ministers should take great personal interest in the background to each case, and there are many cases that come to me which I send back, because I'm not satisfied with the draft. They would be redrafted and then I would add on personal comments of my own.

King: But there is one further point. As it happens, Roy Hattersley is a Labour Member of Parliament, indeed an Opposition spokesman on foreign affairs. Anthony Royle is a

Conservative Foreign Office Minister. Does it make any difference to Anthony Royle whether the MP who writes to him is on his own side?

Royle: Not at all. I'm not interested what the party of the Member is. I write back on the facts of the case, and the question of whether he's a Labour Member or a Liberal Member or a Conservative Member doesn't really come into it. People when they become Members of Parliament act on behalf of all their constituents whatever their party politics, and as a Minister writing back to a Member of Parliament who is approaching the Minister on behalf of his constituents, again the fact of party affiliation doesn't enter into it.

King: The funny thing, though, was that in writing to the Foreign Office Roy Hattersley had inadvertently written to the wrong department. He should have got in touch with the Home Office, which deals with immigration and nationality matters. How did he happen to do this?

Hattersley: Simple mistake. I believed the initial application for an immigrant to come into this country, assuming that they're not Commonwealth immigrants, was taken by the Foreign Office, and I frankly wrote to the wrong department.

King: But it was not a serious mistake, since the Foreign Office simply passed the letter on to the Home Office and said that Mr Hattersley could expect to hear from them. And from this point onwards the main characters in our story are Civil Servants. Constitutionally, almost all decisions taken by government departments are taken in the name of, and on behalf of, Ministers of the Crown. But of course Ministers do not begin to have the time to look in detail at every case. They have to rely on the experience and good judgement of their permanent officials. It is the permanent officials who go into the cases in detail and make recommendations to their political masters. The Civil Servant on whose desk Flora's file eventually arrived was John Hamilton, a Senior Principal in the Home Office's Immigration and Nationality Department. We talked to Mr Hamilton in his office in Holborn. By what route had the file reached his desk?

Hamilton: Well, it arrived on my desk after going through a number of offices. Mr Hattersley, as you know, wrote to the Foreign Secretary in the first instance, and when the subject was not one for the Foreign Secretary or his department, the private office of the Foreign Office sent the correspondence to the private office of the Home Office Secretary of State.

King: The private office being the Minister's own personal staff.

Hamilton: Being the Minister's own personal staff, where it would be sorted out as being a matter for the Immigration and Nationality Department to advise and present the facts. The papers would then come to the Immigration and Nationality Department, where the file of Flora would be found from where it would be resting in our registry; and the whole case would then be considered at what one might call an intermediate level and submitted to me for onward transmission to the Minister of State with a recommendation.

King: When the file did arrive on your desk, what roughly was in it?

Hamilton: Obviously there is the correspondence from Mr Hattersley to the Foreign Secretary and the replies which had been sent on behalf of the Foreign Secretary. But there is also our own file on Flora, which goes back some years since she first came here under the auspices of the organisation for helping children. And the subsequent visits that she paid here were all noted and recorded in her file. So that we did have considerable evidence about her background and her association with someone in this country.

King: On the basis of this information, Mr Hamilton decided that, at the very least, Flora could be allowed to stay in Britain until the end of last year. The reason was that . . .

Hamilton: . . . She had in fact been invited to submit another offer of employment which the Department of Employment might approve. But as she had not done so, it seemed reasonable to me in the background of the close connection with the English family for many years that she had a safe home here for a time, that she could be allowed a reasonable time in which perhaps to find employment which the Department of Employment could approve.

King: Who actually took the decision. Yourself or Lord Windlesham, the Minister?

Hamilton: Intrinsically, it must be Lord Windlesham who took the decision, although I should say that, if the case had come to me to deal with in the ordinary way, I would have taken exactly the same decision and I would in fact have taken the decision.

King: In the event, Mr Hamilton drafted a letter for Lord Windlesham, which Lord Windlesham signed and sent off to Roy Hattersley. It said that Flora was being given an extension and suggested that she get in touch with the local office of the Department of Employment in Birmingham. At this point Roy Hattersley could have done either of two things. He could have given Flora news of the extension and, as far as getting a job was concerned, left her to get on with it; or he could get in touch with the Department of Employment on her behalf. He chose to do the latter, but this time, instead of writing to the Minister, Robert Carr, he wrote directly to the Midlands Regional Controller, Mr Winter, a Civil Servant. We asked him why.

Hattersley: Well, for two reasons. One was that I knew Winter, I knew Winter very well, and the second was that we wanted things to move quickly. I knew Winter because I had been Minister in the department in which he served, and it's very sensible, I think, if one knows a local official, one has some *rapport* with him and one is able to talk with him on much more friendly terms, than writing to the rather faceless, and rather amorphous, central ministry in Whitehall.

King: Bill Winter, as Regional Controller, is in charge of a huge organisation covering the whole of the Midlands. He could hardly be expected to help Flora find a job himself. So he did the natural thing: he arranged for her to go and see Mr Bob Cook, the manager of the employment exchange for the Small Heath part of Birmingham where the Whitehouses live. Bob Cook takes up the story.

Cook: The first thing was to find out if we had any details about Miss Ginetio. We hadn't in fact. And we were asked, knowing what had previously happened, whether there were any other suitable vacancies possible for her to take. At that particular moment there were two possibilities. We wrote to her asking her to come in and see us and discuss this. Well, she did so, but some little time later, by which time the matron thought that the vacancy had been filled; this was subject to the selected candidate passing a medical examination. So there was nothing more to be done. A couple of days later we asked the children's home if the vacancy had, in fact, been filled. The answer was no; the candidate had not started work. So at this point we reported to my regional office that the vacancy was still open and asked whether permission could be given for her to take the job.

King: Who dealt with this in your office? Was it yourself or somebody working under you?

Cook: I was told about it in the first place, and I then asked the officer who is in charge of my women's section to deal with it. She found out the facts and interviewed Miss Ginetio herself.

King: Would it have been dealt with at such a high level if the original inquiry hadn't come from an MP?

Cook: Yes, it would because the officer concerned is one of the comparatively few in the office who would be thoroughly familiar with the regulations in such cases and she would need, if not to do the interview herself, certainly to oversee the whole affair.

King: As Mr Cook says, he found that, although by now several weeks had gone by, the position at the Warwick House Short-Stay Unit that Flora had originally been offered, was still vacant. Somebody else had accepted it but then not turned up for work. The matron was getting pretty desperate. So Bob Cook reported the situation to his superior, who concluded that, after all, even though the Warwick House job wasn't a living-in job, Flora should be allowed to take it. First she couldn't have it; now she could. I put it to Bill Winter that he or somebody had a certain amount of discretion.

Winter: We had, I think, discretion in recommendation, in the sense that the matron of the home had had considerable difficulty in filling this job, and the system anyway is flexible, you know, in the sense that if we cannot find people to fill the job, then it is possible for a girl from abroad to take the job. So it's a question really of the regulations, and flexibility, if I may say so, is admirably illustrated in this case.

King: How many cases of this general sort come up?

Winter: Oh, it's very difficult to give any kind of number to this. I think I can say that we do deal with considerable numbers of these cases throughout the year in the West Midlands Region.

King: Who took the final decision? Was the decision taken in Small Heath, in your office, or in London?

Winter: The area of report, if I may call it that, was in the Small Heath Employment Exchange. The area of recommendation was my office, the Regional Office, but the area of decision was in London. In other words, I made the recommendation from here in Birmingham. The decision was taken in London.

King: You know the position here on the ground. Would you take it for granted that most of your recommendations, in this sort of case, would be accepted once they got to London?

Winter: Generally, yes. I think my headquarters realise that we've a great deal of practical people in the regions, who know what they're talking about, and their recommendations are looked at and listened to very seriously.

King: The formal decisions in these matters are taken by senior Civil Servants and ultimately by Ministers in Whitehall. But, as Flora's case makes clear, the permanent officials working with these problems day-to-day do have an enormous responsibility. I asked John Hamilton, when he sits in his office in Holborn, far away from somebody like Flora, how conscious is he that he is taking decisions that are actually going to have a very substantial effect on people's lives?

Hamilton: I don't think that you can do any sort of case work which involves people without automatically thinking about the background of the person and what the information you have on him or her reveals about their background and personality and indeed their present position and predicament. And I think it's true and honest to say that we regard all applicants to us as human beings and members of the public.

King: Does this degree of responsibility ever worry you? Do you find yourself lying awake at night wondering whether you've done the right thing?

Hamilton: Yes, indeed, because so often the balance of public interest and policy against the wishes of an individual may be very finely balanced. If it is as close as that, the interest may be something much more important and, of course, has to be decided at a much higher level than mine.

King: So Flora Ginetio got the work she wanted: working with mentally handicapped children. And she got what she wanted even more: the right to stay and live in Britain. And another typical Home Office/Department of Employment case had been dealt with, to everybody's satisfaction. Flora is working at the moment at the Warwick House centre.

But there is one question you have probably been asking yourself. How lucky was Flora Ginetio? How lucky was she to have as forceful a backer as Mrs Whitehouse? How lucky was she that a Member of Parliament took up her case? I asked Bill Winter in the Midlands Regional Office what would have happened to Flora if she had been on her own in this country, if she had not had a Mrs Whitehouse behind her.

Winter: This is a very difficult question to decide. It is true that in her backer she had an articulate and intelligent champion who did the right thing in going to Mr Roy Hattersley, although, as I said earlier, she could in fact have come to us, and we should have put her on the right lines. But I think it would have been extremely difficult for Miss Ginetio, with her perhaps limited command of English and her limited knowledge of how government departments work, to make her way on her own after having had her original application rejected.

King: But Mrs Whitehouse did go to her local MP. How much difference did it make that Flora's cause was now being championed, not by an ordinary member of the public, but by a Member of Parliament? The Civil Servants we talked to were emphatic that it made very little difference, if any. Bill Winter in Birmingham.

Winter: I don't know that it made a great deal of difference, except that it was very helpful that Mr Hattersley had written to me because I know him and he knows me. But, having said that, I think I ought to make it perfectly clear that, if the case had been brought to our notice through other channels, the result would have been exactly the same.

King: Likewise John Hamilton in London.

Hamilton: I think I can say with complete honesty that there would have been no different decision in this case, whether Mr Hattersley had taken it up or not, provided that a second approach had been made, and indeed it would not have been dealt with at my level; it would have been dealt with at a lower level in the Immigration and Nationality Department.

King: Roy Hattersley, perhaps predictably, is not so sure.

Hattersley: I accept a general view that very often constituents come to their Members of Parliament when they could do the job for themselves, in theory. In practice, of course, it's a great deal easier simply for a Member of Parliament to have a conversation with a bureaucrat than it is for the man in the street. But I think that, as far as this case is concerned, the proof of the pudding is really in Flora's continued presence here. The letter she got said she had to go home. The letter I obtained said she could stay. And I think it's difficult to argue in the face of that that a Member of Parliament's interceding didn't make some sort of alteration in the judgement.

King: What it seems to come down to is this. MPs don't influence the *content* of decisions; they do not have pull or 'influence' in that sense. But they do know their way round Westminster and Whitehall better than the rest of us, and at the very least, when a Member of Parliament intervenes, Civil Servants and Ministers do pay attention. An MP may not get the outcome he wants but, if he raises a problem, he can be sure that it will be taken pretty seriously. And most MPs seem to be convinced that they and their constituents can expect reasonable and fair treatment. I asked Roy Hattersley what he would have done next if the Department of Employment had said that Flora could not have the job she particularly wanted and had also said that there was not another job for her.

Hattersley: It never struck me that the Department of Employment would not find her another job. Had they not done so, I would have gone and seen them, and I would have argued with them pretty fiercely because of my strong views about the nature of the case. Had they continued to refuse, I would have raised it in the House because it would have been the result of a silly bureaucratic mistake, and the Minister would not try to support that kind of mistake. In fact, the fact that I call it a mistake does not imply that I thought the Department would do it; it implies that I was sure the Department would not make that sort of mistake and would find her a job.

King: How much time does Roy Hattersley reckon he spent on the Flora Ginetio case?

Hattersley: It's certainly hours rather than days. It's probably two or three hours. It's an hour in their presence talking to them on three Saturday mornings, twenty minutes each time, it's half a dozen letters written, it's four phone calls made, and it's a few minutes worrying. It's two or three hours.

King: Taking all the time he spends on constituency work, how much does it add up to over the average week?

Hattersley: About two-thirds of my week is done on parliamentary work of one sort or another, most of which is now constituency work. I've got a constituency with a lot of individual problems and therefore I have an uncharacteristically high load of constituency cases, and certainly rather more than three days a week is spent in the constituency doing political things or dealing with individual cases concerning the constituency.

King: Anthony Royle as a Minister puts a lot of effort into answering the letters MPs write on behalf of constituents. We asked him whether, as a member of Her Majesty's Government, he ever gets impatient having to spend so much time on details of this kind.

Royle: Oh no, certainly not. I've been a Member of Parliament for twelve years, and one of the jobs of a Member of Parliament, as indeed one of the jobs of a Minister, is to keep in touch with the public, and if the public have complaints and they come to a minister through a Member of Parliament, it is the duty of a Minister, and a duty which I find interesting and valuable, to make certain that this member of the public receives as much satisfaction as it's possible to obtain.

King: How much time does he have as a Minister to deal with his *own* constituents' complaints?

Royle: Well, quite a lot. I get out to my constituency once a month for advisory sessions, in Richmond, and my constituents come to see me with their worries and I write in the normal way to other colleagues who are Ministers taking up their complaints. After all, a Minister would not be a Minister if he wasn't elected there by his constituents and, naturally, as a Minister one's constituency comes first in one's life. It must always do.

King: Anthony Royle implies that as a Minister he gets no more favourable treatment, as far as his constituency work is concerned, than any other Member of Parliament. Roy Hattersley was until a year ago a Minister himself; now he is a private Member on the Opposition side. Does he feel that the cases he raises are taken less seriously on account of this?

Hattersley: Not on this sort of case at all. Clearly on policy matters which affect one's constituents one has less influence. But on these matters of individual interpretation I have no doubt at all that the Civil Service treat Opposition members and members of the Government with equal fairness. Indeed one of the great difficulties when I was a Minister in the DEP was dealing with Civil Servants who were determined to lean over backwards to give my constituents no greater favours than anybody else. I think it's a great objectivity in the Civil Service and I think it's a very healthy thing.

King: But in the end doesn't all this constituency work, doesn't the writing of all these letters, the holding of surgeries and advisory sessions, boil down to an effort to win votes, to make sure of getting in next time? Roy Hattersley, and I think most MPs, would deny this vigorously. How much, I asked Roy Hattersley, do you think your constituency work is going to help towards your re-election when the time comes?

Hattersley: Very little indeed. My re-election when the time comes depends on the standing of the two parties. I hope I shall poll about nineteen or twenty thousand votes. If two or three hundred of those are the result of my constituency work, I shall have done rather well.

King: Why then does he do the work?

Hattersley: I do the constituency work, not for a political bonus, because there isn't a political bonus in it. I do it because it's part of the job.

King: Part of an MP's job. The non-partisan, non-speech-making, little-publicised part that goes on week in and week out, even when, as last week, Parliament is in recess.

Oh yes, we almost forgot. Flora Ginetio is to be married in June – to a Birmingham boy she first met visiting the Whitehouse family when she was sixteen; so she'll probably be spending the rest of her life in Britain. Roy Hattersley has been invited to the wedding.

6. Whips and Backbenchers

MARTIN REDMAYNE interviewed by NORMAN HUNT

IN this interview* with Norman Hunt, Martin Redmayne, a former Government Chief Whip, reveals a number of ways in which the Whips function as a communication channel between backbenchers and the Government. In addition, Redmayne describes how the Whips' Office is organised so that contact can be kept with each of the party's backbenchers. The former Chief Whip hints at the way backbenchers can shape policy as a result of representations made to the Government by the Whips, and shows the part played by both backbenchers and Whips in October 1963 when Sir Alec Douglas-Home replaced Harold Macmillan as Prime Minister.

Norman Hunt: *The Government Chief Whip is invariably a man of the utmost discretion, for he is privy to so much confidential information. He shares many of the Prime Minister's innermost thoughts; at the same time he has to know the personal views, strengths and weaknesses of all the government supporters in the House of Commons. At times of crisis, as in the Profumo affair, or when the party is evolving a new leader, the Chief Whip's role is often crucial.*

In this conversation the Government Chief Whip, the Rt Hon. Martin Redmayne, reflects on the part he played in these recent moments of high drama and also on the day-to-day nature of his job. I began by asking him which he regards as his more important function – to maintain party discipline or to keep the party leadership fully aware of the views of its own backbenchers.

Martin Redmayne: Certainly the first function must be the flow of information from the backbenchers to the leadership –

---

* Reprinted from *The Listener*, 19 December 1963, pp. 1011–12, with the permission of Norman Hunt and Lord Redmayne of Rushcliffe.

that is either to the Prime Minister or to other ministers, depending on what the subject of any particular comment may be. Discipline really flows from the success with which the first function is performed. You never get discipline unless the backbenchers are happy that the Whips are performing the function of communication properly.

Hunt: How much is it part of your job to explain the policy of the Government to your backbenchers?

Redmayne: The explanation of policy is properly done by ministers. It has always been my habit as Chief Whip to get the minister concerned to talk to the backbenchers who have a complaint or a criticism, because after all he is the man responsible for policy. My job is to see that the two sides are brought together.

Hunt: How are you organised as a Whips' office to do this job of conveying the views of the backbenchers to the Government?

Redmayne: I have thirteen Whips plus my deputy, and each of those has first of all what we call an area – a geographical area of the country in which there are thirty or forty Conservative members. His business is to keep contact with them, and not merely to keep contact with them but to know them so well that he may in emergency be able to give a judgement as to what their opinion will be without even asking them. Then each Whip is allocated to one or more party committees; he keeps in touch with the chairman and the officers of those committees, attends their meetings, and reports to me anything of interest – that is anything that is likely to be the subject of adverse comment. And every Whip in his ordinary round of the House – and they live in the House most of the time when it is sitting – has his own contacts with those who are his friends or those he may dine with, may meet in the smoking room, and so forth. He is always ready to pick up anything which may be useful to the Government – and equally useful to the backbenchers, because no party can succeed unless it works as one in matters of opinion.

Hunt: How much notice does the Government take of the information which they give you and which you pass on to the Government?

Redmayne: A great deal. The Chief Whip sits on various

government committees. He is always there to make comment when asked by the chairman of the committee, maybe the Prime Minister, maybe other ministers. Or, if he thinks that ministers are taking a view which will not be acceptable to the party, then he speaks on his own account. Of course, these things are not always done in committee; as the information flows into my desk, literally hour by hour throughout the day, I frequently write notes to this minister or that, to say that the party or this member, as the case may be, takes this view or that view, and that in my opinion the policy ought to be amended accordingly; and these things are always taken into account. Obviously my suggestion or advice is not always accepted; but it is always taken into account.

Hunt: How much personal access do you have to the Prime Minister?

Redmayne: At any time a Chief Whip can see the Prime Minister, and indeed one of the charming things about Mr Macmillan, as Prime Minister, was that never in the four years in which I served him – and I know this was the same in the case of my predecessor – did he ever show the least sign of annoyance or irritation if I went in with some particular niggling problem, even though he might be busy with things of far greater importance in a national sense.

Hunt: Is it significant in this respect that one of your bases is No. 12 Downing Street?

Redmayne: Yes, I suppose it is; this is traditional. It does mean that I can go to No. 10 unobserved whenever I wish, and this has its advantages.

Hunt: This is because there are intercommunicating doors?

Redmayne: There are in fact intercommunicating doors, yes.

Hunt: How often does the Prime Minister ask you how the backbenchers will react to a particular proposal?

Redmayne: I see the Prime Minister every day; this is routine. He may ask me many things, or if he doesn't ask me, I may tell him that this or that subject is topical, and this or that will be the backbench reaction to it.

Hunt: But have there really been changes in policy as a result of the representations which you have made?

Redmayne: Oh yes, this is constant. I don't think any

advantage is served by my giving you examples of it, but you must accept my assurance that there are changes – though not necessarily major changes, because a government ought to try to put across its policy in a complete form which will be acceptable. That is where half my function comes in, to look for the snags in advance.

Hunt: So you are consulted at the early stages of policy formation to assess the likely views of backbenchers.

Redmayne: The word consulted, I think, puts it in too much detail. As Chief Whip I am there the whole time, and my function is to be there and to be on the watch as best I can – in my limited knowledge and wisdom – to see what the snags are and to point them out.

Hunt: And to say whether future lines of policy are likely to be acceptable to the party?

Redmayne: Just so.

Hunt: When you have a government with a large majority as you have at present, does this produce a situation in which the Government backbenchers have got more influence on government policy than when the Government has only a small majority?

Redmayne: Yes, although I would put it in a slightly different way. There is no question at all that when you have a government with a small majority you get a much more automatic loyalty. I of course, for my sins, have been in the Whips' Office since the Conservative Government started in 1951; and in those days we had a majority of 18, and even the most junior Whip could use the argument: 'Well, old boy, you mustn't rock the boat.' It isn't much use using that argument when you have a majority of 100 because the boat takes a good deal more rocking.

Hunt: So Conservative backbenchers have had more influence on government policy since 1959 than in the years between 1951 and 1959?

Redmayne: Provided the Government wants to listen to its backbenchers, and in recent years it always has done so. I think it is true to say that the larger the majority the greater the power of the opinion of the backbenchers.

Hunt: Under Mr Macmillan's leadership as Prime Minister was he particularly amenable to the views of backbenchers?

Redmayne: He was a great House of Commons man, and delighted in the contacts which he got in the Commons, both in the House and in the smoking room and so forth. He used to be in often and enjoyed it; you could see, even when he was tired, that he blossomed in the House of Commons and therefore his personal contacts were excellent.

Hunt: So here was a Prime Minister much influenced by back-bench opinion?

Redmayne: Certainly, but at the same time with a strong sense of his own duty to govern and to lead.

Hunt: But if, as you say, he was strongly influenced by back-bench opinion, then in this vital question of the Conservative Party leadership that we have been witnessing over the last few months, it didn't seem so much to outsiders that Conservative backbenchers were really having much influence here. For one thing, although a substantial number of Conservative MPs rather earlier in the summer were clearly anxious that Mr Macmillan should resign, these views probably would not have prevailed had it not been for Mr Macmillan's operation.

Redmayne: It is true that we had our troubles during the summer and there has been much criticism on that account. A party gets depressed, and when it gets depressed it shows its feelings in one way or another. One thing is certain in my own mind, that any question of Mr Macmillan's resignation would never have stemmed as it were directly from those pressures because parties don't work in that way, and it would be wrong that they should. But time passed and the question obviously came whether Mr Macmillan should go on or not. I would like to say straightly that if he had announced that he had decided to go on, and had launched again into a drive to re-establish the party's morale before an election, I don't doubt that would have had solid support, unrelated as it were to the discontents and troubles of the summer.

Hunt: So what you're saying in part, then, is that backbenchers perhaps really cannot force out a sitting Prime Minister, even if they want to.

Redmayne: I think from a party point of view they are stupid if they try to do it. They have their tempers, they have their distempers if you like, but any idea that a party can find profit in forcing its leader to resign is nonsensical, and there was never that purposeful offensive thought in the troubles of the summer.

Hunt: You wouldn't say that backbenchers in fact have this amount of power to be able to force their leader out of office?

Redmayne: Of course they have the power. If the backbenchers choose by abstention on a division, or by voting against the Government, on a vote of confidence, of course the Prime Minister, or the Government, in some cases has to resign. What I was saying was that it would be wrong to think that a Prime Minister can be simply forced out by weight of opinion which is not brought actually into real effect by a positive vote in the House.

Hunt: But although in theory they have this power of ousting a government, or a Prime Minister anyway, by a positive vote in the House, there is really no example of it this century, apart from forcing Chamberlain out in 1940?

Redmayne: But it is no good saying 'except for that' because that was an occasion on which a Prime Minister was forced to resign not of course by a vote which was in the end adverse, but by one which was so significant that he could not carry on.

Hunt: But here was an extraordinary crisis affair.

Redmayne: That's perfectly true.

Hunt: You wouldn't expect it to happen except under extraordinary situations?

Redmayne: I would hope not, certainly.

7. The Chief Whip's Clothes

By ANTHONY KING

IN the light of the extraordinary number of back-bench Labour revolts that took place in the Commons from 1966 onwards (these are discussed in some detail by John P. Mackintosh on pages 244–58 below), Anthony King examines* the amount of power that the Whips have over backbenchers, and the bases on which this power rests. He points out that John Silkin, the Government Chief Whip, and Richard Crossman, Leader of the House of Commons, had adopted a self-consciously permissive style of discipline, which led them to being blamed for the Labour revolts: at the time it was said that a tougher style of discipline would bring the revolts to an end, or at least reduce their number. This article was written to counter the suggestion that it was somehow all Silkin's fault and that a tougher Chief Whip could do anything very different.

The Government Chief Whip, John Silkin, must be feeling a bit like St Sebastian these days. Arrows from the left began to rain on him the moment he took over from Ted Short nineteen months ago. Now he is being pierced too by volleys from the right. The ultra-loyalists have threatened in future to match left-wing abstentions man for man. Earlier this week Will Howie, a deputy Whip, allowed himself to be sacked rather than adopt Mr Silkin's permissive disciplinary style.

Whether Mr Silkin finally achieves martyrdom depends not on himself (he shows no sign of resigning) but on the Prime Minister, who may decide in the end that the Chief Whip must give way to someone sterner. Yet, if Mr Wilson does make Mr Silkin the scapegoat for Labour's recent troubles, he will be making a mistake. The turmoil of recent weeks owes far more to

---

* Reprinted in a slightly expanded form from *The Spectator*, 9 February 1968, with the permission of the publisher and the author.

the decisions of Mr Silkin's colleagues than to Mr Silkin himself. There is every reason to suppose that harsher discipline would only result in the parliamentary party's becoming even more ill-tempered than it is. It might also give the left some of the cohesion and sense of purpose it now so notably lacks.

All the same, Labour since polling day in 1966 has been more rebellious than any government party since the war – perhaps in modern times. Consider the facts. In July 1966, thirty-two backbenchers abstained on Vietnam. The following month, twenty-two refused to back the Government's first Prices and Incomes Bill. In October, twenty-eight abstained when Part IV was brought into force. Early in 1967, sixty-two MPs refused to support the Defence White Paper. In May, thirty-six Labour Members voted against entry into Europe and another fifty-one abstained. In July of last year, there was another revolt against the incomes policy. And now open war over the cuts.

Certainly, the Tories during their thirteen years had rebellions too. One has only to recall Suez, the Rent Act, and the abolition of resale price maintenance. But Labour's troubles have lasted far longer and gone much deeper. What should Mr Silkin do about them? That depends on what he *can* do. And that in turn depends on what one believes the root causes of discipline and indiscipline to be.

On the face of it the odd thing about parties in the British House of Commons is not how often they reveal their differences in public, but how seldom. Britain is undoubtedly somewhat more homogeneous politically than, say, France or America, but the two major parties in Britain are nevertheless very fissile indeed. The elements that go to make up the Labour Party alone would be enough for two or three parties on the Continent. In the United States Congress the parties are notoriously divided, with every roll-call a free vote. What, by contrast, holds the British parties together?

The morality of discipline is debated often enough, but seldom its causes. There seem to be five main ones – and none of them has much to do with 'discipline' in the whips-and-scorpions sense. The first is simply that the majority party wants to sustain a government in office; if too many MPs on the Government side rebel, that is the end of the Government. But that does not explain unity on the Opposition side. Nor does it account for the whips' passion for mustering the *full* Government majority; after all, in terms of keeping a ministry in power, a majority of five is as good as fifty. So the usual explanation for discipline can't be the only one.

The second factor is patronage; MPs fall into line, it is said, because they either hold office or hope for it. And this may well be a strong inducement to unity (though one suspects that, given the present Prime Minister's mechanistic balancing of right and left in the Government, an occasional abstention would actually promote an aspiring minister's cause). The trouble is that ambition for office cannot hold in line those who haven't a hope of office or just aren't interested – and such career backbenchers constitute a large fraction of the present parliamentary Labour Party.

The third factor is easy to overlook if one looks only at politics in Britain. It is the absence of positive, constituency-inspired incentives for breaking with the party. In America party lines in Congress are loose partly because local ties are strong. A Southern Democrat is more Southern than a Democrat; whatever his party may say, a Senator like Henry Jackson of Washington cannot afford to neglect the interests of the Boeing Airplane Company. On the one hand, a congressman who bolts his party in the interests of his constituency can expect to be rewarded. On the other, a congressman more loyal to party than constituency will be punished. These powerful local ties are missing in Britain. It is interesting that the rise of party discipline in this country coincided with the emergence of a truly national electorate. It is no accident that some of Parliament's freest spirits have sat for seats in the Celtic fringe, where a maverick Member can still hope to pick up support by standing out for local causes.

A fourth and equally powerful factor is MPs' sense that the public will punish a divided party at the polls. American congressmen's willingness to defy the whip depends on their belief that their voters can – and do – distinguish between them and their parties. A congressman breaks with his party because he believes that voters in his district may break with theirs. Not so in Britain, where most voters vote only for the party and MPs know it. MPs also know, or at least strongly suspect, that voters respect united parties and despise disunited ones. The more rebellious an MP, the more divided his party appears, the less likely he is to be re-elected.

But here we come to the fifth factor – and the rub. A lot of MPs will think unity in the face of the electorate worth preserving only if there is a good chance of winning the next election, and if they think there is a common cause worth fighting for. Rebellions come and go. The unsettling thing for the Government about the present rebellion is that the very foundations of party unity have been undermined. Why be loyal if you are going to lose the next election anyway? Conceivably, the rebels say, if the Government takes some notice of us, the party may actually be better off electorally, not worse. And anyway, why should the fundamentalist socialists silence their conscience for a Prime Minister and Cabinet with whom they no longer feel affinity? No man in politics is more dangerous than the man who has ceased to care what happens to him. Allaun and Mendelson are Labour's Sinyavsky and Daniel.

That crass calculations of advantage do not have much to do with current restlessness is suggested by the composition of the twenty-five who abstained a fortnight ago. Far from sitting mainly for safe seats (which they could hold even if the Government went down) or ultra-marginals (which might be bound to go whatever happened), the rebels are a very fair cross-section of the whole party; for instance, 54 per cent of Labour MPs sit for impregnably safe seats, 52 per cent of the rebels. A slightly disproportionate number of rebels are new to the House, but their number includes several – S. O. Davies, Emrys Hughes, Will Griffiths – who have manned the barricades at every insurrection since anybody can remember. S. O. Davies, the heir of Keir Hardie at Merthyr Tydfil, lost the whip as long ago as 1954.

So what should Mr Silkin do? We know what he has done already. The twenty-five have been suspended from party meetings for a month. But no one imagines that this rap over the knuckles is going to have a lasting effect. The Chief Whip is not headmaster of a suburban grammar school. This is the blackboard jungle.

Mr Silkin's instinct is probably not to do very much; for he and Mr Crossman seem to have hit on a couple of important truths. One is that the occasional rebellion does not matter all that much. The general public is not very sensitive to the niceties of parliamentary politics. An excess of discipline, far from quelling a rebellion, only calls wider attention to it. Better that a dozen backbenchers should abstain from time to time than that there should be endless stormy meetings of the PLP.

But it is the other Silkin–Crossman discovery that is unnerving; even if they wanted to discipline the recalcitrant twenty-five, they simply haven't the means. Chief Whips are in essence confidence tricksters whose success depends entirely on their never having to fire off the weapons locked in their armoury. Perhaps that is why they keep the armoury locked: one is struck by how rarely MPs are threatened with the sanctions theoretically at the whips' disposal. For most of the sanctions are virtually useless. The threat of dissolution? The old textbooks still talk as though such a threat could be credible; but in practice an election which destroyed the rebels would – since so many rebels sit for safe seats – certainly destroy the Government as well. Apparently Mr Wilson still hints darkly at a dissolution from time to time. If so, the threat is hollow and he must know it.

Even the withdrawal of the whip is not very frightening. Whipless MPs continue to draw their parliamentary salaries, they continue to hold their weekly surgeries, they can mix as freely as ever with their colleagues in the tea room. All they lose is the weekly whip, which they can borrow from friends, and the dubious pleasure of attending meetings of the PLP. Moreover precedent suggests that they can be all but certain of having the whip restored as the next election approaches. The whip was withdrawn from five left-wingers in 1961. It was restored in 1963. Four of the five were among those who abstained a fortnight ago.

The only sanction that would give rebellious MPs serious pause would be the threat of non-re-adoption. Even the most wayward Member would hesitate if he thought he might be denied party support at the next election. But this sanction depends ultimately not on the Chief Whip but on the MP's constituency party. If it supports him, the whips and the National Executive have a hard choice. Either they can disown the rebel and hope to rally enough local support to run a rival, orthodox candidate. Or they can do nothing. Since doing nothing is the negation of discipline, one would imagine that the leadership would usually choose to fight. In fact, however, it has almost never fought. The only Labour members expelled since the war were isolated individuals who were thought to be more communists than socialists and whose local parties could easily be split.

From Mr Silkin's point of view, the present position could hardly be worse. In the first place, there is no reason to think that local Labour parties would collaborate with Transport House in repudiating the rebels. On the contrary, the rebels – unlike most of their Tory predecessors – have at least as much support in the country as Ministers. Michael Foot is more secure in Ebbw Vale than Kenneth Robinson in St Pancras. In the second place, there are just too many rebels to deal with. An isolated Zilliacus or Platts-Mills can be got rid of; but the effort to expel all twenty-five current rebels would wreak far more damage on the party than the rebels possibly could by their activities in the House. It was for this reason that Labour drew back from facing a showdown with the Bevanites fifteen years ago.

In short Mr Silkin has almost no room for manoeuvre. A less easygoing Chief Whip might intimidate a fringe left-winger or two. He might succeed where Mr Silkin has failed in convincing the loyalists that everything possible was being done to bring the left into line. But beyond that he probably couldn't go. Mr Silkin's successor would learn what the present Chief Whip must know already: that discipline is easiest to achieve when least required, and is almost impossible to bring about when a party needs it most. If discipline is restored in the PLP in the coming months, it will not be because someone has cracked a whip but because the rebels have come round to the view that Mr Wilson's Government is worth supporting.

Postscript: Mr Wilson did eventually replace Mr Silkin, in April 1969, just over a year after this article was first published. The new Chief Whip, Bob Mellish, had a reputation for being tough personally and a hard-line right-winger politically. He was appointed precisely because it was thought that Mr Silkin had been too 'permissive'. Yet, if the analysis in the article is correct, the difference in Mr Mellish's style should have made very little difference to the discipline or indiscipline of the Labour Party. And this indeed proved to be so. Back-bench rebellions continued to occur, and it was while Mr Mellish was Chief Whip, in June 1969, that a major Labour revolt forced the Government to abandon its projected Industrial Relations Bill. It is at least possible that the golden age of ultra-disciplined parties is past and that, because Chief Whips have been found out for the confidence tricksters they are, parliamentary parties in future will be no more disciplined than the five factors listed above dictate.

Part II

THE BACKBENCHER AND THE WORK OF THE HOUSE

1. Questions in the House

By JOHN ROSE

IN this contribution John Rose examines the current position in relation to oral and written Questions in the House of Commons, taking into account changes made in 1970. After examining the increase in the number of Questions tabled since 1850, the author looks at the main restrictions – such as the length of Question Time, limitations on the number of Questions, the rota of answering Ministers, periods of notice, and rules of admissibility – and on Member's freedom to ask Questions, and refers to changing practices in relation to supplementaries and the special use made of Prime Minister's Question Time in the most recent Parliamentary sessions.

The first recorded Parliamentary Question was asked more than 250 years ago, on 9 February 1721.[1] It is only in the present century, however, that Question Time as we now know it has emerged. The developments since 1945 can best be followed in the four Reports from Select Committees on Procedure which have dealt with questions, in Sessions 1958–59, 1964–65, 1966–67 and 1969–70.[2] These Reports include not only the agreed reports of the Committees but also interesting suggestions and opinions, as well as accounts of current practice, given by Speakers, Members and other expert witnesses. A new edition of Erskine May's *Parliamentary Practice* has appeared in 1971, which includes a rewritten section on Questions. Chester and Bowring's book *Questions in Parliament*, which was published in 1962, gives a full account of Questions up to that date and contains a useful bibliography. Further changes and developments

[1] In the House of Lords. For a brief historical note on Parliamentary questions by K. A. Bradshaw, see *Parliamentary Affairs*, the journal of the Hansard Society, summer 1954, pp. 317–26.
[2] House of Commons Papers 92–1, 188, 410 and 198, and referred to throughout this study as the 1959, 1965, 1967 and 1970 Reports and Committees.

were taken account of in Chester's chapter on Questions in *The Commons in Transition*, which was published in 1970 (too soon to take account of the 1970 Report). While referring frequently to the past for perspective, the main purpose of the present study is to state the current position in relation to oral and written Questions in the House of Commons as I write in June 1971, to take account of the 1970 Report, its general acceptance by the Government, and its implementation by the House after a nine-minute debate at 1.08 a.m. on 8 April 1971.[3] I am not qualified, and I shall not attempt, to comment on the quality of questions and answers, or on the work they involve for Civil Servants, or on the motives that prompt them.

Numbers of Questions

Statistics of the numbers of Questions tabled and answered, orally or in writing, are assiduously recorded and analysed.[4] Despite fluctuations from year to year they show an obvious long-term trend to greater productivity by Members, both in written and oral Questions and in supplementaries at Question Time. The daily average of Questions on the paper has risen from 2 in 1850, to 41 in 1900, to 123 in 1950–51, to 147 in 1968–69, and to 151 in 1969–70. The average so far for the 1970–71 Session is 178. In Mr Speaker King's words in 1970 'there is a far keener House of Commons, man for man, than ever before, all seeking their place in the sun'.[5] On particular Mondays to Thursdays,[6] dependent on the Ministers open to questioning ten sitting days ahead,[7] and on other factors, the number of Questions tabled changes violently: on one recent Monday 411 notices were given[8] and on the Wednesday, two days later, only 81.

[3] Hansard, cols. 640–3.
[4] See, for example, the statistics given in evidence to the Procedure Committees.
[5] 1970 Report, Q.193.
[6] Fridays are almost always quiet days, particularly for the tabling of Questions in view of the operation of the twenty-one day or ten sitting day rule (see later).
[7] See later.
[8] A record, apart from the 740 given on 2 July 1970 in exceptional circumstances at the start of the Parliament.

Not all Members, however, devote equal time and energy to Questions. Evidence in the 1970 Report[9] showed that of the 538 potential questioners in Session 1968–69, 86 tabled no Questions whatever, 23 tabled more than 100 each (in total 33 per cent of all the notices given), and 55 per cent of all the notices received were given by 74 Members.

Restrictions on Members' freedom to ask Questions

The history of Question Time has been a history of increasing restrictions on Members' freedom to ask Questions. Originally any Member could ask almost any Question to any Minister who happened to be present on almost any subject at almost any time. Changes were inevitable and necessary if Question Time was to become an orderly and well-regulated proceeding, with adequate notice for all concerned. Seventy years ago an oral Question accepted at the Table one day would almost certainly be reached the next. Now, in view of the mass of Questions and the pressure of other business, limits in relation to oral Questions have been placed on the time available and on the numbers each Member may ask on any one day, and a rota of answering Ministers and periods of minimum and maximum notice have been introduced. Furthermore, in relation to both oral and written Questions, a detailed and intricate set of rules relating to form and content have been built up. I will deal in turn with each of these restrictions on a Member's freedom to ask Questions.

(a) The length of Question Time

The first limit on the time for oral Questions was included in the Balfour reforms of 1902, when a maximum period of forty minutes (from 2.15 p.m. to 2.55 p.m.) was allowed on Mondays to Thursdays. This was increased in 1906 to the maximum period of fifty-five minutes which still obtains.

Proposals were made to the 1970 Committee that 'Question Time should run for sixty minutes from the calling by Mr Speaker of question No. 1, i.e. that proceedings such as unopposed private business, which are taken after Prayers, should

[9] 1970 Report, Appendix 1 (II) (continuation of former Appendix 9).

not intrude upon time for questions; that Prayers be taken at 2.20 p.m. and that, when the Prime Minister answers questions, Question Time should extend until 4 p.m. and, on other days, until 3.45 p.m.; and a further proposal was made that questions should be taken for one hour after Prayers on Friday mornings.'[10] The only proposal recommended by the Committee to the House was that Question Time should commence ten minutes earlier, at 2.20 p.m. This proposal had been supported by Mr Speaker King, but opposed by written evidence from the Parliamentary Lobby journalists that 'because many journalists, like MPs, have important business engagements over lunch, an earlier start would not be welcome'.[11] In the debate on the Report, Mr (now Sir Robin) Turton[12] explained that it was perhaps wiser not to implement this recommendation until it could be seen how the new Speaker found Question Time.[13] Question Time therefore still commences at or soon after 2.35 p.m. on Mondays to Thursdays, and no further Questions are started after 3.30 p.m.[14]

(b) *Limitation on numbers of Questions*

Members have always been able to table as many oral Questions, and to table and ask as many written Questions, as they may wish. Severe limitations, however, have been placed on the number of oral Questions which they may actually ask on any one day. This number has been reduced from eight in 1909[15] to four in 1919[16] to three in 1920[17] to two in 1959.[18] The 1964 Committee recommended that no Member should be permitted to table more than eight Questions a month, but this idea was

[10] 1970 Report, para. 7.
[11] 1970 Report, Appendix (VII).
[12] Who is now Chairman of the Procedure Committee, but was then only a Member of it.
[13] Hansard, 7 April 1970, col. 642.
[14] With the exceptions of private notice Questions, Questions a Minister seeks to answer or to answer more fully (e.g. Hansard, 10 June 1971, col. 1237) and Questions which were not answered earlier due to the Minister's absence.
[15] Hansard, 1909 (1), col. 1108.
[16] Hansard, 1919 (112), col. 1382.
[17] Hansard, 1920 (125), cols. 1050–1.
[18] Hansard, 1958–59 (92), p. xxii.

never implemented, so that a Member's right to table as many Questions as he likes remains uncurtailed. The 1970 Committee, despite being 'always reluctant to countenance further restrictions upon Members' freedom to seek answers to their Questions',[19] recommended a proposal made by Mr Speaker King. This was to print the second oral Question of any Member to the top Minister on the rota, or to the Prime Minister, below all first Questions received up till the last day on which they could be tabled, in order to allow many more Members to put an oral Question to the first Minister of the day and to the Prime Minister.[20] It was agreed to by the House on 8 April 1971, and appears at this early date to have had the effect intended.[21]

(c) The rota of answering Ministers

An order of oral Questions was first printed in 1929. It now appears regularly on a large yellow sheet (and in a small and handy booklet form for Members), usually covering the maximum likely period between one recess and the next. The 1964 Committee recommended that this rota should be reorganised 'so as to give a larger proportion of the time available to the larger departments'.[22] The usual channels (i.e. the Whips of the major parties) are now consulted before its publication and the Government changes it in order to reflect as far as possible the changing appetites of Members to question particular departments, as responsibilities change or interest in them alters. I have appended to this chapter a Table showing the changing numbers of Questions to departments (which have themselves been changing), for Sessions 1964–65, 1968–69 and 1969–70.

The present rota works on a three- or four-week cycle for major departments (except for the Prime Minister[23]). Minor departments are currently included on a three-week cycle commencing not later than question thirty or thirty-five (or

[19] 1970 Report, para. 23.
[20] 1970 Report, para. 14.
[21] But for one resulting difficulty, see Hansard, 24 May 1971, col. 29.
[22] 1965 Report, para. 5.
[23] See later.

immediately after all Questions to an earlier Ministry). Questions on overseas aid are at the moment treated in a special way; although addressed to the Secretary of State for Foreign and Commonwealth Affairs, they are answered, when his Questions are first in the rota, in a special batch beginning not later than No. 30. No such treatment is as yet afforded to Questions to individual Ministers within such large departments as Trade and Industry and the Environment, with the result that oral Questions to them embrace a particularly wide variety of subjects and involve a particularly large number of answering Ministers.

Although Ministers on the rota for oral Questions on a particular day answer first, there is nothing to prevent a Member from tabling a Question to any Minister on any day. In fact Members frequently table oral Questions for an early day without wishing or expecting to receive an oral answer, but purely to ensure a written answer on that particular day.[24]

Although the number of Questions down for oral answer normally precludes the possibility of Questions to other Ministers being reached, there is no certainty of this, and strict precautions are taken by Government Whips to ensure that Ministers are available to answer, for attendance in the House is regarded as one of a Minister's highest priorities.[25] Indeed on one recent Monday the last Question was reached,[26] and on a Thursday Questions to Ministers other than the Prime Minister were exhausted altogether and the sitting suspended for eight minutes until Prime Minister's Questions could begin at 3.15 p.m.[27]

[24] Since an answer must be prepared in case the Question is reached, it has become routine that a written answer must be given on the same day to all oral Questions which are not reached. This practice is not altogether popular with the Civil Servants preparing the answers (see e.g. 1970 Report, para. 22).

[25] See Hansard, 7 July 1970, cols. 484–5, for an example of when a Minister was late.

[26] On 19 May 1971, when a Question to the Prime Minister was answered in his absence by an Under-Secretary of State in the Foreign and Commonwealth Office.

[27] Hansard, 13 May 1971, col. 610. Up to the last war a second round of Questions (i.e. Questions by Members not present when their Questions were called the first time) would have followed in this situation.

(d) Periods of notice

Notices of Questions handed in after 10.30 p.m. are now, by Sessional Order [28] made on 8 April 1971, treated for all purposes as if they were notices handed in after the rising of the House. This change was made to help the printer, who has the unenviable task of printing all the Commons' working papers overnight.

A minimum period of notice of two sitting days for oral Questions has been in force since the early 1900s. A Question tabled on a Monday or Tuesday before 2.30 p.m. may, however, be set down for oral answer on the Wednesday or Thursday respectively. These 'expedited' questions as they are called, together with any tabled on a Thursday (before 10.30 p.m.) for the following Monday, even if they constitute the Member's first Question to the top Minister on the rota or to the Prime Minister, are printed after all second questions of Members to the top Minister received on earlier days. Their chances of receiving an oral answer are therefore even that much more remote.

A maximum period of notice for oral Questions was first recommended by the 1959 Committee, but was not adopted until October 1965 after the same recommendation had been repeated.[29] A twenty-one day period was provided to prevent excessive advance notice being given to ensure an oral answer. For abuse had resulted in a Question Time almost totally devoid, except by accident, of topical Questions. Fears were expressed to the 1965 Committee that, taken in conjunction with the rota, a Department's list might be effectively filled within seconds of the opening for bookings twenty-one days in advance.[30] These fears were to quite a considerable extent realised, and Members often complained that Questions tabled on the earliest possible day (before 4 p.m. when the first Questions are sent to the printer) were still not reached at Question Time three weeks later. These complaints gave rise to suggestions for an alternative system to that whereby the printer prints

---

[28] I.e. the change requires renewal each Session to remain in force.
[29] 1970 Report, para. 11.
[30] 1965 Report, para. 6.

questions in a random order, which Members often distrust.[31] However, the 1967 and 1970 Committees both concluded that 'printers' pick' is preferable to a system of time-stamping or of first come first served.[32] The deadline of 4 p.m. also caused difficulties between the Table Office and Members from time to time when Questions had to be held back because of difficulties over their form or content.[33] A proposal to the 1970 Committee to defer the despatch of the 'four o'clock pouch' until six, to allow two extra hours for decision on the admissibility of such Questions, was not recommended to the House.

The 1970 Committee, however, did recommend that the maximum period of notice for oral Questions should be reduced to ten sitting days,[34] and this recommendation was implemented on 8 April 1971. It seems to be generally agreed that it will provide for greater topicality in the Questions reached.[35]

In relation to written Questions there is no maximum period of notice, and such a Question may be tabled at any time before 10.30 p.m. for answer next day. Departments are not obliged to answer a written Question on the actual day on which it is set down for answer, although by convention they are expected to provide an answer within three days of the date for which they are put down. On the occasions on which this is not done, Members are permitted, if an answer is not quickly forthcoming thereafter, to table the same Question for oral answer.

(e) *General rules of admissibility*

The increase in the numbers of Questions has been accompanied by increasingly strict rules of order to govern their form and content. These rules, although they apply equally to written Questions, are largely based on, and justified by, a common sense need to ensure that the time available for oral Questions is wasted as little as possible. Rules cannot of course distinguish between less and more important Questions, between those of

[31] Some Members still have a fixed but erroneous idea that certain Members regularly come out much nearer the top than themselves.
[32] 1967 Report, para. 2; 1970 Report, para. 15.
[33] See e.g. Hansard, 27 May 1971, cols. 589–90.
[34] 1970 Report, para. 13.
[35] It has incidentally reduced the size of the order book of future questions (and all that that involves to the printer) by almost a third.

local and those of national and international importance, but they can and do prevent the trivial, the ironic, the vague, those already answered in substance, those for which there is no Ministerial responsibility, those giving rather than seeking information, and many other classes of Question which for one reason or another would not or could not normally receive a worthwhile answer.[36] The rules, which are founded on Speakers' rulings over the years, are not always easy to interpret. They cause the Table Office considerable intellectual and philosophical problems (aggravated by the sheer bulk of Questions received and the need for speed in processing them) in deciding where to draw the line. Members are naturally annoyed if their rejected Questions appear similar to others which have been allowed, or if their interpretation of the rules differs from that of the Office. If disagreements cannot be resolved – and normally they can be in an amicable fashion – appeal is made to Mr Speaker for a final decision. At one time or another almost every Member is likely to find his Question in conflict with the rules, and a high proportion of Questions are altered in minor ways by the Table Office to conform with them, usually without the need to consult or inform him, before they are printed on the notice paper.

Some of these rules have been considered by the recent Procedure Committees,[37] but no changes have been recommended. Since the rules are founded on precedent it is often possible for them to be modified by later rulings and for their harsher implications to be avoided by favourable interpretation. The scope for admissible Questions shows interesting but minor change between one Government and another, in so far as one may assume responsibility for subjects and by its practices be willing to disclose information which another refuses to do.

Table Office machinery

The Table Office is conveniently situated close to the Chamber behind the Speaker's Chair. Among its other duties it receives and processes all Questions, and makes the necessary administrative arrangements in the House in relation to Question Time.

[36] The rules are set out in May, 18th ed., pp. 323–29.
[37] E.g. 1967 Report, paras. 11 and 14; 1970 Report, paras. 17–21.

It is staffed by four House of Commons Clerks, under the supervision of the Principal Clerk, who are served by a supporting staff (one of the chief functions of which is to maintain a fully comprehensive and up-to-date filing system of all Questions asked and answers given[38]). All House of Commons Clerks are independent officers of the legislature, recruited by the Clerk of the House of Commons through the Civil Service examination (administrative class[39]) and answerable only to him. Their duty is to interpret and administer the rules and practices of the House to the best of their ability and with complete impartiality as between one Member and another. The machinery of the Office remains basically simple in the face of such a complicated set of rules and procedures, and of such a diverse mass of Questions. The system relies largely on the memories, efficiency and attention to detail of the Clerks involved.

Questions are brought in by hand or by post to the Office, on any size or shape of piece of paper, and sometimes in very difficult handwriting;[40] they are checked and edited, put into the pouch for the printer or reserved for further consideration or consultation. Once on the Order Paper they are read for printing or other errors, and can be corrected or removed if necessary. Thereafter the Member retains flexibility to withdraw, amend, defer or bring them forward, or to star or unstar[41] them, until 10.30 p.m. on the last day but one before they are due for answer.[42] Similarly government departments have absolute freedom to transfer them to whichever Minister wishes to answer.[43] By this time they are marshalled by the printer in accordance with the rota, and on this day oral Questions additional to the final ration of two are unstarred and pairs of

---

[38] Mainly so that the rule concerning the inadmissibility of a Question already answered in substance during the same session can be enforced.

[39] Now called administration group (administration trainees).

[40] Though large yellow sheets are now provided, and typed Questions are encouraged.

[41] I.e. change them from written to oral, or vice versa.

[42] Until 8 April 1971 he had this freedom until the rising of the House on the day before the Questions were set down for answer. 1970 Report, para. 14.

[43] Transfer often causes difficulties for Members, chiefly in relation to the rota for oral Questions. See e.g. 1967 Report, para. 13 and Hansard, 23 June 1971, cols. 1427–9.

Questions by the same Member to the first Minister and Prime Minister are divided.[44] Thereafter only withdrawal, unstarring or deferment is possible, and this is open to the Member up till the very last moment before the Minister is due to answer the Question.

Supplementary Questions

The importance and popularity of oral Questions stems largely from the supplementary questioning which can flow from them. Whereas a Minister can read out from a prepared brief an answer to the initial Question which Civil servants have had up to two weeks to consider, he must attempt to answer immediately every supplementary questioner whom Mr Speaker calls. Civil servants provide full briefing to meet likely supplementaries (and this explains why oral Questions cost more money to answer[45]), but a Minister can rarely know exactly what their terms will be. Scope exists therefore for cases to be pressed and for Ministers to be discomfited.

Large numbers of supplementary Questions are now taken almost for granted, and the value of Question Time lies largely in their effectiveness. But it was not always so. Up till 1939 'the Chair regarded a Question to a Minister as a matter between the Minister and the Member'.[46] It is of course the number and length of supplementary Questions and answers since the war which have so drastically affected the number of Questions reached. The right balance between further supplementaries and more original Questions is extremely hard to strike, and much sympathy has been expressed with successive Speakers in their duty to control the numbers and content of supplementaries. The temptation to stray wide of the original Questions, to make short or even not so short speeches and to raise inadmissible aspects[47] are often as hard for Members to resist as for Mr Speaker to control.

All the Procedure Committees referred to have concerned themselves with the reduced number of Questions reached

[44] See earlier and 1970 Report, para. 14.
[45] See my concluding paragraph.
[46] 1970 Report, para. 3.
[47] Which the Table Office have assiduously disallowed in the Question originally submitted to them.

during Question Time since the war. The 1959 Committee urged a return to pre-war practice.[48] The 1965 Committee thought it was 'clearly undesirable ... that only between thirty and forty questions should be reached in a day', although they did not regard the total number of questions answered as the only test of a successful Question Hour.[49] The 1967 Committee were able to report an improvement in progress at Question Time of on average seven or eight more oral Questions being reached and nine more supplementary Questions being asked.[50] The 1970 Committee recommended the strict enforcement of brevity, the denial of some first supplementary Questions, the curtailment of supplementary (and original) answers, and support for intervention by Mr Speaker in cutting short anything irrelevant to the original Question, no matter who the Member.[51] They considered also however that when a Minister's answer was unsatisfactory, the Member asking the Question should have an opportunity to put a second supplementary Question.[52]

Prime Minister's Questions

Questions to the Prime Minister have always been of particular importance and interest. Ministerial responsibility to Parliament is seen at its most clear and obvious in the requirement of the Prime Minister of the day to leave his other pressing duties to come to the House to answer oral Questions and supplementaries put to him by any backbencher or Opposition Member.

Oral Questions to the Prime Minister were the first to have a special place – last on each day's list before 1902, then altered to number 51 and then to number 45.[53] The 1959 Committee understood the reason for this to be that 'they might all be certain of an oral reply towards the end of the question hour'.[54] By 1959 the rate at which Questions were answered had been much reduced, and the Committee's recommendation to take Prime Minister's Questions at the fixed time of 3.15 p.m., on

[48] 1959 Report, para. 38.   [49] 1965 Report, para. 2.
[50] 1967 Report, para. 1.   [51] 1970 Report, paras. 2–6.
[52] 1970 Report, para. 6.
[53] Chester, *The Commons in Transition*, p. 97.
[54] 1959 Report, para. 42.

Tuesdays and Thursdays only, was accepted and implemented. A proposal to the 1970 Committee that time for Prime Minister's Questions should be extended to twenty minutes (from 3.40 p.m. to 4) was not recommended by the Committee.[55] The Prime Minister therefore continues to answer oral Questions for not much more (and occasionally even less) than half an hour a week.

The desire to ask supplementary Questions has always applied with particular force to Prime Minister's Questions, and has resulted in recent years in frequent verbal skirmishes and battles between leading adversaries, 'often on some topic that is not raised at all' in the original Question.[56] As a recent, and not altogether untypical example, a question about official visits to other Heads of Government in the EEC was followed by eight supplementaries, three of them by the Leader of the Opposition.[57] Such confrontations are welcomed and expected by Members generally, by the public and the Press, and provide an almost guaranteed highlight of the Parliamentary week. It is quite rare for there not to be one or more very general Questions on the paper on which the most topical political issues of the day can, with more or less relevance, be raised.

Private Notice Questions

A Member cannot table what he considers to be a particularly important or urgent Question for oral answer less than two days ahead, and even then he is extremely unlikely to have his Question reached. A written Question can be tabled for answer on the following day, but there is no absolute guarantee that it will be answered even three or four days later. In either case the Question can be answered orally by a Minister at the end of Question Time, but totally at his own discretion, and such a proceeding is not common. Separate provision therefore is made for oral Questions of an urgent character relating to matters of importance to be taken after Question Time at 3.30 p.m. (or at 11 a.m. on Fridays), so that they can be answered

[55] 1970 Report, paras. 7–8.
[56] 1970 Report, para. 3.
[57] Hansard, 10 June 1971, cols. 1229–33. For a complaint about this at 3.30 p.m., which is also not uncommon, see col. 1235.

after the minimum possible notice. Notice of such Questions must reach Mr Speaker's Office before 12 noon on Mondays to Thursdays (or before 10 a.m. on a Friday). It is solely within his discretion whether to allow them or not, and no reasons for decision can be given (nor should the disallowance of a Question be referred to in the House at all).

A PNQ, as it is commonly called, can be asked of any Department on any sitting day. A Minister of each Department must therefore be available in London in case a Question is submitted and allowed by Mr Speaker. When a Question is allowed, the Department and the Member involved are immediately informed, and the TV annunciators round the House list PNQs as well as Statements, so that all Members may have advance notice of them.[58]

Business Questions

Oral Questions to the Leader of the House about the business of the House for the following week (or for the first week after a recess) are taken regularly once a week after Question Time and PNQs, usually on Thursdays. They afford a convenient and popular occasion for Members to put without notice a wide variety of points, which often in the past have borne only the most tenuous connection with 'next week's business'. The 1970 Committee referred to Mr Speaker King's anxiety on this score; they rejected a proposal for a time limit on such Questions, but thought that Mr Speaker would be supported in confining them 'narrowly to those on next week's business'.[59] They also felt that he should not feel obliged to call every Member wishing to ask a business Question.

Use of Questions by Backbenchers, Opposition and Government

This book is primarily concerned with backbenchers, but the needs of the Opposition front bench and of the Government are also relevant to Questions. Before the war, Question Time was much more of a backbenchers' occasion. I have already referred to changing practice in relation to supplementaries, and to the special use made of Prime Minister's Question Time.

[58] See Hansard, 16 December 1970, cols. 383-4 w.
[59] 1970 Report, para. 10.

Mr Speaker King, in evidence to the 1970 Committee, thought that the House desired the change, whereby a Question now 'belongs to the House and it is part of the battle of Parliament, and the other side can either back up or try to make a counter-stroke'.[60] Opposition spokesmen now regularly attend Question Time and many of them take a considerable part in it. Some table Questions themselves, on national as well as constituency points, and ask PNQs. Traditionally the Leader of the Opposition does not table Questions himself,[61] although he can ask PNQs,[62] but he has a predominant right to be called to ask supplementaries.

Answering Questions provides the Government, when the House is sitting, with an almost daily platform to expound and justify its policies and its administration, and to give new information in answer to Questions which happen to be on the Order Paper. When a Government wishes to give specific information in an answer on a particular day, it is able to give it in answer to an 'inspired Question'. This is drafted by the Government and handed to a Member, normally for written answer the following day. The extent to which the practice is used is difficult to establish. In answer to a series of Questions on the point in the 1969–70 Session, it was stated to be a 'long standing practice for the general convenience of the House', of which no departmental records are kept since it is an entirely informal procedure.[63] Although some Members are critical of it,[64] it would appear to be relatively harmless in relation to written Questions.

It is not unknown, however, for series of oral Questions to be tabled (whether handed in to the Table Office separately or *en bloc*) as a result of a concerted campaign in some quarter or other. These may originate in a government department, among its supporters, on the Opposition side, or on the back

---

[60] 1970 Report, para. 5.
[61] The Opposition Chief Whip, who is also paid a salary from public funds, asked a written Question on 28 April 1971 (Hansard, col. 110).
[62] He normally asks the introductory business Question on Thursdays.
[63] E.g. Hansard, 26 March 1970, col. 549 w.
[64] See, for example, early day motion No. 601 of 1970–71, in which a Member expressed the view that information which a Minister wishes to supply in this way should be provided under a new system of written statements.

benches. Although there is a rule against campaigns conducted by individual Members,[65] it is not possible to prevent, even if it should be thought desirable, any such use of Questions. There is no rule even against the tabling of identical Questions.[66] It is hard to argue that the use of Question Time by groups of Members with a common purpose is not legitimate, although any abuse (for example, by backbencher supporters of the Government to shield a Minister from hostile Questions) would very soon be spotted and could prove highly embarrassing to him.

The future

How long the current practice outlined in this study will endure is anybody's guess. The unpredictability of the House of Commons is one of its most fascinating features, and as an insider I am in no better position to anticipate future developments than any other informed person. Truly a week is a long time in politics, and although procedures are rather more permanent than this they can be changed very rapidly, depending on their importance, by administrative action, by Speaker's ruling or by decision of the House. On 8 April 1971 the Leader of the House hinted at consideration of more fundamental changes if necessary after allowing some time to judge Question Time on its new basis.[67]

Broadcasting and television, if they come, are bound to make an impact, and Question Time, suitably edited, would provide extremely interesting material for them. British entry to the Common Market, too, if it takes place, is likely to affect the scope and range of Questions. One personal hope, perhaps naïve, is that many of the rules restricting the form and content can be removed, leaving Members with full freedom. Such a change, while enabling Members to table the exact Questions they really wish to ask, would place fully and plainly on them responsibility for their substance and responsibility not to waste any of the valuable time of the House by abusing this freedom. The very powerfulness of the right to ask Questions imposes

[65] Which is itself rarely capable of enforcement.
[66] See, for example, Hansard, 27 April 1971, cols. 235–8 and 29 April, cols. 709–11.
[67] Hansard, 7 April 1971, cols. 640–1.

upon Members a proportionate responsibility in its use, and Members and their constituents will obtain the Question Time they deserve.

Postscript

Re-reading this in January 1972 I have made no alterations. The one significant development has been the promise of a Select Committee in 1972 to consider 'the whole problem of Questions and Question Time procedure'.[70] This followed the allegations and admissions[71] of question 'rigging' by the Department of the Environment, which provoked widespread public interest and comment.

Conclusion

Criticisms of the shortcomings of Question Time are as easy to make as constructive suggestions to enable more and more quarts to be poured into the pint pot[68] are difficult. Certainly the history of Question Time in the last seventy years is a history of increasing restrictions placed on the use of the starred question. Nevertheless it remains an impressive proceeding, and rarely a day passes without something of great interest. The numbers of Questions tabled show how much use is made and value placed on Question Time and on written Questions by many Members. The threat of Questions must also be a powerful stimulus to good government and efficient administration. The 1971 changes should help to improve further the topicality of oral Questions.

Inflation has not passed Questions by. In 1965 the average costs of answering oral and written Questions were estimated at £10·55 and £7·82 respectively. In May 1971 they were estimated to have risen to £15 and £10.[69] I personally think that this represents good value for taxpayers' money. Mr Speaker Clifton Brown in 1946 regarded 'the question hour as a vital part of our proceedings'. If there is still a British Parliament in another 250 years' time, I like to believe that Question Time will remain one of its most cherished and important institutions.

[68] See *The Commons in Transition*, p. 95.
[69] Hansard, 20 May 1971, cols. 357–8 w.
[70] Hansard, 14 December 1971, col. 273.
[71] Hansard, December 1971, cols. 65–77.

TABLE

Numbers of Questions tabled to particular Departments

	Oral 1964–65	Oral 1968–69	Oral 1969–70	Written 1964–65	Written 1968–69	Written 1969–70	Totals 1964–65	Totals 1968–69	Totals 1969–70
Agriculture, Fisheries and Food	601	499	393	317	389	351	918	888	744
Attorney-General	77	53	53	27	102	58	104	155	111
Aviation	429			208			637		
Church Commissioner	0	0	0	0	1	0	0	1	0
Civil Service		102	34		68	58		170	92
Colonies	215			91			306		
Commonwealth Relations	227			61			288		
Defence	538	624	519	427	599	411	965	1,223	930
Duchy of Lancaster	87	0	8	22	5	2	109	5	10
Economic Affairs	394	333		121	118		515	451	
Education and Science	576	659	547	530	602	462	1,106	1,261	1,009
Foreign (later 'and Commonwealth')	507	853	628	190	457	265	697	1,310	893
Health	712			625			1,337		
Home	633	679	559	455	667	505	1,088	1,346	1,064
Housing (and Local Government)	704	730	789	435	698	788	1,139	1,428	1,577
Kitchen Committee, etc.	15			10			25		

Labour (later Employment and Productivity)	385	660	621	283	762	443	668	1,422	1,064
Land and Natural Resources	186			40					
Lord President of the Council		60	61		65	53	226	125	114
Overseas Development	218	179	195	106	115	62	324	294	257
Paymaster-General	54	24	0	3	14	2	57	38	2
Pensions	274			218			492		
Minister without Portfolio	20	0	5	13	0	6	33	0	11
Posts, etc.	565	493	181	420	501	128	985	994	309
Power	329	510		165	317		494	827	
Prime Minister	1,146	1,207	865	156	173	124	1,302	1,380	989
Public Buildings and Works	308	280	266	139	181	98	447	461	364
Scotland	612	906	812	412	944	722	1,024	1,850	1,534
Social Services		958	685		1,196	1,041		2,154	1,726
Technology	250	407	866	80	356	495	330	763	1,361
Trade	738	911	700	476	734	529	1,214	1,645	1,229
Transport	1,048	761	630	814	840	552	1,862	1,601	1,182
Treasury	745	941	710	623	1,005	833	1,368	1,946	1,543
Wales	83	149	118	93	210	232	176	359	350
Totals:							20,236	24,097	18,469
Sitting days in Session:							178	164	122

N.B. Blank spaces indicate non-existent Departments.

2. Adjournment Debates in the House of Commons

By VALENTINE HERMAN

PARLIAMENTARY Questions have been closely studied as a device through which the backbencher seeks to check the actions of the executive. Another device, and one which scholars have not investigated so thoroughly, is the Adjournment debate. In this chapter* one hundred and seventy-five Adjournment debates moved in the House of Commons in the 1966–67 session are examined from the positions of the backbencher and of the Government. Following an intensive analysis of these debates, Valentine Herman concludes that, Adjournment debates, 'are one of the few devices the backbencher can use in the face of increased front-bench control over the content and timetable of the House, and increased government involvement in the lives of the people'.

Adjournment debates are considered neither the most attractive nor the important parts of Parliamentary business and as a result are usually ignored completely or receive only sketchy treatment in works on Parliament.[1] Comparisons between Adjournment debates and Parliamentary Questions are inevitable; however although the value and importance of Question Time has long been recognised – for vastly different reasons which are beyond the frame of reference here – by the backbencher, the Government, the academic commentator, the Press and the public, Adjournment debates have not attracted similar attention to date. Reasons for this neglect are not obvious to locate. On the one hand scholars of Parliament

---

* Reprinted from *Parliamentary Affairs*, Vol. 25, Number 3, 1972, with the permission of the publisher and the author.

[1] See, for example, Ivor Jennings, *Parliament* (Cambridge U.P., 2nd ed., 1957), pp. 110–21, and A. H. Hanson and H. V. Wiseman, *Parliament at Work* (London: Stevens & Sons, 1962), pp. 97–9.

see them as a natural and desirable extension of Question Time. Chester and Bowring for example noted that:

> The device of Question and Answer, strictly interpreted, is sometimes unsatisfactory, for both parties would like a little more elbow room – the questioner to explain the background of his question or complaint, the answerer to give more information and a fuller explanation. Two post-war developments illustrate this desire for something fuller and yet still reasonably specific. First there is the greatly increased use of the daily Motion for Adjournment for the purpose of a very short debate on a specific issue, during which usually only the opener and a Minister take part. Second, there is the use of Ministerial statements followed by questions.[2]

Peter Richards writes in a similar vein, 'Much fuller ventilation of a grievance is possible than can be secured at Question Time, although it is rare for a Minister to concede anything in an Adjournment debate that has already been refused publicly. This device also permits consideration of policy matters that could not otherwise find a place in the crowded parliamentary timetable. It is a most valuable part of the proceedings of the Commons.'[3] On the other hand, there is little evidence that leading parliamentarians place a high value on them. The leader of the House of Commons, Richard Crossman, in a debate on procedure in 1966 referred to them as 'lonely little affairs often related to parochial issues'.[4]

This paper, part of a larger study presently being conducted on Parliament, examines Adjournment debates in the House of Commons in 1966–67. This analysis has been conducted through a reading of these debates in this Parliamentary session: no attempts have been made to view Adjournment debates through an historical perspective, neither have any

[2] D. N. Chester and Nora Bowring, *Questions in Parliament* (Oxford: Clarendon Press, 1962), p. 282. See also Neville Johnson, 'Parliamentary Questions and the Conduct of Administration', *Public Administration*, Vol. 39 (1961), pp. 131–48.

[3] Peter G. Richards, *Honourable Members* (London: Faber & Faber, 2nd (new) ed., 1964), pp. 125–6. See also A. Barker and M. Rush, *The MP and His Information* (London: Allen & Unwin, for PEP and the Study of Parliament Group, 1970), pp. 173–89.

[4] HC Debs, Vol. 738, col. 491.

interviews been conducted with MPs, Civil Servants and Ministers involved.

The Backbencher and Adjournment debates

One hundred and seventy-five Adjournment debates were moved in the House of Commons in 1966–67: 80 of these by Labour MPs, 91 by Conservatives, 3 by Liberals, and 1 by the Plaid Cymru Member.[5] Movers of Adjournment debates, with one minor exception, were typically backbench MPs raising matters of constituency, regional, and in some cases party interest. The exception were the five Adjournment debates moved by Opposition Spokesmen and a further four moved by Opposition Whips. However, eight of these nine debates were concerned with constituency problems and were divorced from major party differences, and only one, on Selective Employment Tax, involved a debate between the parties on policy lines. It does not appear that members of the Shadow Cabinet personally use Adjournment debates as an additional way of opposing the Government. This however does not mean that Adjournment debates do not involve clashes between the Government and Opposition over either the substance or the application of policy; many debates do contain such conflict, but this is introduced by backbench Opposition MPs not the Shadow Cabinet directly.

The focus and subject-matter of Adjournment debates fall into two distinct groups: on the one hand are debates which arise from an earlier government decision and take up individual constituents' complaints of bad administrative decisions or requests to intervene with authority, or which focus on general constituency problems of an economic nature. On the other hand are debates which are neither constituency-oriented nor related to a previous government decision. A large number of matters raised on the Adjournment originate from constituency complaints received by the backbencher through his mail, from his 'surgery',[6] or from visits to the constituency.

[5] In the remainder of this paper the Adjournment debates moved by the Liberals and the Plaid Cymru Member are grouped with the Conservatives to facilitate analysis.
[6] See pages 45–61 above.

When a constituency complaint is received by an MP his normal strategy is,

> ... to use first a letter to the Minister concerned crystallising the complaint, sending the documents, and asking the Minister for an explanation. In many cases the Minister's reply and explanation will settle the matter, the department either having changed a decision or persuaded either the complainant or the MP (or both) of the desirability of the action complained of. If the MP is not satisfied with the reply he has various methods to continue to press the complaint; he can write another letter, he can put down a Parliamentary Question for written or oral answer (or) he can try to get an Adjournment debate. ... Parliamentary Questions are mainly used as follow-up measures to put pressure on a department. Adjournment debates are generally thought of only as a last resort.[7]

How the MP uses these various methods, and how he feels about using them when the normal techniques fail to achieve results, become evident when Arthur Blenkinsop (Lab., South Shields) took up a constituent's complaint about the timing of driving tests.

> I regret that I have had to waste the time of the House, in a sense, in raising a matter of this sort. As I say, I had hoped that a polite note to the local office would have been sufficient. I then hoped in my innocence and naïveté that a note to my Hon. Friend would have been sufficient, or even a second one. I regret that I have had to go through the process of a Question in the House and now this Adjournment debate.[8]

In taking up a constituency complaint an MP frequently uses other techniques, in addition to the ones outlined above, personally involving himself with the authorities concerned by for example talking to members of the local council, meeting organisations in the constituency, leading delegations to the Minister, and so on. Two examples from the Adjournment

[7] Karl A. Friedmann, 'Commons, Complaints and the Ombudsman', *Parliamentary Affairs*, Vol. 21 (1967–68), pp. 38–47.
[8] HC Debs, Vol. 751, col. 1168.

debates under analysis of the way such techniques were used are interesting. When the matter of industrial noise in Walton was raised on the Adjournment, Eric Heffer (Lab., Liverpool, Walton) told the House that he had visited two of the three firms concerned and talked to the management, had made numerous representations to the local authorities, had written to and visited the local medical officer, as well as receiving letters and petitions from constituents.[9] On the day that the closure of Blyth Shipyard was debated on the Adjournment, Edward Milne (Lab., Blyth) introduced shop-stewards from the shipyard to Roy Mason who, as Minister of State for the Board of Trade, was replying to the Debate: previously Milne had accompanied a deputation from the Board of Trade to the shipyard.[10]

Many Adjournment debates do not originate from constituency complaints. It seems likely that many members ballot for subjects on the Adjournment because of a specialised and long-standing interest in the subject they hope to raise in order to bring a considerable amount of specialised information to the Debate. When for example, Harry Randall (Lab., Gateshead, West) secured an Adjournment debate on the European Campaign for World Refugees in 1966, the information he called on and introduced the House to had been obtained by him in his capacity as a Member of the Conference of British Organisations for Aid to Refugees, and the Government representative at Geneva on the Executive Committee of the United Nations High Commission for Refugees.[11] As Chairman of the all-party Parliamentary Committee on Tourism, W. R. Rees-Davies (Con., Isle of Thanet) was well armed with facts when he raised the subjects of Tourism, Sport and Sunday Entertainment on the Adjournment.[12]

MPs frequently undertake considerable amounts of research before raising matters on the Adjournment, contacting, or in some cases being contacted by, interest groups, research organisations, private firms, or individuals to obtain facts, figures and opinions which are then presented to the Minister

[9] HC Debs, Vol. 735, col. 421.
[10] HC Debs, Vol. 734, cols. 569–74.
[11] HC Debs, Vol. 734, cols. 175–80.
[12] HC Debs, Vol. 738, cols. 1475–81.

concerned in the debate, or undertaking private and original research, seeking material which is not readily available so as to make their arguments more convincing. Examples of the latter are especially interesting. Dr David Owen (Lab., Plymouth, Sutton) conducted a survey of London medical teachers to provide information for an Adjournment debate on the salaries of University Clinical Teachers.[13] The day before the House debated Racial Discrimination in Insurance on the Adjournment, David Marquand (Lab., Ashfield) phoned a number of insurance companies asking for quotations for English and Indian car-owners; the discrimination he apparently found increased the viability of his argument.[14] When Selective Employment Tax was debated on the Adjournment, David Mitchell (Con., Basingstoke) presented before the House an impressive array of figures obtained from what he believed was, 'the largest private survey carried out in the United Kingdom on the effects of SET. Over 500 firms were contacted and asked how SET affected their business.'[15]

Not only do MPs differ in the amount of pre-constituency contact, specialised knowledge and research they undertake prior to a debate, they also differ in the geographical context they choose to place the debate in. It is possible to classify Adjournment debates into four general categories according to their geographical focus.

The first category is comprised of debates which focus on problems in the MPs constituency. These problems are generally of one of three types: firstly, they can draw the attention of the House to matters affecting particular constituents; secondly they can be concerned with a part of the constituency; or thirdly they can relate to the constituency as a whole. The second category of Adjournment debates are those which focus on regional problems, that is issues particular to regions, or the whole, of England, Scotland, Wales or Northern Ireland, but not common to the whole of the United Kingdom. The third category is, as expected, an extension of the second, covering Adjournment debates which focus on problems or issues which are relevant to the whole of the United Kingdom. The final

[13] HC Debs, Vol. 739, cols. 384–90.
[14] HC Debs, Vol. 739, cols. 384–90.
[15] HC Debs, Vol. 744, cols. 198–204.

category encompasses those whose focus is international, where the matters which are raised are external to the United Kingdom and where a British Minister has responsibility.

TABLE 1

Geographical Focus of Debates

	Labour No.	Labour Per cent	Conservative No.	Conservative Per cent
Constituency	30	37·5	36	37·9
Regional	16	20·0	18	18·9
National	27	33·7	34	35·8
International	7	8·7	7	7·4
Total	90	99·9	95	100·0

The distribution of Adjournment debates in 1966–67 among these categories is shown in Table 1. Differences between the parties are few and insignificant; however three features relating to the overall distribution deserve some comment. The first and perhaps the most notable, is that slightly less than 40 per cent of the debates focus on constituency problems. Although Adjournment debates provide an MP with a rare opportunity to bring the problems of his constituency to the floor of the House, on many occasions he chooses not to do so. This leads to a second observation. As much as a third of the debates have a national focus, and provide backbench MPs with chances to discuss national issues which they may not get because the front benches take up a considerable amount of time available to discuss such matters in ordinary debates and also because the setting of the House's business in advance by the front benches often restricts issues from being debated when some MP feels they ought. The general impression given of the parochial nature of Adjournment debates is not an accurate one, national and international issues receiving as much attention as constituency ones. Finally, it is important to note that although the geographical focus of Adjournment debates probably does not mirror the focus of the rest of the House's business – over-representing constituency matters and under-representing the national and international – such debates do perform a very useful function, drawing attention to local problems and policy applications and away from major current issues of national policy.

We turn now from the geographical perspective of Adjournment debates to a classification of the matters raised in them; from 'where' a particular thing is wanted, to 'what' it is that is wanted. The 'what' in this instance can conveniently be seen as 'demands' that are made by backbenchers on the Government. These demands fall into four general categories. The first contain demands on the Government to reverse previous policies on the specific applications of such policies: Peter Wolrige-Gordon (Con., Aberdeen, East), for example, asked the Government in an Adjournment debate[16] to reverse its decision to close Ellon Hospital. The second demand financial assistance from the Government in certain cases, an example occurring when Ednyfed Hudson Davies (Lab., Conway) sought to increase the financial resources of the Welsh Tourist Board.[17] A third category demand statements from the Government either of an explanatory nature and relating to the past ('why did the Government do so-and-so?'), or seeking information about what the Government is doing at the present ('what progress has the Government made in its discussions with such-and-such?'), or concerned with the future plans of the Government ('what does the Government intend to do about the following?'). The fourth category of debates place demands on the Government to widen its activities: when he raised the matter of television reception in Scotland on the Adjournment John Brewis (Con., Galloway) wanted the Government to extend television coverage to his constituency.[18]

The distribution of the Adjournment debates in 1966–67 according to these categories is presented in Table 2. A number of differences between the parties are evident. It can be seen that Conservative MPs concentrate more on challenging previous policies than do Labour MPs. This is as would be expected, the Opposition opposing the Government more than its supporters. Two slightly less obvious facts explain why this is so. The first is related to the geographical focus within which Adjournment debates of this nature are cast, and reveals an

[16] HC Debs, Vol. 735, cols. 616–20.
[17] HC Debs, Vol. 743, cols. 2006–12.
[18] HC Debs, Vol. 750, cols. 2087–92.

important difference between the parties. A large number of Adjournment debates moved by Conservative MPs which contain demands to reverse policies are focused at the national level, while a far smaller number seek reversal of policy applications at the constituency level. On the Labour side the pattern is reversed; Labour MPs challenge previous local policy applications frequently, and very rarely challenge national policies. When they do challenge the latter, in the majority of cases the policies criticised were those introduced by the previous Conservative Government and 'inherited' by the current Labour administration. A second difference between

TABLE 2
Demand Nature of Debates

	Labour No.	Labour Per cent	Conservative No.	Conservative Per cent
Policy reversal	13	16·2	31	32·6
Financial assistance	16	20·0	20	21·1
Government statement	25	31·2	22	23·1
Widening activities	26	32·5	22	23·1
Total	80	99·9	95	99·9

the parties is in the way each challenges the Labour Government's policies: Conservative MPs use Adjournment debates to challenge government policies, while Labour MPs use them to challenge specific applications of such policies. Drawing these two points together it can be seen that the Opposition and the Government's supporters use Adjournment debates in much the same way as they use Parliamentary Questions and speeches: in Adjournment debates not only does the Opposition oppose more, but it opposes in a different manner – criticising government policy at a national level – than the Government's supporters – who restrict their criticism to specific policy applications at the constituency level.

This however does not mean that Labour backbenchers in the period under study did not use Adjournment debates as vehicles to challenge government policy, or to suggest that they did not place such challenges in a national perspective. Labour MPs did achieve both these ends through Adjournment debates, but went about doing so in a different manner from Conservative MPs, who, as we saw above, criticised the Government through Adjournment debates on a considerable number of occasions. Labour MPs were (and perhaps had to be) more subtle in the way they went about this – using Adjournment debates to obtain general statements from the Government about why it was doing what it was doing, and at the same time suggesting that it either was not doing enough or could be doing things better. Thus while the Opposition had no hesitations about criticising both the content and application of government policy at both national and constituency levels, the Government's backbenchers criticised only policy applications at the constituency level, and sought general statements from the Government asking it to explain the content of its policy at the national level.

Another way that Labour backbenchers differed from the official Opposition in how they opposed the Government was in the way they used Adjournment debates as a way of pressing demands on the Government to widen its activities. Here the tactic of opposition was, broadly, 'Not enough is being done with respect to this problem, and I advocate increased Government activity along the following lines. . . .' Similar statements were, of course, made by Conservative MPs on a number of occasions, but far more frequently – and especially when the geographical focus was national – the line of opposition was, 'The wrong approach is being taken to this problem; the policy involved should be rejected and replaced by an alternative one.'

The large number of Adjournment debates used to obtain general statements from the Government is interesting. Such debates it will be recalled seek explanations of past, present or future government activity and are tied to no particular benefit which the backbencher hopes to obtain. It appears that the Government and backbench members of both parties welcome such debates. From the backbencher's point of view it is likely that they serve a valuable purpose as a means of bringing certain matters to the attention of the House, matters which might otherwise not be raised in the foreseeable future, or which have not been looked at closely enough in the past. Explaining why he chose to raise the subject of the Telephone Service on the

Adjournment, Henry Clark (Ulster Unionist, Antrim, North) stated,

> I have chosen this occasion because the subject of all-figure telephone numbers has barely had a mention on the Floor of the House. The first announcement was made in a written answer in July 1965, when we had other things to think of, and any other discussion has been largely in the form of Written Answers. The only reference I can find is one Question in another place, and that did not seem to produce any very valuable discussion or conclusion.[19]

From the Government's point of view Adjournment debates of this nature provide a useful means of fulfilling one of the basic functions of Parliament – informing the country of the business of the Government – and do this without making heavy inroads into the House's limited time.

The Government and Adjournment debates

The analysis so far has primarily viewed Adjournment debates from the position of the backbencher: we have examined the pre-debate background of the MP, and the geographical perspective and subject-matter of each debate. This section will concentrate on Adjournment debates from the position of the Government, looking at the Ministries involved in replying to debates, the Government's response to each debate, and an evaluation of how these responses meet the requests of the backbenchers concerned.

The number and percentage of Adjournment debates moved to the various Ministries, and a ranking of the general 'importance' of these Ministries, are reported in Table 3. An approximation of the importance of the various Ministries can be obtained from the ranking of Ministries and Members of Her Majesty's Government included in each volume of Hansard. This enables one to assume that Ministries represented in the Cabinet are more important than those excluded from it, and to list the various Cabinet and non-Cabinet Ministries in descending order of importance.[20] This does little more than reveal the

---

[19] HC Debs, Vol. 746, col. 1927.
[20] Portfolios numbered from one through fifteen were represented in the Cabinet in 1966–67, those numbered between sixteen and twenty were not.

obvious (for example, the Treasury appears more important than the Ministry of Transport which, in turn, is more important than the Ministry of Public Building and Works, and so on) but its purpose will soon become evident.

TABLE 3

Ministries Replying to Debates

	No. of Debates	Per cent	Importance of Ministry
Health	21	12·1	17
Transport	20	11·5	13
Housing and Local Government	17	9·8	10
Education and Science	16	9·2	9
Home	13	7·5	6
Scotland	12	6·9	8
Board of Trade	12	6·9	7
Labour	10	5·8	11
Treasury	8	4·6	1
Defence	8	4·6	5
Foreign Affairs	6	3·4	2
Post Office	6	3·4	19
Agriculture, Fisheries and Food	5	2·9	12
Commonwealth Affairs	5	2·9	4
Technology	4	2·3	15
Overseas Development	3	1·7	16
Wales	3	1·7	14
Social Security	3	1·7	18
Economic Affairs	2	1·1	3
Public Building and Works	1	0·6	20
Total	175	100·0	

The rank-order association between the number of Adjournment debates moved to a Ministry and the importance of that Ministry produces a weak negative relationship ($r_s = -0.21$). While this is not statistically significant the general direction of the relationship is interesting for mainly two reasons. Firstly, an impressionistic survey of the House's debates over the last few years suggests a positive relationship between the general importance of the various departments and the amount of time the House spends debating their activities, questioning their Ministers, and passing their legislation. In all these ways it is interesting to observe the manner in which the House appears to divide its time; the more important a Ministry, the more important is its business, the more the House focuses on it. Adjournment debates in general reverse this trend, concentrating on the activities of the less important departments: thus only one less Adjournment debate was moved to the Ministry of Health in 1966–67, than to the total moved to the Treasury, the Foreign Office and the Ministry of Defence. Viewed in this light Adjournment debates act as a counterbalance to the House's tendency to deal primarily with matters of major importance, acting as a potential check on those Departments which attract the attention of the House less frequently than others, in the majority of other forms of business.

A second point needs to be made. While the preceding paragraph argued that the activities of less important Ministries come before the House infrequently in other forms of business, it is necessary to explain why Adjournment debates focus on such Ministries at the expense of others. Although less important Ministries were identified above as those which the House focused on infrequently, it does not follow that the *activities* of these Ministries lack importance to the Government, the House or the constituent. Indeed the opposite is likely to be the case in all three instances. While little work has been undertaken to date on measuring the importance of legislation,[21] it appears that legislation originating from less important departments has two distinguishing characteristics; firstly, such legislation is likely to be low in quantity, and, secondly, its effects are likely to be considerable. Major Education Acts, for example, are passed infrequently, but their consequences are far-reaching not only in the long-term effects they have on society, but also in the way they bring the constituent into contact with the Government. In his day-to-day life the constituent is more likely to be affected by, and have some understanding of, his routine dealings with the Government in matters of health, housing, transport and social security, than he is to be affected by or understand the Government's activities in the area of defence, or foreign or commonwealth affairs. The distribution of Adjournment debates in Table 3 then reflects the constituency character

[21] However, see Jean Blondel, Paul Gillespie, Valentine Herman, Paul Kaati and Dick Leonard, 'Legislative Behaviour: Some steps towards a Cross-National Measurement', *Government and Opposition*, Vol. 5 (1969–70), pp. 62–85.

rather than the importance of the Ministries in the Government.

The next step in this analysis is to examine the way the Government replies to Adjournment debates. On the one hand, these replies are important for they allow us to view debates from the position of the Minister concerned – revealing how much or how little the Government is willing to take up the points raised by the backbencher. On the other hand, viewing debates from the position of the backbencher, the Ministerial reply – what is 'got' – is related to the subject-matter raised – what is 'wanted'.

Replies to Adjournment debates fall into the following nine general categories:

(1) the Government denies responsibility for the matter raised on the Adjournment, passing this to other authorities (a local council, a regional board, a nationalised industry, etc.) and regretting it cannot intervene;

(2) the Government believes that existing arrangements which it has responsibility for are satisfactory, and refuses to make any changes in them;

(3) the Government defends the general policy challenged by a matter raised on the Adjournment, either refusing to change or reject the general policy, or to adapt it or make exceptions in it to meet specific cases;

(4) the Government cannot take any action to remedy a complaint as the necessary procedures (usually of appeal) have not been completed as yet, and government intervention before such completion would be improper;

(5) the Government cannot take any action at present, as it is either studying the results of a report, or is waiting the completion of one, and will eventually take action when it has had sufficient opportunity to consider the findings;

(6) the Government gives a general statement, as requested by the backbencher, on matters for which it has responsibility;

(7) the Government is unable to remedy a situation immediately but announces its intention to do so when the legislation, orders, etc., it is either drafting or considering are passed;

(8) the Government gives its assurance that it will look, and in some cases re-look, at the matter raised on the Adjournment, and take a decision which may produce benefits in the immediate future;

(9) The Government announces that it will remedy the matter raised on the Adjournment: benefits will be apparent immediately.

In terms of what the backbencher gets compared to what he wants, these nine categories can be grouped into three more general ones. The first four categories are 'negative' – the backbencher receives no benefits from the Government as a result of raising matters on the Adjournment. For example, when Sir John Eden (Con., Bournemouth, West) sought extended parole for a constituent jailed for receiving, the spokesman for the Home Office could find no grounds to recommend a remission of the prison sentence.[22] The last three categories are 'positive' – the benefits to the backbencher are what he sought, even though there may be some time-lag before the benefits accruing from these become apparent. The Under-Secretary of State for the Army gave an assurance to Miss T. M. Quennell (Con., Petersfield) that NAAFI officials and the Southern Command would come to a satisfactory agreement with a private trader who, it was claimed, was being forced out of business.[23] The remaining two categories are of an 'intermediate' nature, neither negative nor positive – the Government does not deny the backbencher any benefits but does not provide any either.[24] For example when Robert Howarth (Lab., Botton, East) raised the matter of Derelict Industrial Sites on the Adjournment, the spokesman for the Ministry of Housing and Local Government outlined several activities that the Ministry was already engaged in to clear away these sites.[25]

Table 4 shows the distribution of Adjournment debates among these categories. The most noticeable difference between

[22] HC Debs, Vol. 735, cols. 1277–80.
[23] HC Debs, Vol. 741, cols. 581–4.
[24] Irrespective of the Government's response, all Adjournment debates provide some pay-off to the backbencher in terms of a limited amount of publicity he receives, and the opportunity he has to develop an argument in some detail and receive a ministerial reply.
[25] HC Debs, Vol. 745, cols. 1567–72.

TABLE 4
Ministerial Responses to Debates

| | Labour || Conservative ||
	No.	Per cent	No.	Per cent
Negative	36	45·0	97	60·0
Intermediate	25	31·2	20	21·1
Positive	19	23·7	18	18·9
Total	80	99·9	95	100·0

the parties is that Conservative MPs receive negative response from the Government more often than Labour MPs. To understand why this is the case we need to return to two differences between the parties outlined earlier – differences in the geographical focus and demand nature of matters raised on the Adjournment by the Opposition and by the Government's supporters. In general Conservative MPs made greater demands on the Government than Labour MPs. It will be recalled that Conservative MPs frequently challenged governmental policy at the national level, while Labour MPs emphasised policy applications at the local level and sought explanations of governmental policy at the national level. As it appears to be the case in Adjournment debates that the more a backbencher (whatever his party) asks for the less he will receive, it follows that Conservative MPs (who asked for more) received less than Labour MPs (who asked for less). Negative answers were usually given by the Government when its national policy was challenged; replies tended to be more positive when matters arising from local policy applications were raised. When the Government was asked to give a statement of its activities or asked to widen its existing activities (providing the widening sought was perceived by the Government as realistic) it usually responded in a manner which was at least intermediate and often positive.

Differences in the apparent motives of Labour and Conservative backbenchers in raising matters on the Adjournment are also related to the types of pay-offs received. Conservative MPs often pressed demands which they must have known the Government would not agree to. The tactic involved in these instances appears to be a general tactic of opposition – when in Opposition one seeks opportunities to draw the Government into debate, criticise its policies, present alternative policies of one's own, and attempt to get the views of both the Government and the Opposition on the record. Knowing that its chances of defeating the Government are negligible the Opposition can attempt only to act as a check on the Government and hope that its efforts attract the public's attention. The demands pressed in Adjournment debates by the Government's own supporters tend to be, by the Government's standards, more realisic. Here the tactic used by Labour MPs appears to be mainly that of publicising the work of the Government in a favourable manner, and challenges to it tend to be of a minor nature: major differences within the Government party are not often brought to the floor of the House, and rarely brought out in Adjournment debates.

Conclusions

Adjournment debates play an important part in the Parliamentary process. Like Questions they are one of the few devices the backbencher can use in the face of increased front-bench control over the content and time-table of the House, and increased government involvement in the lives of the people: in both these areas Adjournment debates function as a counterbalancing mechanism, returning an element of control to the backbenches.[26] More specifically they are valuable to the Parliamentary process for the following reasons. Firstly, they offer the backbencher an opportunity to raise anything he likes and in any manner he chooses on the Adjournment, subject to few procedural restrictions and the luck of the ballot. The range of topics debated in 1966–67 illustrates this: their geographical focus ranged from a flooded street in a Northern constituency to the Banaban Islands, their subject-matter ranged from a constituent's pension appeal to the work of the United Nations, the tactics used ranged from hard-hitting attacks on the Government's policies to enthusiastic support of them. Secondly, Adjournment debates provide an MP with a further and in

[26] As Dr M. P. Winstanley (Lib., Cheadle) commented in a debate: 'The opportunity of raising matters on the Adjournment is surely evidence, whatever some may say, that Honourable Members still possess valuable powers which they can use on behalf of their constituents.' HC Debs, Vol. 737, col. 1529.

some cases final, chance of bringing an issue to the attention of the Government, after letters, Questions, petitions, etc., have failed. While the Minister can avoid or dodge these if he chooses, he cannot get around Adjournment debates so easily. Thirdly, they allow specialised and in some cases topical issues to be raised in the House, when for various reasons these cannot be accommodated in other parts of the Parliamentary timetable. Fourthly, they serve as a counterbalance to the geographical focus of the remainder of the majority of the House's business, frequently drawing attention away from the national and the international and placing it on the constituency and the region. Fifthly, they focus attention on certain Departments which do not frequently attract the attention of the House, even though they may affect the daily lives of millions of people. Finally, and this is perhaps their most valuable function, they serve to make the workings of the Government and the administration more open.

Many of the above advantages are, of course, common to Questions and it is futile to search for fine distinctions in evaluating each one's contribution to the work of Parliament. Although Adjournment debates lack much of the glamour of Questions, we should not be forced to evaluate either on the basis of glamour alone. Both are valuable and essential parts of the Parliamentary process: the fact that one contains glamour and one is noticeable by its absence reveals a very satisfactory balance.

3. Private Members' Bills since 1959*

By DICK LEONARD

BACKBENCH Members of Parliament have limited opportunities to make their mark as legislators, but over two-thirds of them usually participate in the annual ballot for Private Members' Bills. The 214 Bills introduced under the ballot between 1959–69 are scrutinised, and markedly different behaviourial patterns between Labour and Conservative backbenchers emerge, as well as differences in the attitudes of Labour and Conservative Governments towards backbench legislation. In a postscript, the Bills introduced during the 1970–71 session are examined, and the conclusion emerges that those distinctions between Labour and Conservative members resulting from differences in their social and educational backgrounds are diminishing rapidly, but that those which stem from personality and ideological factors remain as wide as ever.

Sir Alan Herbert, Sydney Silverman, Leo Abse, David Steel – the list of MPs whose fame rest largely on their sponsorship of Private Members' Bills is short, and few if any of the 27 Members successful in this year's ballot are likely to be added to it. For every Bill that makes the headlines, there are scores which remain in semi-obscurity. Little noted by the public, they are also largely ignored by most academic writers on Parliament. Those authorities who have taken notice – Sir Ivor Jennings,

---

* A shorter version of this study appeared in *New Society* on 15 January 1970 while material included in the Postscript appeared in *New Society* on 25 November 1971. The author wishes to acknowledge the support of the Social Science Research Council, under whose auspices he held a Senior Research Fellowship at the University of Essex in 1968–70, when the research was carried out. The full findings may be consulted on request in the University of Essex Library under the title *The Private Member as Legislator 1959–69* (typescript).

Peter G. Richards and, in particular, P. A. Bromhead[1] – have all contributed to a consensus that inter-party differences in the treatment of Private Members' Bills are minimal, or have become so in the post-war period.

To test this view, I recently made a survey of the 214 Private Members' Bills (including 85 Acts) introduced under the annual ballot between 1959 and 1969, a period made up of two equal spells of Conservative and Labour Government.

The first significant point to emerge was that Conservative MPs have been far more active than Labour Members in this form of legislative activity. No fewer than 135 of the Bills were introduced by Tories, as against 75 by Labour MPs, the remaining four being Liberal Bills. Table 1 shows that Conservatives were more than twice as likely to enter the annual ballot in the 1959 Parliament, and since 1964 have been one-and-a-half times more likely to do so.

TABLE 1

Proportion of Eligible Members Participating in Annual Ballot

	Conservative (*per cent*)	Labour (*per cent*)
1959 Parliament	71	34
1964 Parliament	81	60
1966 Parliament	84	56

The reason for this was put to me by a Labour Whip: 'Some of our people think they are not up to introducing a Bill and piloting it through the House. They feel inhibited because of their lack of education. They have less experience than the average Tory – who is often a professional or businessman. It's difficult, for instance to imagine someone like . . . [a Yorkshire miner] introducing a Bill.'

This view is corroborated by an analysis of the names of those entering the ballot in the 1968–69 session. Only 35 per cent of Labour Members elected before 1964 took part, compared to

[1] P. A. Bromhead, *Private Members' Bills in the British Parliament* (London: Kegan Paul, 1956); Sir Ivor Jennings, *Parliament* (Cambridge U.P., 2nd ed., 1969); Peter G. Richards, *Honourable Members* (London: Faber & Faber, 2nd ed., 1964).

73 per cent of the post-1964 intake, whose average educational attainment is much higher than their predecessors' and whose economic and social background more closely resembled that of Conservative Members. A subsidiary reason for the higher Tory participation is that most members of the then Shadow Cabinet had recently taken to entering the ballot (Hogg, Joseph and Boyle were all successful during the 1964 and 1966 Parliaments), whereas Labour frontbenchers before 1964 seem to have regarded this as a sphere of activity reserved for backbenchers.

The greater activity of Tories is also reflected in the statistics for speeches and amendments. Fifty-seven per cent of all Second Reading speeches (other than those by ministers) were made by Tories, while Conservatives moved amendments to 25 per cent of the Acts passed, compared to the 16 per cent which Labour Members sought to amend. But here, too, the behavioural gap between the two parties has narrowed since 1964.

More lasting differences emerge when the subject-matter of the Bills is scrutinised. The Bills were divided into ten subject categories, five of which (accounting altogether for 46 per cent of the Bills) yielded no significant differences between the two parties. The party split of the remaining five is shown in Fig. 1.

That Tories produced many fewer pro-worker Bills than Labour and were responsible for all the pro-employer ones will cause little surprise. What may need explanation is that they promoted relatively few of the latter. The reason for this may well be that *every* Bill in this category was unsuccessful, while the overall success rate was 40 per cent (Table 2). It is clear that most Tory MPs have realised that this was an unprofitable field of activity, and have consequently looked elsewhere for likely legislative topics.

At first glance, the inter-party differences on animal welfare Bills do not appear very great, but half of the Labour Bills were anti-blood sports, and if these are excluded it emerges that Tories produced six times as many Bills as Labour in favour of 'our dumb friends'.

Perhaps the anti-blood sport Bills should have been introduced in the category of controversial social and moral issues. If this had been done it would have further increased the Labour predominance in this field. In fact this is greater than the bare figures reveal, as the Labour Bills have, on the whole, tended to

Table 2
Subject Classification of Balloted Bills, 1959–69

Subject	Passed	Not passed	Total	Proportion of All Bills (per cent)	Success rate (per cent)
1. Pro-worker	8	19	27	13	30
2. Pro-employer	—	8	8	4	—
3. Criminal Law	5	3	8	4	62
4. Animal welfare	6	10	16	8	38
5. Constitutional and Local Government	6	15	21	10	29
6. Amenity and Safety	25	21	46	22	54
7. Professional, etc. regulation	12	7	19	9	63
8. Social and Moral issues	7	13	20	9	35
9. Social Security and Family	7	23	30	14	23
10. Miscellaneous	9	10	19	9	47
Total	85	129	214	100	40

be more controversial than those introduced by the Tories. Apart from Humphrey Berkeley's Sexual Offences Bill in 1965–66, which was eventually piloted through by Leo Abse after the 1966 election, the Tory Bills in this category have mostly been minor amendments to the gaming laws. The Labour Bills have,

FIGURE 1

Proportions of Conservative and Labour Bills Dealing with Certain Subject Categories*

▨ Conservative ▮ Labour

pro-worker
▨ 5%
▮ 25%

pro-employer
▨ 6%

animal welfare
▨ 9%
▮ 5%

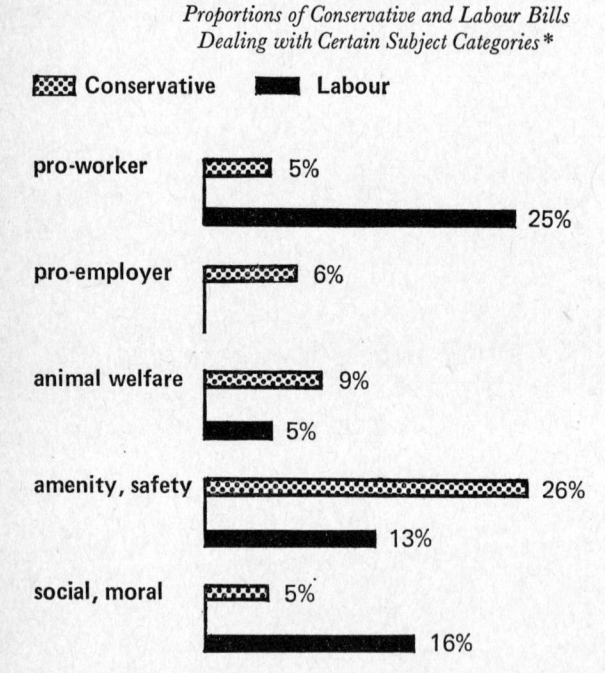

amenity, safety
▨ 26%
▮ 13%

social, moral
▨ 5%
▮ 16%

* Five other subject categories – criminal law, constitutional and local government, professional regulation, social security and miscellaneous Bills – revealed no significant inter-party difference.

by contrast, overwhelmingly been concerned with more contentious issues.

The most intriguing inter-party difference is the Tory predominance in the amenity and safety category – a large classification accounting altogether for over a fifth of the Bills introduced. Some of the Bills in this category are complex measures, such as Duncan Sandys' Civic Amenities Act 1967 or Robert Maxwell's Clean Air Act 1968, which respectively occupy 24 and 16 pages in the Statute Book. More typically however, they have been modest proposals of a largely technical nature to improve the quality or efficiency of some small element of the national environment. The category is, in fact, largely co-terminous with that characterised by Jennings as 'useful non-controversial legislation'.

A fair number of these Bills are prepared inside government departments and are given to Members successful in the ballot, who have no Bills of their own to introduce. The exact proportion cannot be determined, as steps are often taken to disguise the origin of such Bills, and even the Whips are not always in the know, as Parliamentary Private Secretaries are sometimes used as go-betweens. But it seems likely that around one-half of the amenity and safety Bills emanate from the Government, and in most cases these Bills would be given to its own supporters.

When these amenity and safety Bills are divided into those introduced before and after 1964, a sharper contrast emerges (Table 3). Labour Members appear to be willing to introduce such Bills only when their party is in Government, and they are pressed upon them by the Whips. But Conservative MPs continued to introduce a steady stream of such Bills even when they went into opposition. Personality differences between Labour and Tory Members may explain this variation. Tories seem happy to promote small, unexciting Bills which secure limited improvements in the law, whereas Labour Members, unless prompted by the Whips, tend to concentrate on larger, more flamboyant enterprises, which may have considerably lower chances of success.

TABLE 3
Amenity and Safety Bills, by Party

	Number of Bills	
	Conservative	Labour
1959–64	20	1
1964–69	15	9

Another effect of the change of Government in 1964 was the variation in the success rate of Labour and Conservative Bills (Table 4). It is evident that Bills introduced by Government supporters are much more likely to be passed. Up to 1964 Tory Bills were more than twice as likely to be successful as Labour Bills; between 1964–69 the ratio was reversed. The overall success rate declined too from 58 per cent in the 1959 Parliament to 31 per cent in the first three sessions of the 1966 Parliament, in spite of the decision in 1967 to provide an extra six days per session for Private Members' Bills, and the additional provision of time (during all-night sittings) for the Report Stages of a handful of important Bills such as the Abortion and Divorce Reform Bills. But the increased flow of such controversial measures placed greater pressure on the time available and had the unintended consequences of producing a higher casualty rate for less contentious Bills.

TABLE 4
Success Rate of Bills

		Bills introduced	Bills passed	Success rate (per cent)
1959–64	Conservative	69	48	70
	Labour	28	9	32
	All	97	57	58
1966–69	Conservative	36	6	17
	Labour	38	16	42
	Liberal	4	2	50
	All	78	24	31

Although more Bills fell by the wayside, one welcome development was a decline in the practice of 'talking out' Bills, much favoured by Tory Whips in the 1959 Parliament. The proportion of Bills talked out was more than halved after 1966, as a direct result of a change in tactics by Labour Whips, one of whom told me: 'If we don't like a Bill we think it's more honest to vote it down rather than to block it by procedural means.' Table 5 shows the relative increase in the number of Bills negatived and the decrease in the proportion 'talked out' in the 1966 Parliament, and also clearly indicates that both these tactics are employed primarily against Bills proposed by Opposition Members.

Divisions are still infrequent, but their incidence has trebled since 1966, reversing a forty-year downward trend (Fig. 2). Even so, divisions in which a substantial number of Members

TABLE 5
Progress of Balloted Bills in House of Commons, 1959–69 and 1966–69

Stage reached	Labour Bills No.	Prop. (%)	Conservative Bills No.	Prop. (%)	All Bills No.	Prop. (%)
1959–64						
No 2R debate	4	14	7	10	11	11
2R Adjourned ('talked out')	10⎫	36⎫	7⎫	10⎫	17⎫	18⎫
2R – negatived	4⎬14	14⎬50	2⎬11	3⎬16	6⎬25	6⎬26
2R – withdrawn	—⎭	—⎭	2⎭	3⎭	2⎭	2⎭
Committee	—	—	3	4	3	3
Report	1	4	—	—	1	1
Passed	9	32	48	70	57	59
1966–69						
No 2R debate	12	32	13	36	26	33
2R Adjourned ('talked out')	1⎫	3⎫	4⎫	11⎫	5⎫	6⎫
2R – negatived	—⎬8	—⎬8	10⎬15	28⎬42	11⎬19	14⎬24
2R – withdrawn	2⎭	5⎭	1⎭	3⎭	3⎭	4⎭
Committee	2	5	—	—	2	3
Report	5	13	2	6	7	9
Passed	16	42	6	17	24	31

take part are rare – only five issues have produced divisions in which more than 200 Members have taken part. Figure 3 shows how Labour and Conservative Members voted in important divisions on these five topics, two of which were on Ten-Minute Rule Bills.

On average, in these five divisions some 52 per cent of Labour Members participated, of whom 90 per cent voted on the 'liberal' side. Tory participation was somewhat lower – 40 per cent voted, of whom 69 per cent cast their votes on the 'anti-liberal' side. This is the only aspect in which Tories have been found to be less active – the reason being either a greater reluctance by Tories to commit themselves on controversial issues or a feeling of resignation by opponents of these 'permissive' measures, who realised in advance that they were likely to be passed.

Although it has been widely recognised that Labour MPs are predominantly supporters, and Tories opponents, of such reforms, it seems to have escaped notice that the 'anti-liberal' fringe of the Labour Party is markedly smaller than the Tories' 'pro-liberal' faction. In the five divisions noted, 34 per cent of all Tory MPs voted at least once on the 'liberal' side; whereas only 19 per cent of Labour Members found their way on one occasion or more into the 'anti-liberal' lobby.

The characteristics of the 'liberal' Tories have already been described by Anthony King.[2] They tend to be younger, wealthier and better educated than their fellow Conservatives. An analysis of the fifteen Labour MPs who cast two or more 'anti-liberal' votes in the 1966 Parliament reveals them to have exactly contrary characteristics. Elderly, working-class, poorly educated, they are predominantly trade unionists representing industrial constituencies in Scotland and Lancashire.

Moreover they are fast disappearing from the Parliamentary scene. One, Mrs Cullen, is already dead, and several others announced their retirement. Less than half of them survived the 1970 general election: their replacements are in general younger, better educated and consequently less likely to adopt an anti-liberal posture. A similar process of replacement is concurrently taking place in the Conservative Party, but as younger Tories

[2] *New Society*, 2 May 1968, p. 631.

PRIVATE MEMBERS' BILLS SINCE 1959   135

FIGURE 2

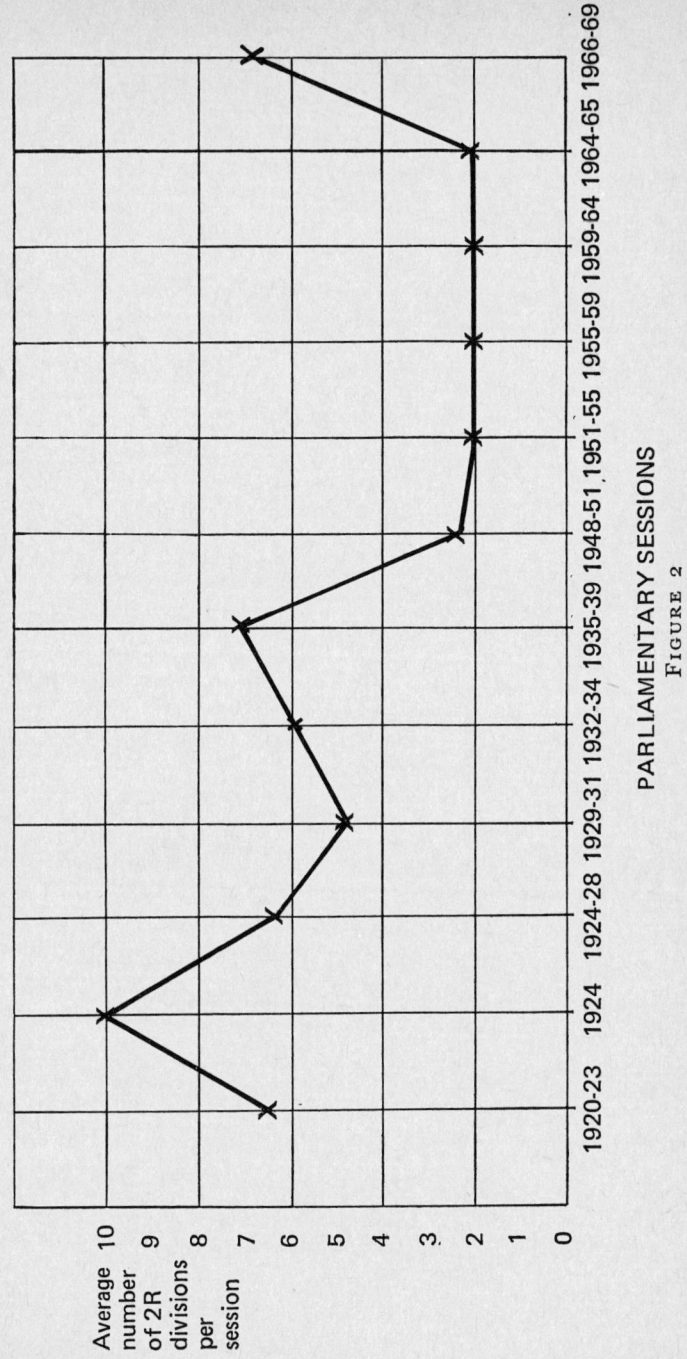

Average Number of Second Reading Divisions per Session – 1920–69

Conservative ▨▨▨ Labour ▇▇▇

ANTI-REFORM   PRO-REFORM

MPs voting 100   0   100   200

abortion

homosexual
law reform

divorce

Sunday
entertainment

capital
punishment

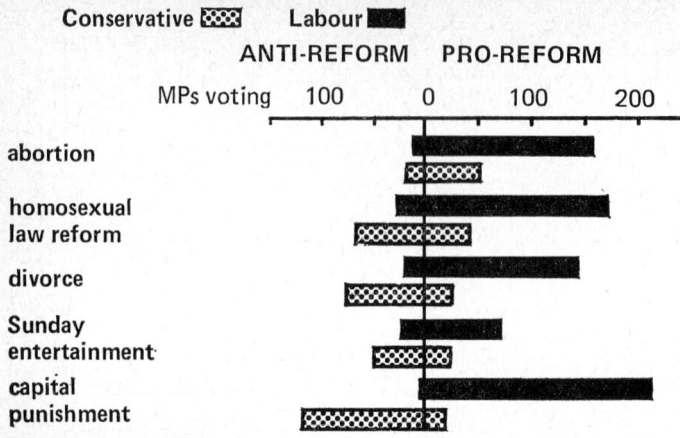

The five divisions were:
1. David Steel's Abortion Act, 2nd reading (Lab, 162–12; Con, 51–17)
2. Leo Abse's Sexual Offences Act, 1st reading (Lab, 187–32; Con, 47–68
3. Alec Jones's Divorce Reform Act, 2nd reading (Lab, 153–19; Con, 22–83)
4. John Parker's Sunday Entertainment Bill, 2nd reading (Lab, 82–25; Con 21–67)
5. Duncan Sandys's Capital Punishment Bill, 1st reading (Lab, 228–4; Con 21–121 — votes against given first)

FIGURE 3

*Party Votes in Five Important Divisions
1966–69*

are less uniformly liberal the balance within the party is changing more slowly.[3]

It is evident that *both* parties are becoming more 'liberal', but the Labour Party is doing so at a more rapid rate. Despite the arguments of Samuel Brittan and Christopher Mayhew,[4] there is no evidence of a reduction in the size of the gap between

---

[3] A more detailed analysis of intra-party voting on these five issues is included in Peter G. Richards, *Parliament and Conscience* (London: Allen & Unwin, 1970), Chapter Nine.

[4] See Samuel Brittan, *Left or Right – The Bogus Dilemma* (London: Secker & Warburg, 1968); Christopher Mayhew, *Party Games* (London: Hutchinson, 1969).

them. In the future, the Labour Party is likely to be even more monolithically pro-liberal than at present, while the Conservatives will be increasingly split between an anti-liberal majority and a slowly waxing liberal minority.

Postscript 1971

The period of the Wilson government was characterised by a significant widening of the scope of Private Members' Bills – important reforming measures such as the abolition of capital punishment and of theatre censorship and divorce, abortion and homosexual law reform all reached the Statute Book through the initiative of backbench Members. The Labour Government, while not collectively adopting an attitude towards the merits of these Bills, held that it was right that Parliament should be able to decide for or against them, and facilitated this by the provision of drafting assistance and of crucial additional Parliamentary time for their Report stages. The general attitude of the Government towards Private Members' Bills was encouraging – partly because most Ministers were personally sympathetic to many of the proposed reforms, and apparently also because they calculated that such activities would usefully absorb much of the surplus energies of their frustrated backbench supporters which might otherwise find more disruptive outlets.

At the end of the first Parliamentary session of the Heath administration, it is evident that this relaxed attitude towards backbenchers' Bills has been replaced by a more restrictive approach. In fact Ministers lost no time in making this clear. On 3 November 1970 William Whitelaw, the Leader of the House, moved a Sessional Order reducing the number of days available for Private Members' Bills from 16 to 12, which had the effect of reducing from 27 to 20 the number of Bills which could be introduced. On 18 February 1971 he told the House, 'I wish to stick to the principle that the Government do not give time to Private Members' Bills'.

The Government held to this firm resolve even to the extent of letting the Divorce (Scotland) Bill founder, although Ministers had indicated their support on Second Reading and even though its failure meant the continuance of inconvenient and indefensible anomalies between the divorce laws of England and Scotland. Mr Whitelaw also proposed to downgrade Ten-Minute Rule Bills by switching them from their 'peak viewing time' of 3.30 in the afternoon to late at night, as had been recommended by the Select Committee on Procedure. But this was defeated by a backbench rebellion in which 47 Conservatives joined with 120 Labour Members and two Liberals in voting down a motion which was supported, on a free vote, by only 48 Tories and six Labour MPs.

The 1970–71 session provided some evidence that Tory Whips were resorting to their earlier tactic of 'talking out' inconvenient Bills rather than continuing the more recent Labour practice of seeking to negative them on a division. As in all recent sessions under both Labour and Tory governments, a higher proportion of Bills introduced by Government rather than Opposition supporters was successful. Of the 20 Bills introduced, seven were passed – an overall success rate of 35 per cent; but five out of nine Tory Bills passed (55 per cent) compared to only two out of eleven Labour Bills (18 per cent).

The figures for Members taking part in the annual ballot in 1970–71 corroborate my earlier finding that the greater propensity for Tory Members to participate was due primarily to social and educational differences in the background of MPs and that, as these narrowed, the gap between the parties was likely to disappear. As indicated earlier, the 1964 and 1966 intake of Labour Members had already contributed to this, and the 1970 election seems to have completed the process. The 365 Members taking part in the ballot for 1970–71 included exactly two-thirds of the eligible Members of both major parties (see Table 6).

TABLE 6

Proportion of Eligible Members Participating in Annual Ballot

	Conservative (per cent)	Labour (per cent)
1959 Parliament	71	34
1964 Parliament	81	60
1966 Parliament	84	56
1970 Parliament	66	66

In the future, as the average educational attainment of Labour MPs continues to improve, the prospect is that Labour Members will become more active than Conservatives in promoting Private Members' Bills. This was foreshadowed in the 1970–71 session by the figures for Ten-Minute Rule Bills, the time for which is allocated on a first come, first served basis. There were 20 Labour Bills and only seven Conservative.

In their choice of Bills Labour Members continued to be more ambitious than Conservatives. The subject-matter of Labour Bills ranged over Divorce (Scotland) and Protection of Human Rights to House of Commons (Conditions of Service). Tory Bills dealt with more mundane topics such as the Interest on Damages (Scotland) Act and the Administration of Estates Act, while only one Conservative Bill – the Shops (Weekday Trading) Bill, which was talked out by Labour supporters of USDAW, the shop workers' union, provoked any serious controversy in the House. In fact, a clear majority of the nine Conservative Bills were taken 'off the peg' – being either Bills which had almost been legislated in the previous session, but had been cut off by the general election, Law Commission Bills or non-controversial measures put up by government departments. Of the eleven Labour Bills only two fell into these categories.

As in the earlier period, the sharpest contrast between Labour and Conservative Members was revealed in their voting behaviour in divisions on Bills raising controversial social and moral issues. In the 1970–71 session there was only one such division on a balloted Bill – the closure vote on Robert Hughes' Divorce (Scotland) Bill but relevant divisions also took place on three Ten-Minute Rule Bills – John Parker's Sunday Entertainment Bill, Kevin McNamara's Hare Coursing (Abolition) Bill and Mrs Sally Oppenheim's Family Law Reform Act 1969 (Amendment) Bill. The purpose of this last Bill was to permit medical practitioners to reveal to parents of patients under eighteen details of their treatment, including prescription of the Pill. Table 7 sets out the voting figures in these divisions.

The figures are striking – Labour Members contributing as many as 472 of the 528 'pro-liberal' votes, while Tories were responsible for 199 of the 243 'anti-liberal' votes. Of the

TABLE 7

Party Votes in Four Important Divisions 1970–71

	'Pro-liberal'			'Anti-liberal'		
	Lab.	Con.	Total	Lab.	Con.	Total
Sunday entertainment	96	18	115	34	81	118
Family law	152	2	157	—	108	108
Hare coursing	167	14	183	—	—	—
Divorce (Scotland)	57	13	73	7	10	17
Total	472	47	528	41	199	243

Labour votes cast 92 per cent were pro-liberal (compared to 90 per cent in comparable divisions in the 1966–70 Parliament), while 81 per cent of the Conservative votes were cast on the anti-liberal side (cf. 69 per cent in 1966–70). On the basis of these figures a case could be argued that the Conservatives are actually becoming *less* liberal on social issues, though in view of the small proportion of Conservative Members who took part in these divisions (only 17 per cent, on average, compared with 45 per cent of Labour MPs), one must proceed with caution. What cannot be denied is that words written twelve years ago by Roy Jenkins in a chapter entitled 'Is Britain Civilised?' remain at least as true today. He wrote then: 'It is ... clear that on a wide variety of libertarian issues the balance of feeling within the Conservative Party is very different from that within the Labour Party.'[4]

[4] Roy Jenkins, *The Labour Case* (Harmondsworth: Penguin Books, 1959), p. 140.

4. Backbench and Opposition Amendments to Government Legislation

By VALENTINE HERMAN

IT has long been argued that certain stages of the legislative process are almost exclusively controlled by the executive. The following paper* focuses on the Government's control of its own legislation during the Committee of the Whole House and Report stages. Valentine Herman examines the fate of Opposition and backbench amendments moved to government legislation in these stages during the 1968–69 Parliamentary session. Although he finds that only a small number of opposition and backbench amendments are accepted, many others are indirectly incorporated or accommodated by the Government into its legislation.

The various stages of the legislative process in Great Britain fulfil two objectives; discussion of the general principles of legislation and scrutiny of its detailed aspects: the Second and Third Readings of Bills focus on the former, while the Committee and Report stages concentrate on the latter. Reviews of outputs of Parliament, the end-products of the legislative process, inevitably fail to cast much light on the way the House deals with these outputs at the different stages of the legislative process. Each stage, or set of stages, has a distinct purpose, and it is valuable to focus on these stages as well as the outputs themselves. This paper examines amendments moved to government legislation in the Committee of the Whole House and Report stages during the 1968–69 Parliamentary session. Before turning to a detailed analysis of these amendments, it is useful to consider reasons why the Government, backbenchers of the governing party, and the Opposition are interested in amending, and attempting to amend, government legislation.

---

* The author is indebted to Dick Leonard and Norma Percy for their helpful comments on the manuscript.

Following this we will look at the volume of amendments moved to government legislation, the amount they changed (or would have changed, if they had been accepted) this legislation, the fate of these amendments and, finally, a detailed assessment of the success that movers of amendments had.

However, before we can approach these matters it is necessary to give some consideration to the reasons why amendments are moved. In particular we are interested in the legislative background of amendments and the motives of Members who move them. A comprehensive treatment of these points would be impossible in a work of this length even if the process of government was completely open, and we can do little more than provide a few generalisations. Whatever their limitations, these generalisations will, it is hoped, be useful in that they will enable us to appreciate some of the constraints behind, and tactics of, the legislative process which will be of some advantage when we turn to the numerical analysis which follows this discussion.

The reasons why the Government of the day moves amendments to its own legislation are illustrated by Walkland:

> Often a Bill will be incomplete at its stage of introduction to Parliament – although, as mentioned earlier, the main deliberative stage of legislation occurs before Parliament is brought formally into the process. But although inter-Departmental consultation will already have taken place at the stage of the initial preparation of a Bill and in the appropriate policy committee of the Cabinet, and although consultation with pressure groups will also have been usually thorough, many representations on the details of the Bill may still remain to be made, as will a number of last-minute drafting amendments. Much of the Parliamentary Committee proceedings is a 'Ministerial' stage where refinements are added and administrative oversight corrected on the basis of the printed and published Bill.[1]

The Opposition, excluded from these often very long and involved initial deliberations, has its first Parliamentary opportunity to examine the details of legislation in Committee and

[1] S. A. Walkland, *The Legislative Process in Great Britain* (London: Allen & Unwin, 1968), p. 76.

Report. Before these stages the Opposition is likely to have given detailed consideration to the amendments it will move. Some of the amendments moved by the Opposition (many of which will be inspired by pressure groups) during these stages can be seen as propaganda exercises designed to attract the Government's and, it is hoped, the nation's, attention to what it perceives as flaws and inadequacies in the details of the Government's policies. Other Opposition amendments (which again may originate from pressure groups) represent sincere and relatively non-partisan efforts to improve the legislation under consideration.

Backbenchers of the governing party have greater access to the Government than the Opposition has and, as a result of this, greater opportunities to suggest changes to a proposed piece of legislation in its pre-parliamentary stages. These suggestions are also likely to be accepted by a Minister in many instances: although government supporters are reluctant to offer important amendments which might be unacceptable in Committee and Report, they do not have the same qualms about advancing them before these stages where the chances of the Government's receiving them favourably are increased. This is especially the case in those instances when Government backbenchers are excluded from the early deliberative stages of legislation and only learn of the details of a Bill immediately before it is published: by that time the main lines of policy will have been determined by the Cabinet. On occasions, the Opposition and backbench members of the Government move amendments, not in the hope that they will be successful and change the content of legislation but to secure from the Government explanations of previous decisions it has taken or to put pressure on the Government to take a decision in the future. In these instances amendments are moved, as are Parliamentary Questions and Adjournment debates, in order to make the workings of the Government more open. This point is returned to below when we examine more comprehensively the various ways in which amendments achieve success for non-Government MPs.

Of the 51 Government Acts passed during the 1968–69 session, amendments moved to 45 of them are included in the present study. Excluded are all amendments which were moved to six financial and perennial Acts, and four Government Bills which failed to reach the statute book. Amendments moved to Bills in Standing Committee are not considered here, nor are amendments which were put down by Members but not chosen. Only those amendments which were selected by the Speaker and moved by a Member on the floor of the House are under analysis.

A total of 768 amendments were moved to these 45 Acts in the Committee of the Whole House and Report stages. Almost 70 per cent of these amendments (533) came from the Government, over a quarter (211) came from the Conservative side of the House, and the remainder were shared almost evenly by the twelve Liberal MPs who moved 14 amendments, and Labour backbenchers who moved 10 of them. In many instances Opposition amendments could not be affectively divided between front- and backbenchers, and are combined in the following analysis. A number of reasons will be advanced below why the Government moved almost two and a half times more amendments to its own Bills than did the Opposition, but before moving to this it is worth considering why only 10 amendments to the Bills under discussion were moved from the Labour backbenches. This small number of amendments does not reflect a lack of interest or lack of involvement in the legislation on their part for they made about as many speeches in the Committee and Report stages as Opposition members did. The main difference lies in the fact that the Opposition's speeches were usually concerned with moving amendments, and speeches from the Labour back benches were usually concerned with arguments against these amendments. By the time government legislation reached the Committee and Report stages it would have been, on the whole, acceptable to Labour backbenchers who would have taken advantage of extra- and pre-parliamentary opportunities afforded to them to put desired alterations in legislation to Ministers in party meetings and other discussions. Most usually Ministers would have accepted these amendments, or put forward sound reasons why they could not be accepted which satisfied a backbencher: in either case it would have been unnecessary for the backbencher to offer the same amendment at a later moment. On occasions, Labour backbenchers were quite obviously not totally satisfied with legislation by the time it reached the Committee of the Whole House and Report stages, but often reasons such as the force of party loyalty, and unfavourable publicity resulting from party splits, overrode their desire to change the details of Bills. In spite of this some amendments were quite clearly 'arranged' between the Minister and the Member; others arose when the Member had no opportunity to approach the Minister in advance; others represent instances where backbenchers continued to press a Minister on matters he had previously rejected; and still others were propaganda exercises to ventilate grievances publicly. Unfortunately the small number of amendments moved by Labour backbenchers does not provide us with many opportunities to develop these points in any detail, although we are able to give them a little more consideration later.

In the meantime however it would be misleading to suggest that all the 768 amendments moved would have had identical effects on legislation had they been carried: some were designed to alter the content of Bills significantly, while others were concerned with 'tidying-up' legislation, dotting i's and crossing t's. Although it is very difficult to make exacting distinctions between amendments, it is possible to place them into four somewhat crude but analytically useful categories according to the extent of departure, or change, they intended to make from the original text of a Bill. These categories allow us to place amendments on a continuum of 'importance'. The first of these categories – major amendments – contains proposals to make fundamental changes in a Bill, and includes amendments which intend to change the major principles behind a Bill, and amendments intended to negate a Bill. A second category – important amendments – contains proposals to make substantial changes within the general principles of the Bill. The third category – minor amendments – contains proposals to change relatively unimportant details of a Bill, while the fourth category – technical amendments – is concerned with correcting drafting errors, clarifying the original text without altering its content, and bringing later parts of a Bill into line with earlier parts which have been amended.

The distribution of amendments in 1968–69 between these categories is presented in Table 1. What is perhaps most noticeable about this distribution is that less than a seventh of the total number of amendments moved are of a major or important nature. In other words, only about 100 amendments were offered in the session which intended to make significant changes in the Government's legislation: most of the amendments offered were of a minor or textual nature, and most of these minor and textual amendments came from the Government. A closer inspection of these figures reveals further differences between the Government and the Opposition. Three-quarters of the major and important amendments were moved by the Opposition who were more likely than the Government to direct their efforts to attempt to change the major details rather than the

TABLE 1

Importance of Amendments Moved

	Major	Important	Minor	Technical	Total
Government	3	19	81	430	533
Labour	2	2	4	2	10
Conservative	17	56	123	15	211
Liberal	1	5	8	—	14
Total	23	82	216	447	768

technical aspects of legislation. However, although the Opposition appears almost unconcerned with these technical aspects, almost half of its amendments fall within the minor category. As the Opposition, in many instances, is likely to have unsuccessfully attempted to amend the major principles of legislation at earlier moments in Committee and Report, these minor amendments represent their attempts to alter the relatively unimportant and uncontroversial details of Bills. This is more or less as expected; opposition is to the principles and details of legislation, not its wording. That the Government moves relatively few major and important amendments in Committee and Report, and moves less minor amendments than the Opposition, is perhaps less expected. As few of the Government amendments are either major or important it appears that by the time legislation reaches these stages the Government is quite satisfied with the principal parts of its Bills and unlikely to make significant changes in them. Amendments which fall into the minor category and are moved by the Government again represent desires to change the details rather than the principles of legislation. As over four-fifths of the Government amendments are of a technical nature, the Committee and Report stages are mainly used by the Government to tidy-up the more technical aspects of legislation. On the other hand, the Opposition uses these stages to challenge the principles of the Government's legislation.

We turn now from an examination of the various levels of importance of amendments moved to a consideration of their 'fate' – whether or not they were accepted by the House. Amendments to legislation which are successful (and successful in this context implies they are incorporated into the legislation) are made in one of two ways, either they are passed following a Division of the House, or agreed to without a Division. Amendments which are unsuccessful (that is, are not incorporated into legislation) are defeated following a Division, negatived without a Division, or withdrawn. A number of differences between the fate of Government and Opposition amendments which Table 2 highlights are worthy of attention.

TABLE 2
Fate of Amendments

	Passed on Division	Agreed	Defeated on Division	Negatived	Withdrawn	Total
Government	13	520	—	—	—	533
Labour	—	2	4	3	1	10
Conservative	—	12	81	57	61	211
Liberal	—	—	—	7	7	14
Total	13	534	85	67	69	768

Although 547 of the 768 amendments (slightly over 70 per cent) were successful, it can be seen that almost all these were Government amendments. While the Opposition only managed to have 12 (5 per cent) of its 225 amendments accepted, the Government was 100 per cent successful in passing all the amendments it moved: this is one indication of the control the Government exerts over its own legislation. A second is provided by the fact that all 14 of the non-Government amendments (12 moved by the Opposition, and 2 moved by Labour backbenchers) which were successful were acceptable to the Government: the Government resisted all other amendments to which it had objections. A final indication of government control can be seen by examining the amendments which led to Divisions. Of these 98 amendments, 13 (all moved by the Government) were passed, and 85 (81 moved by Conservatives, and 4 moved by Labour backbenchers) were defeated. The Opposition was quite obviously more keen to press its own amendments to a Division than was the Government: on average one in every three Opposition amendments was divided on compared to only one in every fifty Government amendments.

Table 3 examines the fate of amendments by their importance and allows us to expand on two points which have already been mentioned briefly in the analysis to date. Looking first at the Opposition amendments it is noticeable that all twelve of the successful amendments which came from that side of the House fall into the minor and technical categories: not a single major or important Opposition amendment was accepted by the Government. Thus it appears that although the Government was willing on rare occasions to accept Opposition amendments it would only do so if they satisfied at least two conditions: first and most importantly they had to be acceptable to the Government and secondly they had to alter the less important details, rather than the major principles of the Government's legislation. The more an Opposition amendment represented a significant departure from the contents of a Government Bill, the less likely it was to be accepted. The 213 Opposition amendments which the Government resisted failed to meet either or both of the above conditions.

Turning again to the amendments which led to Divisions, from Table 3 we see that 67 per cent of the Government's major amendments were divided on, 35 per cent of their important amendments and 8 per cent of their minor amendments. Comparable figures for the Opposition amendments which led to Divisions are 76 per cent for major amendments, 64 per cent for important amendments and 22 per cent for minor amendments. Not a single technical amendment moved by either the Government or the Opposition led to a Division. These figures suggest that the more important an amendment the more likely it is to be divided on and that whatever the level of importance of an amendment the Opposition is more likely to press it to a Division than the Government.

TABLE 3

Fate of Amendments by Importance and Origin

	Passed on Division	Agreed	Defeated on Division	Negatived	Withdrawn	Total
A. Government Amendments						
Major	2	1	—	—	—	3
Important	5	14	—	—	—	19
Minor	6	75	—	—	—	81
Technical	—	430	—	—	—	430
Total	13	520	—	—	—	533
B. Labour Amendments						
Major	—	—	2	—	—	2
Important	—	—	1	1	—	2
Minor	—	1	1	1	1	4
Technical	—	1	—	1	—	2
Total	—	2	4	3	1	10
C. Conservative Amendments						
Major	—	—	13	1	3	17
Important	—	—	39	8	9	56
Minor	—	7	29	45	42	123
Technical	—	5	—	3	7	15
Total	—	12	81	57	61	211
D. Liberal Amendments						
Major	—	—	—	1	—	1
Important	—	—	—	2	3	5
Minor	—	—	—	4	4	8
Technical	—	—	—	—	—	—
Total	—	—	—	7	7	14

The discussion to date has revealed and emphasised the strength of the Government and the weakness of the Opposition in the passage of amendments to Government Bills in the Committee and Report stages. The Government has been portrayed as 'strong' because it secures the passage of all its amendments and is successful with its amendments which are decided in the Division Lobbies: in contrast the Opposition has been portrayed as 'weak' because only a handful of its less important amendments are successful, and because all its amendments which it divides the House on are defeated. From the essentially numerical analysis so far undertaken these findings can hardly be contested. However, when we look more closely at the sources of Government amendments and the reason why certain types of Opposition amendments are withdrawn, we must make important modifications to a number of our earlier conclusions.

The Parliamentary stages a Bill has to pass through are the last ones in the legislative process. The contents of a typical Bill introduced into Parliament will have been determined on the one hand by politicians and Civil Servants, and on the other hand by spokesmen for various interests in the community. It is unlikely that earlier Parliamentary stages through which a Bill passes before it reaches the Committee of the Whole House and Report stages (unless it has been sent to a Standing Committee) will have significantly altered its contents. However, during these early Parliamentary stages, and earlier in party meetings, consultations with bodies affected by the proposed legislation, and informal discussions, the Minister responsible for a Bill will have heard many suggestions, arguments and alterations designed to change its contents. Some of the points made to him will have been resisted vigorously, others reluctantly, and on still others the Minister will have postponed making an immediate decision whether or not to incorporate them into the Bill until he has had further time to consider them.

In the Committee and Report stages Ministers often acknowledge that amendments to Bills moved by the Government have in fact originated from Labour backbenchers or members of the Opposition during earlier Parliamentary stages of the legislative process. Although the wording of these amendments when reintroduced by the Government is frequently different from the original wording the content is usually very similar. From Table 4, which records the number of amendments moved by the Government which originated with the Opposition or with Labour backbenchers, it can be seen that about one in ten of the total number of amendments moved in 1968–69 have this background. If we exclude the relatively unimportant and non-contentious technical amendments from consideration, this figure is reduced to one in five.

TABLE 4
Government Amendments made on behalf of

	Major	Important	Minor	Technical	Total
Labour	—	3	2	—	5
Opposition	1	8	34	26	69
Total	1	11	36	26	74

Perhaps not too much should be made of the fact that there are few Labour backbench amendments which fall into this category: we have seen earlier that Labour backbenchers move few amendments anyway and, in attempting to change the content of legislation, probably use other methods than the amendment on the floor of the House. In the light of our previous discussion two other points are more important. Firstly, the amendments which are moved by the Government and which originated from the Opposition cover all levels of importance from major to technical. Although it was suggested above that an Opposition amendment would only be agreed to by the Government if it satisfied two conditions (acceptable to the Government and relatively unimportant) it appears that the first of these requires some qualification, and the second does not hold absolutely. Although it remains critically important that an Opposition amendment be acceptable to the Government, the Government will not choose to defeat or negative an amendment from the Opposition when it is first raised if further time is required to consider it. If this is the case then a member of the Opposition moving such an amendment is likely to withdraw it and the Government will reintroduce it in its own name later. As can be seen from Table 4 not all amendments of this type are minor and technical ones: the Opposition is, then, able to make major and important contributions to Government legislation, though these come about in a somewhat roundabout fashion which changes their 'parentage'. These amendments represent Opposition successes as they are accepted by the Government and incorporated into its legislation.

A second point relating to the Opposition's numerical rather than qualitative successes in the legislative process follows from this. We saw earlier, it will be recalled, that only 12 out of 225 Opposition amendments were passed in the Committee and Report stages. Of the Government's 533 amendments, 79 originated from the Opposition and 5 from Labour backbenchers, and it is necessary to subtract these from the total number of Government amendments and to adjust the other figures presented in Table 3 accordingly. If we exclude technical amendments from consideration the number of amendments passed by the Government which did not originate from the Opposition or Labour backbenchers is reduced to 2 major, 8 important and 45 minor. If we add the number of Government amendments moved on behalf of the Opposition to the total number of Opposition amendments passed, the number of successful Opposition amendments is increased to 1 major, 8 important and 41 minor. Although the total volume of non-technical amendments under consideration remains the same, differences between the Government and the Opposition have been considerably reduced. Even though the recalculated number of Opposition amendments has markedly increased, this increase is still ultimately dependent upon the benevolence of the Government. The Opposition, however, can be seen to have a greater influence in determining the content of legislation than was originally portrayed.

A further alteration to our earlier findings regarding the weakness of the Opposition in the amending stages of the legislative process also needs to be made. In the preceding discussion of the fate of amendments it was postulated that amendments either succeeded or failed; in the former instance they were either passed following a Division of the House or agreed to without a Division; in the latter they were defeated in a Division, negatived or withdrawn. This success–failure distinction is rather too clear cut for it rests on the not completely correct assumption that the sole purpose behind these amendments was to alter the content of Bills. Not all amendments however were moved with this purpose in mind. When we examine the reasons why a large number of Opposition amendments were withdrawn we can see what the intention behind them was in more detail, and relate these intentions to the success of the amendments concerned.

It is possible to identify two main reasons which explain why amendments moved by the Opposition were withdrawn. A first category were withdrawn because they appeared unnecessary after an explanation given by a Minister. These probing amendments were initially moved in the hope that the Government would clear up uncertainties and confusions that the Opposition had about the content of the Government's legislation. Following satisfactory explanations about the matters in question by the Minister it was not necessary for the Opposition to pursue the amendments any further and it was logical to withdraw them. A second category of Opposition amendments also led to satisfactory responses from the Government and were withdrawn. The responses in these instances were in the form of assurances given by the Government to points that the Opposition raised. On some occasions these were assurances that the Government would move the amendment later in its own name – although the Government accepted the spirit of the amendment it was unable to accept it at the present time either because it wanted more time to consider the matter, or because the drafting of the Opposition's amendment was unsatisfactory. On other occasions the Government's assurances took the form that the legislation it was proposing was satisfactory and it would meet the Opposition's point when implementing the measure. Amendments which fall into either of these categories represent successes for the Opposition. Their success lies not in the fact that they were accepted, rather in the fact that they were not refused: they realised at least what, and sometimes more than they were intended to achieve even though they were not immediately incorporated into the legislation under consideration. There is a quite distinct similarity between the way backbench MPs move amendments and withdraw them for reasons outlined above, and the way they use Parliamentary Questions and Adjournment debates: through each one of these devices the backbencher can attempt to make the workings of the Government more open.

The number and importance of Opposition amendments withdrawn is presented in Table 5. On the basis of the arguments in the last two paragraphs it is necessary to reconsider once again the conclusions we drew earlier from Table 3 relating to the success of Opposition amendments. Amendments with which the Opposition had definite success are those which were accepted by the Government, and those which were moved by the Government but originated with the Opposition: there were 81 of these, 1 major, 8 important, 41 minor and 31 technical. To these must be added those Opposition amendments shown in Table 5 which were withdrawn when they achieved what they meant to. Altogether 149 Opposition amendments were successful (4 major, 17 important, 86 minor and 42 technical) compared with 145 unsuccessful Opposition amendments (15 major, 49 important, 78 minor and 3 technical) which were either negatived or defeated following a Division.

TABLE 5

Opposition Amendments: Reasons for Withdrawal

	Major	Important	Minor	Technical	Total
Probing	1	4	21	5	31
Assurances given	2	5	24	6	37
Total	3	9	45	11	68

By judiciously reconsidering the figures and conclusions presented earlier the success of the Opposition in the amending stages of Government legislation can be seen in a different light. It is inadequate merely to consider the number of Opposition amendments which are accepted in the Committee and Report stages because the Opposition cannot and does not expect all its amendments to receive the same treatment by the Government. This becomes evident when we consider the content of these amendments. One category of amendments contains policy differences between the Government and the Opposition: these amendments are not accepted by the Government and the majority of them are disposed of in the Division Lobbies. A second category of amendments does not divide the Government and the Opposition so fundamentally: these are amendments which the Opposition is likely to be successful with. This latter category can be additionally divided into amendments which are meant to alter the content of legislation, and those which are not – i.e. probing amendments. By making these distinctions we are able to present a more realistic appraisal of the Opposition's success.

It must, of course, be realised that the analysis presented here has to a very large extent been based on incomplete information as it is impossible to ascertain with any great accuracy the background of and reasons behind every amendment. And the analysis is only partial in that not all the amending stages of the legislative process have been considered. However, in spite of these drawbacks it can be seen that the Opposition has a considerable amount of success in moving amendments to Government legislation: more complete evidence, and the examination of other stages, would probably confirm this conclusion. Only those amendments, as we have seen, which contain policy differences that basically separate the Government from the Opposition are unlikely to be accepted by the Government. All other Opposition amendments however the Government is likely to accept, incorporate, or accommodate in one way or another into its legislation. Although the Government draws up the details of its legislation without consultation with the Opposition and exerts tight control over what amendments are accepted, the Opposition is able to make its mark on both the principles and details of this legislation in the Committee of the Whole House and Report stages.

5. The Select Committee on Science and Technology

By ARTHUR PALMER

ESTABLISHED in 1966 the Select Committee on Science and Technology grew directly from the 'non-party and all-party' Parliamentary and Scientific Committee. Composed entirely of backbenchers, the Select Committee's terms of reference in the fields of science and technology make its powers considerable. In this extract* the first Chairman of the Committee, Arthur Palmer, Labour MP for Bristol Central, illustrates how the Committee has increased the accountability of the executive in the scientific and technological fields since its inception. Palmer examines the role of the Committee by considering the outcomes of recent investigations into the nuclear reactor industry, the National Environmental Research Council, and defence research and development. 'What influence', he asks, 'on government policy and affairs at large has the Committee achieved?'

There appears to be an idea about that to be an advocate (as I am) of the increased use by the House of Commons in a modern context of one of its oldest and sharpest instruments, the select committee, is to decry the continuing value of the floor of the House. This is a mistake.

As a place for the great occasion – or even the little occasion, for boredom has its proper contribution to make to parliamentary government – there is no substitute for the general assembly of the six hundred or any chance fraction of that number who happen to be scattered on the green benches at any given time. There we have the living heart-beat and swelling lungs of the parliamentary system as practised in the United

---

* Reprinted from Alfred Morris, ed., *The Growth of Parliamentary Scrutiny by Committee* (Oxford: Pergamon, 1970), pp. 15–31, with the permission of the publisher and the author.

Kingdom. There the two stage armies of the parties face each other. There Ministers and Opposition leaders take on a special parliamentary shape or stand revealed as hollow shells. There the pompous are deflated, the wits applauded and the tedious left alone to talk to themselves. All this has been told and extolled a thousand times and I would not wish to diminish its glories in the smallest degree. But whether the method of a continuous dramatic performance in fact provides realistic and effective parliamentary accountability has been questioned by many constitutional writers in recent years and the man in the street has had his doubts for even longer.

The root difficulty is that under the Westminster system, as it has evolved, there is no ultimate separation of powers between the executive of the State and the legislature and no written constitution exists to define their powers relative to each other. The struggles between the Crown and the Commons in the sixteenth and seventeenth centuries can be interpreted in a variety of ways: political, religious, social and economic. But constitutionally it was a confrontation of irreconcilables: an executive with an inescapable duty to govern and administer, facing a money-and law-granting assembly isolated from the processes of government and administration.

As every schoolboy knows, or did know, the conflict was resolved finally, with many false starts and several backslidings, by the Crown drawing its Ministers mainly from those in the House of Commons who, commanding a party majority, could guarantee the executive both its funds and its laws. This has resulted in modern times in a close daily contact and conflict, at least when the House is sitting, between the Members who are Ministers and those who are not. This is usually held to be an outstanding advantage of the British system as against, say, the American system, where the relations between the President's departmental Ministers and Congress are distant, formal and closely defined. But is it such an advantage, even allowing that the minority of MPs who constitute Her Majesty's Opposition for the time being will partially perform the critical and checking role that the House as a whole, in the nature of things, cannot do? Do not the scientific, technical and administrative complexities of many of the questions that modern governments are called upon to decide make the general open debate where

Ministers are backed by the vast, expert resources of the Civil Service and innumerable fact-collecting agencies, and individual Members have only their own reading and time-limited research, a contest of David and Goliath? It is true that occasionally the well-aimed dialectical stone fells the front-bench pundit, but only occasionally. As for official Oppositions, they are naturally more interested in propaganda arguments that will help to win the next election than in an abstract parliamentary concern that the Government should prove its case in a particular area of public policy. All too often a Minister's presumptuous cry from the despatch box is in effect: 'I am advised, by those qualified to advise in this matter, that the course I propose is the only correct one, although I admit it involves the daily lives and future prospects of many millions of our people and the expenditure of vast sums of their money.' But is it the correct and only course?

Technology, if not always science, has been with us since mankind took to living in organised societies. It is its extent and complexity, the problems brought about by its acceleration in the last hundred years or so, the increased and increasing specialisation of technology, that now makes things so difficult on democratic assumptions. Even at the start of the industrial age, governments and Parliament could fairly easily make up their minds without too much argument about scientific and technical decisions: for example, the advantages of railways and steam traction over roads and horse carriages, the need for an improved observatory or, say, the desirability of a loading line for ships. But today how is judgement to be made on subjects such as the nuclear reactor programme, the development of carbon fibres, the desirability or otherwise of a European nuclear accelerator and the proper part for operational analysis to play in the choice of weapons systems for the armed forces? What technical methods should be used to stem coastal pollution or to further space research?[1] Here the House of Commons has to make decisions involving great financial expenditure in fields where it is hard for even the most intelligent and hardworking MP to obtain a firm grasp of the issues. How is he, or she, to decide whether the decision is the right one, without some check

[1] These are all subjects investigated by the Select Committee on Science and Technology since it was set up.

beyond the brief moment of a parliamentary question or the uncertain answer to a point raised in debate?

It was to this challenging problem that the Parliamentary and Scientific Committee addressed itself in 1964. I should explain that this influential, unofficial body was established soon after the Second World War on a non-party and all-party basis to provide a two-way channel of communication between parliamentarians and scientific and technical bodies outside. Some hundreds of Members of both Houses of Parliament support its activities and a wide range of learned intitutions and specialist societies of all kinds are affiliated to it. The Parliamentary and Scientific Committee had a great burst of reforming activity in 1960–64 under the urging of several then back-bench MPs who later became Ministers and junior ministers in the Labour Government, aided and abetted by several former Conservative junior ministers among others. They established a sub-committee to consider:

(a) if there is need for improved methods by which Members of Parliament can quickly get information from scientists about matters likely to be raised in Parliament; and

(b) what can be done to improve the existing machinery to ensure that Parliament can establish more effective control over scientific and technological policy.

The establishment of this sub-committee meant that the unofficial Parliamentary and Scientific Committee accepted its own limitations and reflected the growing apprehension of MPs at their lack of control of public policy in Science and Technology. The sub-committee recommended that, to improve parliamentary control, a select committee be established:

> To consider the reports of such bodies as the Research Councils, the Atomic Energy Authority and the National Research Development Corporation, and also the activities of scientific research groups and establishments in government departments, with a view to informing the House on their work and future.[2]

[2] Fourth Report from the Select Committee on Procedure, Session 1964–65. HC 303 of 1964–65. Appendix 3, p. 143. Memorandum by the Parliamentary and Scientific Committee

It will be noted that the Parliamentary and Scientific Committee was cautious in making its suggestions about the order of reference for its desired select committee. It was prepared to accept a limiting formula probably because it felt that limitations would in any case be insisted upon by the managers of the political parties in the House. As it turned out, the parliamentary midwives who brought the Select Committee on Science and Technology into existence in 1966, among them Mr R. H. S. Crossman, who had become Leader of the House of Commons a short while before, threw caution to the wind and gave the new select committee an order of reference which is as wide as the world itself. The order charges the committee '... to consider science and technology and to report thereon'.[3] As chairman of the committee since its inception I must say that these uninhibited terms of reference have been a great advantage to our work. Unlike the late and lamented 'departmental' specialist committee on Agriculture, we have not been confined narrowly to the work of a particular government department but have been able to range about according to our own judgement of need. This fact, I think, has had two useful results. Members of the committee have not felt frustrated; equally, particular government departments have not felt singled out for specially critical treatment.

There are fourteen members of the committee divided by party colour as is the usual practice, according to the relative strength of the parties in the House of Commons. This resulted in the 1966–70 Parliament in our having eight Labour Members (including the chairman), five Conservatives and one Liberal.

There have been some changes but on the whole there has been a fair continuity of membership and there remains, I am glad to say, competition among MPs on both sides to be appointed to the committee.

In matters of science and technology all legislative assemblies are outstandingly amateur. The House of Commons is no worse served in this respect than other free Parliaments. I give in Table 1 some recent figures I have collected on the position in the United Kingdom, from which it will be noted that the 'scientific' professions are out-numbered by the 'non-scientific' professions by roughly 10 to 1. I am not suggesting, of course,

[3] 14 December 1966; HC Debs, Vol. 738, col. 477.

that professional scientific or technical experience should be a necessary qualification for service on the committee, for that would be constitutional nonsense.

TABLE 1

The Professions in the House of Commons Elected in 1966

	Engineers	Scientists	Medics	Managers and economists	Lecturers and teachers	Lawyers	Regular forces
Labour	6	4	6	18	56	51	1
Conservative	2	1	1	9	5	55	17
Liberal	1	—	1	—	1	2	—
Scottish Nationalist	—	—	—	—	—	1	—
Total	9	5	8	27	62	109	18

In any case a cynic might say that if you made knowledge of a subject a requirement for speaking on it you would greatly limit the freedom of parliamentary debate. But the fact that members of the committee are often experts in their own right, or have acquired specialist knowledge by dint of application since their election as MPs, has been of great value to our work. We have had three chartered engineers, one PhD, and other committee Members have served in industry in an executive or administrative capacity. Nevertheless, I should make it clear that the select committee is not out to do jobs which only those with the necessary skill and responsibilities are qualified to do. We might, for instance, pass an opinion upon the choice of a nuclear reactor in the light of the evidence given to us by those in a position to know, but we would hardly presume to design or specify a better reactor on our own account. This is the answer to some of our purist scientific critics who say the committee has been more concerned with the administration of science and technology than with the combined art itself. We are bound to be. It is wise for Members of the committee to know their limitations and to stick to their true parliamentary task. Their task is to select relevant subjects and to investigate them as thoroughly and critically as possible not only for the better guidance and judgement of government and Parliament, but for opinion generally including particularly scientific and technical opinion.

Science and technology have far-flung boundaries if such exist at all, and to cover every subject of a scientific and technological nature which comes before the Parliament of an advanced industrial country would be an impossible task for any organisation, let alone for a group of MPs with innumerable other calls on their time and energy. Yet the committee's work must be topical, relevant and of a standard to command respect. (See Table 2 for a list of investigations completed or still proceeding.) To dart here and there, forming hasty and shallow judgements, would be fatal to the committee's reputation. It is the search for solid achievement, I think, which has led the committee to complete two major investigations. These are:

(a) the nuclear reactor programme in the United Kingdom in the parliamentary session 1967–68; and
(b) the research and development of weapons system for the armed forces in the parliamentary session 1968–69.

The committee's self-imposed criteria for selecting these particular subjects were:

(1) That the subject was of prime national importance.
(2) That the nature of the work involved the spending of large sums of public money.
(3) That the area was one where it was generally accepted that changes in public policy were required to accommodate technical and organisational evolution.

Each of these major inquiries was conducted by the committee as a whole and each inquiry involved many public sittings to take evidence, as well as a few private sittings. In addition to 'home' sittings, there were visits to take evidence at research establishments and at manufacturers' works away from Westminster. For both investigations sub-committees were sent to continental Europe and the United States to bring back reports on the latest developments in those places in order that effective comparisons might be made.

The range of evidence collected, written and oral, with complex investigations such as those into the nuclear reactor industry

SCIENCE AND TECHNOLOGY SELECT COMMITTEE

TABLE 2
Select Committee on Science and Technology Published Reports*

Report	Date of publication	Description of field	Remarks on outcome of report
United Kingdom nuclear reactor programme [4]	27 October 1967	Electrical and mechanical engineering	Ministerial Statements. Debate in House. Some recommendations adopted [5]
Coastal pollution [6]	26 July 1968	Biological and chemical	White Paper issued. Debate in House on Opposition vote of censure. Some recommendations adopted [7]
Carbon fibres [8]	20 February 1969	Engineering and industrial chemistry	Minister's letter sent to Committee. Industrial action taken
Defence research [9]	27 March 1969	Military science	White Paper issued. Debate in House promised [10]
Natural Environment Research Council [11]	27 July 1969	Natural environment and resources	Comment awaited
United Kingdom nuclear power industry [12]	24 July 1969	Electrical and mechanical engineering	Comment awaited

* At the time of writing, Session 1969–70, inquiries have been started into population questions and aspects of the computer industry; the reasons for breakdowns in new electrical generating plant are also being studied.

[4] HC 381 of 1966–67.
[5] Ministerial statement, 17 July 1968; HC Debs, Vol. 768, cols. 1428–9. Debate, 23 May 1968; HC Debs, Vol. 765, cols. 651 et seq.
[6] HC 421 of 1967–68.
[7] Cmnd. 3880, 20 January 1969. Debate, 16 June 1969; HC Debs, Vol. 785, cols. 105 et seq.
[8] HC 157 of 1968–69.
[9] HC 213 of 1968–69.
[10] Cmnd. 4236; December 1969.
[11] HC 400 of 1968–69.
[12] HC 401 of 1968–69.

and into defence research, is necessarily wide, involving careful discrimination in the selection of witnesses and much hard work afterwards in sifting and summarising evidence as a preliminary to the drawing of conclusions and the forming of recommendations.[13]

Select committees have power to compel all subjects of the Crown, including Ministers, to come before them; as the parliamentary phrase has it: 'to send for persons, papers and records'. Whatever the true willingness or reluctance to come, this is in my experience never made apparent, although departmental witnesses – especially I am afraid from the Treasury – show a caution in answering that can amount to near evasion on occasion.

The select committee is under instruction from the House to sit in public unless its Members resolve otherwise. I am much in favour of taking evidence in public wherever possible. Certainly it should be the normal and not the abnormal practice. Apart from the democratic case for public hearings – the right of the public to know – witnesses tend usefully to answer each other as the inquiry proceeds. The process is assisted by the printing of Hansard records of the proceedings as they take place without waiting until the final report is published.

Apart from major investigations into specific subjects, such as those I have described (I shall come to coastal pollution, which was a special case, in a moment) the select committee has been haunted by the fearful thought that the government in power is making important and perhaps irrevocable decisions almost every month in the scientific and technical field. Should not some of these be scanned? The breadth of our terms of reference certainly give us the opportunity if only there were the time to use it.

In an attempt to exorcise our fears, we have set up a general purposes committee to investigate shortly a particular governmental decision – or failure to take a decision – to see if there is on the face of it a case for deeper inquiry. We wish to avoid wasting our resources in time and staff if for the moment the

[13] Select committees now have the useful and necessary power to appoint their own specialist advisers on subjects under investigation. Science and Technology has taken full advantage of this power, but it still rests with the committee to accept or reject the advice given.

Government appears to have taken the right course or as near to it as can be judged. Using this method, we glanced quickly at the decision to reduce nuclear fusion research at the Atomic Energy Authority's laboratory at Culham; examined the decision not to support the 300 GeV European nuclear accelerator; and considered Ministry of Technology involvement in the commercial exploitation of carbon fibres. In this last case, the general purposes committee thought there was a strong case for a deeper investigation and entrusted it to a special sub-committee under the chairmanship of Brian Parkyn, a member of the committee and an industrial chemist. In its report the sub-committee recommended that the Ministry of Technology should encourage the building of a large-scale plant for the production of carbon fibres in the United Kingdom. The recommendation was taken up in principle by a major chemical company, although there have been difficulties subsequently.

The foregoing does not by any means exhaust the activities of the committee in three years of its existence, as the list in Table 2 demonstrates. We have done, for instance, a great deal of work under the leadership of Sir Harry Legge-Bourke on coastal pollution. As I have indicated, the circumstances which led us to embark on this investigation were somewhat special. The House of Commons referred the subject to us in the wake of the *Torrey Canyon*[14] affair at the request of the Government. We did not resent the task as such. Coastal pollution is obviously a good subject for inquiry, but if the Government got into the habit of giving the committee jobs to do, however worthy or necessary, then the Government would be dictating the committee's activity and limiting our freedom of action.

The list of work done shows that we completed in the last session of Parliament two parallel inquiries: one into the progress so far of the Natural Environment Research Council,[15] and the other a further study of the nuclear reactor industry.[16] NERC was looked into because of a feeling in the committee that the detailed examination of research council reports was to

[14] The *Torrey Canyon* was a large oil tanker wrecked off the coast of Cornwall in 1967 causing vast oil pollution on the beaches of south-west England and northern France.
[15] HC 400 of 1968–69.
[16] HC 401 of 1968–69.

be a 'bread and butter' task of the Select Committee on Science and Technology. Because of the pressure of so much else we have not had much opportunity as it has turned out to review research council reports, but we have thought it important to do at least one. Opening a long review of the findings (drawn up by a sub-committee with Sir Harry Legge-Bourke as chairman) the eminent scientific journal *Nature* said:

> The House of Commons Select Committee on Science and Technology has fired several shots across the ambitious bows of the Natural Environment Research Council in the report on the inquiry into the council's operations. Although the general tone of the report will no doubt allow the high officials of NERC to sleep easily in their beds, some of them may also be disconcerted that the committee has uncovered such a great deal of uncertainty in the council's operations.[17]

The second nuclear reactor inquiry (1968–69) came about because of the select committee's impatience with the snail's pace reorganisation after the strong recommendations of the committee for major changes in the industry in the first nuclear report of 1966–67. It was in short a follow-up inquiry. Mr Wedgwood Benn, the Minister of Technology, was closely examined when he appeared as a witness and, in the concluding paragraphs of the subsequent report, these strong words were used:

> Our opinion is that, in spite of all the time and energy that have been devoted to the reorganisation of the industry, very little has been achieved so far to rationalise, strengthen and make it more competitive in world markets. Apart from the elimination of one of the consortia, and with it the departure of its component firms from the nuclear scene altogether, we do not notice much real change. The two new companies are little different from the two previous consortia and there appears as yet to be little change in the functions of the authority. The shift of emphasis in design work, of which much was expected and of which on paper much is made, appears to mean in fact that the companies are doing fractionally more on existing reactor types, whether commercial or not, than they did previously. This situation may of course

[17] 7 September 1968, p. 993.

evolve into something more rational with the passing of time but in view of the stress placed once upon a time on urgency, the present position is loose and confused to say the least.[18]

This quotation touches on a key question: what influence on government policy and affairs at large has the committee achieved? This is not an easy question to answer in precise terms and I will content myself with general observations only.

One outstanding gain from the existence and activity of the committee has been the steady building up of a network of connections, both personal and corporate, with industry, with leading scientific and engineering personalities and with the specialist journals. To them the Select Committee on Science and Technology is an independent centre of power and influence. It is within Parliament but apart from the massive governmental bureaucracy: a centre to which an approach can be made and from which inquiries can come.

Another gain is to be seen in the fact-finding mission of the select committee. Apart from any recommendations the committee make on what public policy in a given field should be, the compilation of evidence on the facts of a situation and the unveiling of the motives behind existing policy is in itself an invaluable service to parliamentary and public opinion. Only a body like the Select Committee on Science and Technology possesses the powers that make the compilation possible; a government department cannot do it. As to the direct effect in influencing or changing government policy, our score of successes cannot be totted up with certainty and in any case these are still early days. With nuclear reactors, coastal pollution and carbon fibres, the recommendations of the select committee have left their mark. For example, there is the promised nuclear fuel company. There has also been the appointment of Mr Anthony Crosland as a senior Minister responsible for all issues affecting the natural environment and the changes in the responsibilities and powers of the National Research Development Corporation foreshadowed by Mr Wedgwood Benn's new Green Paper on government research.

It is true that on an important early recommendation of the

[18] HC 401 of 1968–69, para. 67.

select committee (that the resources of the United Kingdom for the production of nuclear reactors should be concentrated in one national design and manufacturing organisation) the Minister rejected our view and retained two competing groupings. But here the committee itself was divided. In fact, the Labour Minister ended up by agreeing more with, as it happened, the Conservative minority of the committee than with the Labour majority. This incidentally is the only occasion on which the committee has split more or less along party lines, reflecting not sectarian rivalry or a desire to agree with the government of the day, as we have just seen, but an honest philosophical difference. The Conservatives leaned towards a 'market' solution of the industry's difficulties, while the Socialists opted for a 'managed' solution of the same difficulties.

In reply to the select committee's important report on defence research and development, the first-ever parliamentary inquiry in modern times into the technical working and equipment of the armed forces as distinct from the cost of providing equipment, the Secretary of State for Defence, Mr Dennis Healey, has issued a White Paper.[19] In our report we had placed great stress upon the following:

(a) that the close linking of ideal defence research with foreign policy be properly understood;
(b) that operational analysis should be greatly expanded;
(c) that the supremacy of the Treasury in defence matters is not always a force making for economy and efficiency;
(d) that the use of project managers on a wide scale is desirable;
(e) that industry needs to be made conversant with the forward thinking of the defence departments; and
(f) that urgent action be taken to encourage the movement of qualified scientists and engineers between industry and government.[20]

In the introduction to the White Paper, the Government say in reply that they: '... welcome this inquiry, in which departments have co-operated with the committee to the fullest extent consistent with national security considerations, and they have given careful consideration to the report since its publica-

[19] Cmnd. 4236; December 1969. [20] See HC 213 of 1968–69.

tion in May. It makes a valuable contribution to public knowledge of defence research and development and thereby assists a process to which the Government attach the highest importance.'[21]

This statement is, I think, perfectly fair and as far as it goes not unsatisfactory to the committee. Naturally, committee members have examined the sixty-one paragraphs of the Government's answer and they approve where the Minister agrees with the committee and disapprove where he rejects their arguments. But the important consideration is that the dialogue is taking place, that changes are coming about and that no one is holding fast to positions that should be abandoned in the face of argument's attack. Debates on the floor of the House on the reports of select committees are important and more parliamentary time obviously should be given to such debates. But it would be superficial to measure the impact of the work of the Select Committee on Science and Technology on public policy simply in terms of the frequency of debates and favourable ministerial replies. For instance in a confidential comment from an industrial source I have been told recently that 'there has been a considerable increase in the level of communication between the Ministry of Defence and industry since the committee started its investigations'.

I would argue again, as I did earlier, that the root difficulty about obtaining fuller parliamentary accountability of the executive is the lack of an absolute separation of powers between the Government and the legislature under the British constitutional system. I am not suggesting that this situation should be changed, but its continuance means that the extended introduction of open parliamentary committees is an operation of some delicacy until new precedents are established and new methods of working take root. Now we have started however, there is no way back. For science and technology, the select committee experiment is another instalment in the adaptation of that sturdy old social organism, parliamentary government, to the conditions of a complex industrial society. A next stage might well be the reference of Bills in the sphere of science and technology which are agreed by the parties to be non-controversial (and they are many) to the select committee suitably

[21] See Cmnd. 4236.

expanded after Second Reading and not to the traditional standing committees as is the present practice. Under this new arrangement Ministers, Civil Servants and independent experts would be examined by the committee as witnesses to justify the Bill's clauses. In the light of the evidence taken, amendments would be made and the Bill reported back to the House for final approval. This would leave the government still free to have its own way, backed by its party majority, if it wished. But in circumstances where the Bill, by agreement in the first place, did not involve party principle or interest and where amendments made were based on the balance of expert opinion openly expressed, it is unlikely that governments would wish, or would dare, to set aside the committee's findings. This new approach would incidentally reduce one of the strongest present practical objections to the extension of specialist select committees, namely that the Committee of Selection and the Whips already experience difficulty in finding enough Members for the standing committees, which are essential to government business. But the greatest gain of all would be the more intelligent and realistic operation of the House of Commons in the twentieth century.

6. Policy and Self-perception: Some Aspects of Parliamentary Behaviour

By KEITH OVENDEN

THE following study* is concerned with the perceptions that MPs have of themselves and of their work in the House of Commons. The findings of interviews conducted in 1969 with 60 MPs are reported by Keith Ovenden who illustrates how personality characteristics, the influence of party, ideological position, and differing sources of information explain why the subjective efficacy of MPs differs so much. In addition, the author relates the extent to which efficacy helps to explain Parliamentary behaviour with respect to the policy of renationalising the iron and steel industry, and shows that 'the vital precondition for participation in the policy process by the backbencher is the belief that, through his actions, policies will be affected'.

A nickel prospector arrives at the gates of Heaven, but is stopped by St Peter, who says 'sorry. Full up. We have a quota of 100 nickel prospectors, and the places are all taken.' After some thought the prospector says: 'Please tell them that there has been a new nickel strike west-south-west of Windarra, with 12·8 per cent nickel.' At this news there is a stampede of nickel prospectors back towards earth, and St Peter says 'O.K, you can come in now.' But the prospector turns away. 'No thanks – after all there might just be some truth in the story.' (Anon. But see the *Financial Times*, 8 January 1971.)

---

* Drawn from a much larger one of the politics of the renationalisation of the British iron and steel industry, which was undertaken while the author was a student at Nuffield College, Oxford. A longer and more detailed version of this paper is published in the *British Journal of Political Science*, Vol. 2, 1972. My thanks are due to Mrs Lynn Doscher for help in preparing the manuscript.

A recurring theme in recent research into Parliament is that of trying to define the extent to which MPs exercise influence on public policy.[1] This theme is threefold, consisting of a concern with (i) the extent of MPs' influence as perceived by more or less objective observers (in this case, academic researchers), (ii) the extent of their influence as perceived by non-Parliamentary political actors (e.g. members of the Civil Service), and (iii) the extent of their influence as perceived by themselves. The interview schedule on which the findings here are based was designed to tap all of these: to see whether the MPs' evaluation of themselves was at one with an objective evaluation from outside; to see whether they suffered from distortion by proximity, or whether an objective outsider was misguided in his analysis, or both; and to see what status MPs occupied in the eyes of non-Parliamentary actors, whether they were considered to be influential in the policy process or not.

Of these, this paper is specifically concerned with the perceptions that MPs have of themselves and of their work in the House of Commons. As most political actors cannot be said, however, to have a single clear conception of what it is that they are doing,[2] and as many public figures may be engaged in numerous political activities more or less simultaneously, it is important to distinguish exactly what activities and perceptions we are concerned with here. The scale on which the findings

---

[1] See R. Butt, *The Power of Parliament* (London: Constable, 1967), pp. 275–92 and 417–46; P. G. Richards, *Honourable Members* (London: Faber & Faber, 2nd ed., 1964), pp. 263–80; S. E. Finer, *Anonymous Empire* (London: Pall Mall, 1966), pp. 39–74 is lively, as is S. E. Finer, H. B. Berrington and D. J. Bartholomew, *Backbench Opinion in the House of Commons, 1955–1959* (London: Pergamon, 1961), pp. 1–13 and 122–38. For a view from the thirties, see H. J. Laski, *Paliamentary Government in England* (1938); R. J. Jackson, *Rebels and Whips* (London: Macmillan, 1968) gives all the cases since 1945 where efforts to exert influence involved rebellion; see especially pp. 201–52. The best general synthesis is in R. Rose, *Politics in England* (London: Faber & Faber, 1964) at pp. 211–16. For related evidence, see Lord Windlesham, 'Can Public Opinion Influence Government?' in R. Rose, (ed.), *Studies in British Politics* (London: Macmillan, 1966); H. Eckstein, *Pressure Group Politics* (London: Allen & Unwin, 1960), pp. 76–8; and S. A. Walkland, *The Legislative Process in Great Britain* (London: Allen & Unwin, 1968), pp. 68–72 and 77–83.

[2] See, for instance, P. Nettl, 'Consensus or Elite Domination: the Case of Business', *Political Studies*, Vol. 13, No. 1, February 1965.

below are based consists of two related but distinct elements: firstly a measure of each respondent's sense of efficacy as an MP, and secondly, his sense of the efficacy of Parliament as an institution. The first of these is the more complex, and needs some elaboration.

One reason why it is difficult to talk about 'the power of Parliament' is that Parliament is composed of such a wide variety of political elements that it hardly amounts to a single political institution at all. It is, rather, a cluster of political institutions all of which are related to each other, but most of which can be seen to be quite different. For instance there are select committees, some of which play an influential role in policy formulation; there are political parties; there is a government that consists of perhaps as many as 100 MPs; there is the Press lobby, with its important function of interpreting politics to the nation; and so on. One cannot, therefore, talk about 'the power of Parliament' because in the last analysis Parliament has many powers, and one ought to distinguish very carefully among the various possibilities. Similarly, it is not possible to formulate a complete account of Parliamentary powers on the basis of empirical evidence alone, for in constitutional theory Parliament has residual powers which, although only very rarely exercised, are none the less real.

What the interview schedule used in this study was designed to accomplish therefore, was to persuade the respondent, with respect to certain questions, to think of himself simply as an MP. To lay aside all his other many 'hats', and to answer the questions simply as an ordinary Member of Parliament. This was not difficult for some respondents: they were simply back-bench MPs. Others found it slightly more difficult: front-bench spokesmen for the opposition for instance. A very few, one senior and several junior ministers, found it most difficult of all, for they acted as ordinary backbenchers only a very little of the time. But even so they were MPs. Like backbenchers they had constituencies to nurse, constituents to see and correspond with, a party to which they owed loyalty, and a government from which, in common with other backbenchers, they wanted specific policies. Again, one could not be said to have studied 'the power of Parliament' if, in any analysis of the institution, members of the government of the day were excluded. They are after all its most exalted members. In addition, all the ministers interviewed in this study had served as backbenchers themselves, so they had a conception of what it meant to be a backbench MP.

The scale on which the conclusions of this work are based is composed of eleven items.[3] The two elements of which it is composed – the MP's sense of his own efficacy, and his sense of the efficacy of the institution of Parliament – are quite distinct in some questions (numbers 3, 4 and 6 are all directed at the institutional element), but in some cases it is not possible or desirable to make a clear distinction. An MP's sense of his ability to influence legislation (question 8) is bound up with his feelings about the House of Commons – at least in the sense that his membership of the House provides him with a role which he recognises is regarded as of some importance by other political actors, and at most in the sense that such membership permits him to engage in the formal business of debates, questions and committees. How much he engages in this business will depend again to some degree on his view of how worthwhile it is.

Interviews were conducted with sixty Members of Parliament, chosen from a population of about 150. This population consisted of all those MPs who had been involved in some way with the renationalisation of the iron and steel industry. What 'being involved' amounted to was not hard to define, since the issue was one of considerable public controversy, but in choosing the final sample, three principal variables were employed: Party; membership of Standing Committee D (the Committee to which the Bill was assigned after the second reading on 25 July 1966); and membership of the House for steel-producing constituencies. The sample is shown according to these three variables in Table 1 below.

One explanatory word of caution is required. Since the whole sample of MPs interviewed in this study amounted to only sixty, multivariate analysis is constrained. Any kind of moderately sophisticated manipulation of the data brings about a situation in which cell sizes rapidly approach zero. Although the material is full of suggestive insights into the workings of Parliament it cannot be substantiated against statistical tests of significance.

---

[3] The questions, and some information on the interviewing technique employed, are set down in the Annex, at the end.

TABLE 1

Parliamentary Respondents by Party, Membership of Standing Committee D and Representation of Steel-producing Constituencies

		Labour	Conservative	Liberal	Totals
Members of Standing Committee D	Steel Constits.[4]	7	0	0	7
	Non-Steel Constits.	9	13	1	23
Non-members of Standing Committee D	Steel Constits.	6	0	0	6
	Non-Steel Constits.	10	13	1	24
Totals		32	26	2	60

The empty cells under the Conservative and Liberal columns reflect the fact that, after the 1966 election, only 2 of the 55 steel producing constituencies were not represented by Labour members. Neither of these was active over the issue of renationalisation of steel, although one of them, Enoch Powell, does have opinions about the general question of nationalised industries.

It would not take a very considerable degree of non-randomness in responses to a few questions to produce plausible but incorrect results. Some effort was made to overcome this problem by incorporating two checks for reliability, and these are reported below, but great care is required in their interpretation.

The scale itself is a simple interval scale, the answers to each question being coded and allotted a score, the scores being summed. The maximum possible score was 28, although the highest score actually recorded was 21. It was possible to score zero, but in fact nobody did. The distribution of scores is shown in the frequency table and the histogram below. (Figs. 1 and 2.)

How can we be sure that these efficacy ratings do actually measure something? Two questions were included in the interview schedule as a check on the reliability of the data. One was a logical test and the other a catch question. The results of these

[4] After B. R. Mitchell and Boehm Klaus, *British Parliamentary Election Results 1950–1964* (Cambridge U.P., 1966).

two equations, cross-tabulated with the efficacy scores, are shown in Tables 2 and 3.

TABLE 2

Involvement in Parliamentary Activities by Efficacy Scores

		\multicolumn{4}{c}{Efficacy scores}	
		0–5	6–10	11–15	16+	Totals
How much did you get involved in these things in an active capacity?	Continuously/ a great deal	2	9	16	6	33
	A fair amount/ average/no more than usual	1	3	2	2	8
Could you tell me what you think were the most important activities of the House of Commons during this period? (1964–67)	Not much/less than usual/ not at all	0	5	1	0	6
	Don't know/ no answer	5	8	0	0	13

Table 2 shows that all but one of those respondents who claimed they were very little involved with the most important activities of the House of Commons in the period under discussion, or who claimed that they did not know how much they were involved, scored 10 or less on the efficacy scale. Two-thirds of those claiming to be continuously or a great deal involved scored 11 or more. Moreover, all of those scoring 16+ fell into the top half of the self-evaluation as to degree of involvement. This is of course almost exactly what one would predict. It is only logical that those who have a high estimate of their efficacy in the political system should be most active in trying to influence the issues which they consider important. The efficacy scale developed and used here would obviously have had very little to tell us if the results of this test had been substantially different.

The second test involves the catch question shown in Table 3. The catch is that governments do not allocate time for the committee stage of Bills (unless, out of frustration, they introduce a guillotine, which most ministers prefer not to do). The matter of time is negotiated between the leaders of the respective party groups in the committee. In the particular instance

POLICY AND SELF-PERCEPTION

FIGURE 1

Distribution of Efficacy Scores

Median: 10
Mean: 10·33
Standard deviation: 4·41

No. of respondents
Total = 60

Efficacy scores

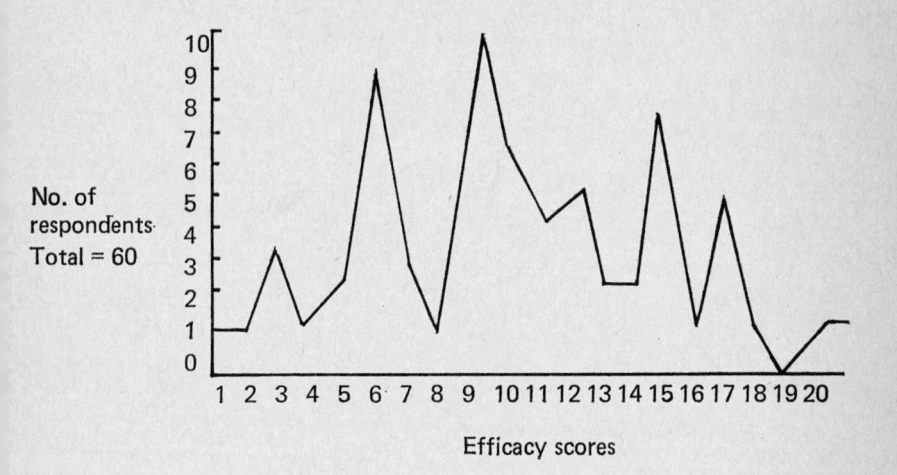

FIGURE 2

Histogram to show the distribution of Efficacy Scores

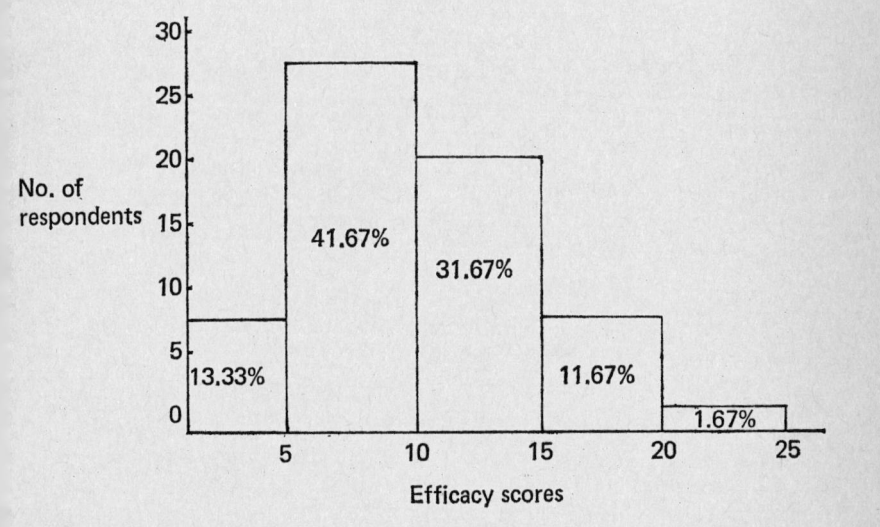

No. of respondents

13.33%
41.67%
31.67%
11.67%
1.67%

Efficacy scores

of the nationalisation Bill, Marsh, the Minister responsible, was thwarted in his attempts to get the Bill through quickly and the Opposition team felt that they had won a major victory by slowing down the Bill's progress. The 'correct' answer to the question, therefore, is that shown in the bottom row, where we also find that all the respondents giving this reply fall into the upper half of the efficacy scale. These are the best-informed respondents with respect to a fairly fine point of Parliamentary

TABLE 3

Beliefs about the Allocation of Time for the Committee Stage of the Bill by Efficacy Scores

		0–5	6–10	11–15	16+	Totals
In its allocation of time for the Committee stage of the Bill (to renationalise the iron and steel industry) would you say that the Government was:	Generous	2	5	8	3	18
	About what one would expect	2	9	4	3	18
	Unreasonable	0	1	2	0	3
	Don't know/ could not remember	4	10	0	0	14
	Thought the question meaningless and explained why	0	0	5	2	7

(Efficacy scores)

practice, and we would have been right to doubt the utility of the scale if these MPs had not scored well on it. It is interesting to note that all of those who gave a wrong answer by saying that they did not know or could not remember performed badly on the efficacy scale. It is hardly surprising that they should have had a low estimate of their own efficacy when they were both badly informed on Parliamentary practice and also confessed to having poor memories.[5] Those who fell into the top three rows were the MPs who gave partisan responses (top row nearly all Labour, those below nearly all Conservative), and they were quite normally distributed. The evidence here permits us to

[5] Those who claimed to have forgotten really had done so. I could find no evidence to show that they were either being modest, or trying to obscure their role in the policy process over steel.

proceed with the use of the scale as a device for predicting variations in efficacy among MPs, but it is perhaps important to bear in mind that, despite the two tests illustrated here, the measure is a simple one judged alongside the complex responses it seeks to summarise.

Why does the subjective efficacy of MPs differ so much? Possible sources of the differences set out in Figs. 1 and 2 can be grouped into four categories: (1) those arising out of differences in the MPs' personal characteristics (age, sex, education, occupation, region represented in Parliament, size of majority, length of tenure); (2) those arising out of the influence of party (which party he belongs to, whether he occupies a position of leadership in it, whether he is conscious of the discipline of the party); (3) those arising out of MPs' differing ideologies; and (4) those arising out of MPs' differing sources of information.

Many personal characteristics of MPs do not seem to be related to their sense of efficacy. Efficacy scores did not vary significantly between MPs according to the type or region of their constituency, or the size of their majority. The interviews were conducted in 1969, coming just before an election, and ought to have picked up any variation resulting from constituency marginality, especially among Labour members. But there was none: the secure differed not at all from the insecure. Two other variables do however provide food for thought. Table 4 shows a cross-tabulation between efficacy scores and the dates when respondents were first elected to Parliament.

TABLE 4

Efficacy Score by Date of Election

		Efficacy scores 0–10	11+	Totals
When elected	Before 1951	15 71·4	6 28·6	21 100%
	1951 and up to 1964	13 61·0	8 38·0	21 100%
	1964 and after	5 27·8	13 72·2	18 100%

What stands out from this table is that, broadly, the longer a man has been in the House of Commons the lower his estimate of his own capacity to influence events. Optimism in this regard seems to be a function of inexperience, the bottom row in the table neatly reversing the pattern shown in the top. None the less, it is interesting to note that, even among those MPs who have served for nearly twenty years, nearly one-third do still score high on the scale. This finding, in turn, leads us to explore the influences of party in explaining MPs' different senses of efficacy.

Table 5 cross-tabulates length of service and party affiliation with efficacy score.

TABLE 5
Length of Service and Party Affiliation by Efficacy Scores

			0–10	11+	Total
	Labour	Before 1951	7	3	10
		1951–64	6	3	9
		1964	3	10	13
Party	Conservative	Before 1951	8	3	11
		1951–64	6	5	11
		1964	1	3	4
	Liberal	1951–64	1	0	1
		1964	1	0	1

The number of Conservatives elected between the 1959 election and 1970 was very small compared with the number of Labour MPs returned. One might predict that backbenchers of the government party, whichever it was, would have a higher efficacy rating than backbenchers on the opposition side. This assumption is reasonable given their greater access to ministers, and given also the unusual circumstances of the 1964–66 Parliament when members of the governing party were in a position to exploit the Government's small majority to achieve their own ends. The figures in Table 5 however, show that, although Labour MPs elected from 1964 onwards were overwhelmingly more optimistic about their efficacy than their more experienced colleagues, three out of the four Conservatives elected in the same period were equally optimistic. The table does not show the further fact that these three had efficacy scores of 17, 17 and 21, among the highest achieved by anyone.

What is the explanation? Much of the answer lies in the

nature of Parliamentary work in opposition, and in particular in connection with a major Bill like steel. The work of opposition is largely hard grind and small rewards in terms of policy accomplishments; governments by and large get what they want. But opposition does provide real opportunities for political advancement. The young Opposition MP, by dint of hard work, especially on the committee and report stages of a major piece of government legislation, begins to tread the path to the top. He experiences first-hand contact with opposition leaders, men who themselves may recently have held high public office, and he assumes responsibility, having to move amendments, to fight matters of detail, and to make life difficult for the government of the day. Clearly, the opposition MP, whether young or not, who chooses not to devote his time to Parliamentary work in this way, will have a low (and appropriately pessimistic) view of his efficacy. But his active colleague can hardly be faulted for feeling that he has, in some sense, 'arrived'. He is the daily confidant of senior party men, and the aura of power, the doing of great deeds, brushes off on him. Since the present sample was chosen explicitly on the basis of the extent to which MPs were involved in the issue of steel, it necessarily 'picked up' a much more substantial number of these 'hopefuls' than would occur in a random sample of all opposition MPs. (I shall return to this point when I come to discuss the relationship between efficacy ratings and leadership positions in the party.)

The influence of education seems likely to be great in any analysis based on self-perceptions, and the findings set out in Table 6 are not, therefore, surprising. They show quite clearly a strong relationship between a high level of education and a more pessimistic view of personal political efficacy.

Twenty-five of the 33 respondents scoring ten or less had had the benefit of a university education, and of those respondents who attended Oxbridge a staggering 82 per cent appear in the lower half of the efficacy ratings. MPs who left school as children or only completed secondary school, on the other hand rate themselves in the upper half of the scale. Two-thirds of them score 11 or more, and not one rates himself at 5 or less. Does it follow that the educated politicians are cynical of their Parliamentary efficacy? The question should probably not be asked in this way. It is probably better to consider what it means to be a poorly educated Member of Parliament. By definition, since an MP is of high social status, a poorly educated man or woman who achieves election to the House has been upwardly mobile socially. Since our culture stresses the virtues of self-reliance and self-improvement, an individual who has achieved considerable upward mobility can be excused for holding a fairly imposing view of his ability to influence the world around him. And in a very real sense, he is quite justified in doing so. He *has* influenced

TABLE 6
Education and Efficacy Scores

Education	\	Efficacy scores			Totals
	0–5	6–10	11–15	16+	
Elementary school only	0	1	1	2	4
	0·0	25·0	25·0	50·0	100%
Elementary school and up to secondary school	0	5	7	2	14
	0·0	35·7	50·0	14·3	100%
University: Oxbridge	5	14	3	1	23
	21·7	60·9	13·1	4·3	100%
University: Other	2	4	7	3	16
	12·5	25·0	43·8	18·7	100%
Other	1	1	1	0	3
	33·3	33·3	33·3	0·0	100%

the world in which he 'moves and has his being'. A young person educated at Oxford, on the other hand, could similarly be excused for believing, on becoming an MP, that he had, as it were, inherited his birthright. This was what his education had fitted him to do. It is hardly surprising therefore if, other things being equal, less well-educated MPs feel themselves more 'efficacious' than their better-educated colleagues.

Once again however it may be that party membership is intervening between the educational backgrounds of respondents and their efficacy scores. It may be in other words that those MPs with few years of formal education are drawn uniformly from the Labour Party and that what the efficacy rating is capturing is their optimism as members of the governing party rather than optimism born of poor education coupled with high social mobility. Table 7 explores this point, and shows it to be false. Of respondents with little formal education (elementary or secondary school only) 7 are Conservatives and 11 Labour.

Further, Table 7 shows that respondents had obtained university education by a ratio of two to one, and that this ratio was constant within parties. Of the 37 university-educated MPs investigated here, 18 were Conservative and 19 Labour MPs. Clearly the issue of steel was fairly attractive to highly educated men; the proportion of university graduates in the whole House

TABLE 7
Education, Party and Efficacy Scores

Education and Party		_____ Efficacy scores _____					
		0–5	6–10	11–15	16+	Totals	
Elementary	Labour	0	1	0	2	3	
only	Tory	0	0	1	0	1	18
Secondary	Labour	0	3	4	1	8	
	Tory	0	2	3	1	6	
Oxbridge	Labour	1	6	0	0	7	
	Tory	3	8	3	1	15	37
Other	Labour	2	3	6	1	12	
university	Tory	0	0	1	2	3	
Totals		6	23	18	8	55*	

* Excludes 'other' educations (3) and Liberals (2).

of Commons after the 1966 election was 58·6 per cent, compared with 67·3 per cent in the steel sample. Moreover, relatively poorly educated MPs who spoke up on steel were drawn much more evenly from the two major parties than their relative distribution in the House as a whole. Where the variable of party did intervene significantly however, was in the relative distribution of university graduates between Oxbridge on the one hand, and Redbrick universities on the other. Among the MPs active over the steel issue twice as many Tories went to Oxbridge as did Labour men; and Labour respondents who went to Redbrick universities outnumber the Conservatives by four to one.

We have already dealt with some aspects of the influence of party. Those that remain to be explored have to do with 'discipline' and 'hierarchy'. These two variables are linked, but it is possible to treat them separately as long as the fact that they are linked is borne in mind. The extent to which the two principal Parliamentary parties are disciplined is shown by the events surrounding the Labour Government's handling of the steel issue from 1964 to 1966. The failure of Donnelly and Wyatt to support the party line by threatening to abstain in crucial divisions, and the party leadership's reaction to their behaviour in bringing pressure to bear on them to conform, is evidence enough of the crucial role that discipline plays in organising both collective patterns and individual behaviours in British Parliamentary life. But how aware are MPs of the Whips, and how free do they feel to dissociate themselves from their party's proclaimed position? When they abstain, or even vote against their party, do they do so with fear in their hearts? And, if we could distinguish between them on this group of variables, would it help us to explain the variance in efficacy scores? A number of questions in the schedule were designed to draw out respondents on these points, both by encouraging them to reveal how often they *had* deliberately abstained from voting with their party, and by offering them opportunities to reflect aloud on their perceptions of the power and role of the Whips' offices. The results are interesting, but they do not help to explain the distribution of efficacy scores. MPs who did well on the efficacy scale did not behave more or less independently of their party, and neither did they have a different perception of the Whips' offices. Where we do find interesting differences is in connection with leadership.

It is possible, by concentrating one's attention solely on Parliament, to think of the back-bench MP as the lowest of the low. In fact of course he is a political leader of almost, if not quite, the front rank. His standing in the party outside Westminster is high. He has frequent opportunities to affect the nature and level of public opinion on matters of national importance. He may be the most important citizen in his constituency, and his time and energies are in constant demand. He has unique opportunities of access to Whitehall, both at the ministerial and the Civil Service levels, and he has opportunities

POLICY AND SELF-PERCEPTION 185

for assembling, receiving and transmitting information far in excess of most other political actors outside Parliament. To talk, then, of a party hierarchy which places the back-bench MP at the bottom is to emphasise the nature of his low standing *vis-à-vis* the Parliamentary leadership at the expense of his high standing *vis-à-vis* others. All the same, Cabinet Ministers, members of the National Party Executives and the opposition front bench spokesmen rank higher in whatever hierarchies one identifies. One would expect the ordinary backbencher to have a lower sense of efficacy both of himself as an MP, and of Parliament than say the Cabinet Minister. Distributions of efficacy scores by leadership position are shown in Table 8.

TABLE 8
Efficacy Scores by Leadership Position

	0–5	6–10	11–15	16+	Totals
1. Members of the Cabinet or Shadow Cabinet at any time since 1959	5	4	1	0	10
2. Non-Cabinet members of the Govt. including PPSs, and non-Shadow Cabinet opposition front-bench spokesmen at 25.7.66	1	5	3	2	11
3. Members of Party Executives; House of Commons Select Committees, Party Whips at 25.7.66	0	6	2	3	11
4. Holders of positions under 2 and 3 in the past, but not doing so on 25.7.66	1	4	5	1	11
5. Backbenchers	1	8	8	2	19
Totals	8	27	19	8	62*

* Total is greater than the sample owing to multiple memberships.

One of the most striking things about these figures is the numbers of MPs concerned with steel who held some position of great public importance. Only a third of all the MPs interviewed could be described simply as backbenchers. These respondents bunch together almost exclusively within the range 6–15 on the efficacy scale. The extremes of the curve are filled by current or recent office holders (as measured on 25 July 1966, the date of the second reading of the Bill). Top party leaders are especially interesting in this regard. Nine of the ten score less than 11, and half of them five or less. From these scores we get the clearest indication of the contempt in which backbenchers and the general power of Parliament are held by politicians of Cabinet rank: they are almost uniformly sceptical of the ability of Parliament to effect policy outcomes. To have experienced the real opportunities to determine policy that go with a seat in the Cabinet must make Parliament taste like very small beer indeed.

By contrast we find that the MPs one step away from Cabinet rank or in positions of party or Parliamentary authority are skewed one cell to the right along the scale. The men responsible for substantial areas of government under a Cabinet Minister or Shadow Cabinet spokesman, or who have recently held positions of this kind, perhaps because they can see decisions being made while also having a keen sense of commitment to the Parliamentary institution, share a uniformly higher efficacy rating. There is indeed just the merest indication in the fourth row of a stronger sense of Parliamentary efficacy among those who once held these second-rank positions but now no longer do; almost as if, having experienced the taste of power elsewhere, they have returned to the back benches with their sense of their own power enhanced. No statistical test shows a relationship here, but the raw scores are suggestive.

Questions relating to party discipline did not influence efficacy scores. The same is true of ideology. Questions related to the specific issue of renationalisation and to respondents' general perceptions of political issues, yielded some useful information on levels of ideological commitment among MPs, but none of this helped to explain the efficacy ratings. MPs with decidedly ideological views of politics performed no differently on the efficacy scale from their pragmatic colleagues or opponents. This perhaps reflects the fragmentation of the left in the politics of the Labour movement over the past fifteen years. Perhaps if this study had been conducted in the immediate post-war Parliament one would have found a strong measure of congruence between age, kind of constituency, educational background, ideological commitment and efficacy score.

What was the relationship between efficacy and information? MPs who were associated with the steel renationalisation measure were not particularly well-informed, and appeared to rely on a very narrow range of sources for their information. Almost half of the respondents named only two or fewer sources of information. When these figures are cross-tabulated with efficacy scores we get the outlines of an interesting picture. These are shown in Tables 9 and 10. These tables show a remarkably neat reversal of proportions. Respondents who named three or more sources accounted for 63 per cent of all respondents who scored 11 or more on the efficacy scale. Similarly, of all those naming two sources or less, 65·5 per cent

TABLE 9

Efficacy Scores and the Number of Sources of Information (by number of respondents)

		Efficacy scores 0–10	11+	Total	Percentage of all respondents
No. of sources named	0–2	19	10	29	48·3
	3–6	11	17	28	46·7
	N.A.	—	—	3	5·0
	Totals	30	27	60	100·0

TABLE 10

Efficacy Scores and the Number of Sources of Information (by row and column percentages)

		Efficacy scores 1–10 (%)	11+ (%)	Totals (%)
No. of sources named	1–2	65·5 / 63·3	34·5 / 37·0	100
	3–6	39·3 / 36·7	60·7 / 63·0	100
	Totals (%)	100	100	

scored 10 or less on the efficacy scale. This is nice, but of course unsurprising: it would have been remarkable if those with the fewest information sources had none the less contrived to have a higher sense of efficacy than those with the most such sources.

So much for the correlates of efficacy. An MP's sense of his efficacy as a political actor able to influence policy outcomes is connected, through his party membership, with his length of tenure, his education and his location in the party hierarchy, and, independently of party, to the nature and number of his sources of information. But the question remains: can this measure of subjective efficacy be related to some objective measure of political influence or impact? Given that an MP has this sense of his ability to influence policies, and given also that the degree to which he holds this sense of subjective competence will change both through time, and from issue to issue, what can our measure tell us about the policy-making activities of the House of Commons?

Firstly, it is trivially true that what an individual perceives about his situation will determine his behaviour. And if it is his behaviour that one is interested in, then it does not matter whether his perceptions are right or wrong. A batsman may perceive the ball floating towards him as an off-break and play an elegant drive, but if he has been deceived, and is the victim of a 'wrong 'un', he may well be dismissed. His behaviour is unalterable, whatever the consequences, because it is firmly based on his perceptions of the environment to which he must react. In this sense then it must be fairly clear that the level of efficacy that an MP feels with respect to policy formulation will largely dictate his behaviour in the pursuit of specific policy objectives.

Whether he is successful in his attempts to influence policy outputs will depend on the accuracy of his perceptions. If those are accurate he will succeed: if they are not, he will most likely fail, and, as a consequence of meeting failure, alter his general perceptions about his efficacy. A Member of Parliament with a lot of Parliamentary experience and a high sense of efficacy, is either a stubborn fool or a successful politician. The latter is probably more often the correct explanation.

Do the efficacy scores recorded here help to explain Parliamentary behaviour with respect to the policy of renationalising the iron and steel industry? To a limited extent, they do.

As the measure to renationalise the steel industry went through its various stages in Parliament, and as the organising

POLICY AND SELF-PERCEPTION

committee outside Parliament set about the task of creating the British Steel Corporation, the minister responsible for the measure altered his own attitude to his responsibilities (his recognition of his responsibility for the whole industry, not just the public sector of it, was crucial here) and, as a result, altered several specific aspects of the original policy objectives. Not all the changes were incorporated in the legislation, but the minister was driven or persuaded to make public commitments and to give public assurances on a whole range of policy matters. Many of these adjustments came from the organising committee, which took up uncompromising positions on some questions. But it is also clear that a few of the major changes stemmed directly from Members of Parliament. Three of these changes – to lower compensation payments, to conduct a limited experiment in workers' participation, and generally to tighten up the legislative position regarding the divisions between the public and private sectors – were all substantially the work of Parliament. It is interesting to note in this regard, therefore, that the three MPs most closely associated with these changes (O'Malley on compensation, Mikardo on workers' participation and Jenkin on public and private sector provisions) all score well on the efficacy ratings. Indeed, two of them (O'Malley and Jenkin) fall into the top decile on the frequency distribution.

It is not possible to draw grand conclusions from this. It is not clear for instance that MPs who have a high estimate of their efficacy can as a result participate in the policy process, either easily or frequently. There were, after all, six respondents who scored 16 or more on the efficacy scale who do not appear to have influenced policy outcomes over steel in the slightest. It may be that they had influence on other measures of policy that are not included in this study; but it may also be that they simply have an inaccurate perception of their abilities and opportunities. Similarly, since the interviewing for this study was conducted in 1969, it is possible that those MPs who did influence the steel legislation score well on the efficacy scale because they know that they did influence steel. In other words, the casual link may be in the opposite direction – from steel to a high sense of efficacy, and not from a sense of efficacy to nfluence on steel. But what is fairly clear is that the vital precondition for participation in the policy process by the back bencher is the belief that, through his actions, policies will be affected. Without this belief, participation in the determination of policy would be pointless. In the politics of policy-making, as in so much of life, it is those who work hardest and longest, and who have a firm belief in their own abilities, who create opportunities in which they can be influential.

Annex
Questions:

Could you tell me what you think were the most important activities of the House of Commons during his period? (1964–67).

How much did you get involved in these things in an active capacity?

1. Do you think that it did any good?

Apart from the things that you have mentioned as 'the most important' were you involved in any other activities in the House during the same period?

2. Do you think that *they* did any good?
3. Do you think that there should be more free votes?
4. Do you think that Parliamentary Questions have any effect?
5. Did this reaction have any effect on your subsequent behaviour? (After a series of questions probing the number of times the respondent had abstained from voting with, or had voted against, his own Party, and the way in which his Party had reacted to his 'rebellious' behaviour.)
6. Do you think that the facilities of the House of Commons are adequate for you to carry out your job properly?
7. You were a great deal involved in this whole business of the renationalisation: would you say that you influenced the kind of legislation finally enacted?
8. Do you think that this is normal? That you can usually expect to have that amount of influence?

Do you have any technical knowledge of the iron and steel industry, or of finance in the area, that you think might have been useful in devising the legislation?

9. Did you have an opportunity to use it?

10. Do you think that it was heeded?

11. Do you think that the Minister took what he expected to be your personal reactions into account when he was drawing up the legislation?

The eleven questions which are numbered in this Annex are those used as the basis for building the efficacy scale. Other questions have been included in the list published here when it is essential to know them in order to understand the questions designed to measure efficacy. The eleven questions were asked in the order shown here, but were scattered fairly far apart in an interview schedule that, in addition to these matters, involved another 110 variables.

The general interview technique employed was that of an open format. Questions were always asked in the same order, but respondents were allowed great freedom to respond as they saw fit. This meant that interviews took on the form of a structured conversation. Clearly some rigour is sacrificed by adopting this procedure, for respondents fit much less easily into coding categories: the data are not so hard. The advantages of such an approach, however, seem to me far to outweigh the disadvantages. Firstly, there is a much higher degree of *rapport* when the respondent is not being organised into answers he might not *exactly* want to give, and secondly it is possible, by adopting the open-ended technique, to pick up nuances and subtleties that are essential to an understanding of the mechanisms at work in society, but inappropriate for quantitative analysis.

Part III

VIEWS FROM THE BACK BENCHES

1. A Day in the Life of an MP

By DAVID MENHENNET and JOHN PALMER

IN this study* David Menhennet and John Palmer show how a typical backbencher is occupied on an average day. The range of subjects dealt with in this average day include hospital policy towards visits by children, the development of a small town in the Member's constituency, government policy towards the dates of the Easter holidays, his party's East of Suez commitments, and the improvement of a trunk road in his constituency. The authors show that the job of an MP has many parts to it – keeping abreast with local and national news, attending meetings of Standing and Select Committees, answering constituents' mail, meeting delegations from the constituency, being present in the Chamber to ask questions and to vote at the end of debates, and so on. As the authors suggest, the life of an MP is certainly varied.

To give an idea of the parliamentary day we shall have to mingle fiction with fact. As neither Hansard nor any other printed record gives an adequate idea of what a Member of the House of Commons actually does, we will invent a 'hero' and outline a day's activities. Our aim is to indicate the possible scope and variety of a Member's work and of the proceedings in the House, and we cannot suggest that the day we describe is typical or 'average' – we rather hope indeed that no Member is ever quite so busy as our man, whom we will call Mr William Ember.

He is in his forties, a backbench member of the party in opposition, and he first entered the House three years ago. He represents a mixed urban, rural and seaside constituency in Dorset, and still devotes part of his energies to the family

---

* Reprinted from *Parliament in Perspective* (London: The Bodley Head, 1967), pp. 99–112, with the permission of The Bodley Head Ltd, and the authors.

timber-importing business, based on a small port within the constituency. He is a director of the firm along with his brother and two others.

Ember's working day begins over breakfast at the flat in Pimlico which he shares with an MP for a Scottish constituency. For both of them it is rather more than a *pied-à-terre* but less than a home. Ember is not happy to be separated from his wife and two children for most of the week, and they have agreed that when his children finish schooling, in a few years' time, and if he is still an MP (which is never certain!) the main family home will have to be moved to London.

As he breakfasts, he glances through the *Daily Express* and *Daily Mirror* and works rather more carefully through the *Guardian, Times* and *Financial Times*. Keeping abreast of the news and noting developments of interest to himself, his constituency and his party is one of the most onerous of a Member's duties. The main home news is a report on the aircraft industry, which is of direct interest to Ember because one of the big companies has a subsidiary factory in his constituency. The matter is to be discussed at a party sub-committee the next day which Ember will attend.

Another article which catches his eye appears on the *Guardian*'s women's page. It says that although it is official policy to allow unrestricted visiting of children in hospital, a large number of hospitals still refuse in practice to allow it. This subject has interested Ember and his wife ever since one of their children, at an early age, had to go to hospital for a week. He remembers, as he reads the article, the various stages in the campaign to improve the welfare of children in hospital – the setting up of the Platt Committee of the Central Health Services Council, its recommendation (among many others) in favour of unrestricted visiting for parents, the Minister of Health's circular to hospitals which advised them to adopt the suggestions made by the Committee. He had thought that this particular battle was over, but now he resolves to draft a Parliamentary Question on the subject – something like 'Whether the Minister is satisfied with the progress that has been made in implementing the policy of allowing unrestricted visiting hours for parents of children in hospital; and whether he intends to issue any further advice to hospital boards.' Rather clumsy, he feels, but the Clerks in the Table Office may suggest a better wording. Ember mentally rehearses a Supplementary Question referring to the successful arrangements which have been made at the hospital in his constituency, and asking for pressure on hospitals to be kept up.

After absorbing the main news in the various papers, Ember turns to his copy of Hansard. He was not at Westminster the previous day because, as a member of one of the sub-committees of the Select Committee on Estimates, he was visiting the central office of the Ministry of Social Security situated at Newcastle-upon-Tyne in the course of the sub-committee's inquiry into the work of the Ministry. He skims quickly through the speeches in the main debate – on foreign affairs, and he felt that he knew pretty well what every speaker would say – and then he reads through some of the Questions more carefully.

The newspapers give a lively and vivid account of a rumpus in the House during the Prime Minister's Questions – apparently a mock-solemn Question on when the Government would introduce legislation to abolish the House of Lords sparked off a good deal of hilarity and indignation – but the Hansard account seems disappointingly tame; the hubbub and interjections are all reduced to an occasional '(interruption)' or 'Hon. Members: No!' Ember hopes that if the proceedings in the House are ever televised these moments of light relief will still be possible.

At about 9.45 Ember drives to the Palace of Westminster. He collects his mail – he always gives his official address as 'The House of Commons' and so only receives personal letters at his flat – and takes it up to the room where he and two other backbenchers have desks. Ember has only the part-time services of a secretary whom he shares with another Member, and he wishes that she had time to undertake a preliminary sorting of his post. Newsletters and duplicated hand-outs from the North Vietnam Liberation Front, the League Against Cruel Sports, the Free Cuba Association, the Income Tax Payers' Society and about a dozen others go straight into the wastepaper basket. They may be important, but they aren't among Ember's particular concerns.

There are a number of letters with various postmarks in

Ember's constituency, but first of all he opens the copy of the previous day's local newspaper which is regularly mailed to him. He finds, as he suspected he would, that there have been further developments in the saga of Fettlebridge, a small market town in his constituency which the Greater London Council has selected as a possible site for a scheme under the Town Development Act. The GLC has already entered into discussions with the urban district and county councils and proposes that the town be expanded from its present population of 6,000 to around 40,000 over the course of about five years. A number of London firms – including a fairly small but world-famous manufacturer of hypodermic needles – are interested in moving their businesses and their employees to Fettlebridge. Ember, who is a member of his party's New Towns Committee, is whole-heartedly behind the plan, but there is some strong local opposition. Ember feels sure that it is only a minority, but quite a powerful one.

The local paper has a long letter from a local Councillor whom Ember knows quite well. He retired five years ago to a pleasant house on the outskirts of Fettlebridge and is an active member of the local council and, what is more awkward, worked hard for Ember at the election. Ember reads this letter carefully: *Fettlebridge as it has existed for hundreds of years would be ruined – influx of people not used to country or small-town life – good agricultural land sterilised – traffic difficulties: poor roads, railway line already closed – duty to preserve our diminishing countryside – what do the people really want?* And so on. Ember begins to draft a suitable reply to send to the Editor of the paper, and also resolves to dictate a personal note to the Councillor suggesting that they meet to discuss the matter next week-end.

Ember is a member of Standing Committee A, which this morning is meeting at 10.30 to discuss clause 2 of the House Purchase (Temporary Provisions) Bill. Ember gathers up his constituency correspondence and goes down to the Committee Room at about 11 o'clock, looks in, and in a whisper asks the Whip if he is needed this morning. He is relieved to hear that no divisions are expected and that he needn't stay. As Ember looks around he hears his party spokesman arguing about interest rates, and he sees the Parliamentary Secretary in charge of the Bill conferring in undertones with his advisers; he turns away, goes down in the lift and crosses Old Palace Yard to meet his (half!) secretary.

Together they start to go through the constituency letters. One is unusually bulky – a petition from (as it is headed) The Parents of Fettlebridge. Ember can guess the contents: he has already been in correspondence with a number of parents over the issue of school provision for the expanded town. The Local Education Authority has proposed a system of fairly small primary schools with two comprehensive schools for the secondary stage, the post-war buildings of the existing secondary modern school to form the basis for a new technical college. Fettlebridge has no grammar school, but a number of children go to grammar schools in another town ten miles away. The petition demands grammar school provision within the expanded town. Ember has already discussed this matter at length with the chairman of his party's Education Committee and he dictates a reply in terms which echo his previous correspondence on the subject: *This is a matter for the Local Education Authority; ministerial policy in favour of comprehensive education is well known and although he is opposed to it in many respects he feels that new communities are a special case. Grammar school education will be provided within the comprehensive school. The LEA scheme is a workable one. They will have ahead of them in Fettlebridge a great task in building a happy and integrated community, and the sharing of all types of children in the educational process can be a decisive influence. He doubts if a petition to Parliament will really be useful, and suggests that he arrange a meeting of the parents and members of the County Education Committee and its chief officer with himself in the chair.*

The other letters are more individual. One is an invitation to speak in his home town ('ten minutes only!' it says) at the showing of an Oxfam film. Ember will be in London that day, but he replies that he knows his wife will be delighted to speak and that he will ask her to contact his correspondent. Most of the other letters raise personal problems. One is from a council-house tenant who needs a larger home, another from a private tenant whose landlord refuses to carry out repairs to the roof. Ember wishes that council tenants would realise that he can't dictate to the officials in the Town Hall or somehow magically get a name to the top of the housing list. However there seems to be a case here (the tenant has a two-bedroomed flat and has just had a third baby), so Ember tells his secretary to make a copy of the letter and send it to the council's Housing Manager with a covering note. At the same time he dictates a reply to his correspondent suggesting a meeting at the 'surgery' he holds in the party committee rooms in his constituency every alternate Friday evening. Ember is unsure about the legal position of the private tenant with the unco-operative landlord. He pockets this letter intending to look up the legal points in the Library. This, he feels, is another case where it would be as well to meet the person concerned at his 'surgery'.

A long letter denounces the war in Vietnam and demands that Ember vote against the Defence Estimates. Ember sighs, and dictates a reasoned reply which takes up a valuable quarter of an hour. He doesn't expect to convince his correspondent and doubts if the writer expected to convince him either.

A letter from a retired Civil Servant sets out with a meticulous wealth of detail the decline in the real value of his pension. He must have missed the announcement in the House three days before that public service pensions are to be increased. Ember asks his secretary to get the relevant Hansard and send it off with a short note. Another letter is concerned with the writer's entitlement to industrial injury benefit: it sets out all the facts carefully and makes a convincing case; Ember suspects that the correspondent's trade union may have helped in the drafting. He asks his secretary to take a copy of the letter and send it on to the Minister of Social Security, together with a request for investigation. There must already be quite a bulky file at the local insurance office. He dictates a stereotyped reply to his constituent, saying that he has asked the Minister to look into the matter and that he will pass on the result. If the Minister's reply should be unsatisfactory, Ember will have to go over the case with the individual concerned and perhaps pursue it further by means of Parliamentary Questions, or, if the decision can be challenged, in an Adjournment Debate.

By the time he has dealt with a number of other letters, it is 12.30, and Ember walks across to the Central Lobby. He has arranged to meet for lunch two officers of his local party association who are in London for the day. At lunch in the Strangers' Dining Room, looking out over the Thames, they give Ember an account of the previous week's local elections, where some wards returned disappointing results. Conversation ranges freely over the always absorbing topic of electoral prospects. Ember brings up the subject of Fettlebridge and points out that the expansion scheme would eventually mean that constituency boundaries would have to be redrawn, with all the electoral uncertainty that that involved. His guests give an assessment of the attitude towards the scheme within the local party. They believe that opponents are now a fairly small minority. At about 2.15 they all return to the Central Lobby to watch the Speaker's procession pass on its way into the House to open the day's proceedings. Ember's guests go up to the Strangers' Gallery, for which he has given them tickets, and Ember himself walks through the Members' Lobby into the House just as Prayers are finished, and goes to his usual place on the back row of green benches on the Opposition side.

The Home Secretary is answering Questions this afternoon and Ember put down a Question some weeks before. As it stands on the Order Paper it reads:

> 7. Mr Ember (Dorset, East): To ask the Secretary of State for the Home Department what is the policy of the Government regarding the making of some change in the variable dates of Easter.

This subject has a long parliamentary history, and Ember has been encouraged to take it up by the holiday trade in his constituency. When the Speaker calls 'Mr Ember' he rises in his place and says 'Number 7, Sir'. The Joint Under-Secretary of State for the Home Department gets up at the despatch box, opens his folder of Answers, and reads out: 'We are awaiting the outcome of the consideration being given to this question by the World Council of Churches.' Ember is prepared for this reply and he rises again, is called by Mr Speaker, and asks his Supplementary: 'Is the Joint Under-Secretary aware that it is 39 years since the Easter Act, 1928, was passed allowing for the fixing of the date of Easter? Cannot we get agreement with the churches? Failing that, cannot we go ahead on our own and fix our own Easter?'

The Minister has envisaged a come-back on these lines and does not need to glance at his notes as he replies: 'The churches in this country, both Protestant and Roman Catholic, are agreed on the question of a fixed date, but it would be highly undesirable if the festival of Easter was on a different date in this country from that operating in the rest of the world.' Ember does not rise again and there is a rustle of Order Papers as the Speaker calls the next Member to ask Question No. 8. A fellow-Member leans towards Ember and mutters, 'Try again in five years' time.'

Ember sits on through Questions – they are concerned with the usual Home Office mixed bag of Commonwealth Immigration, crimes of violence, the prison conditions of the train robbers, police manpower, prevention of drug addiction, conditions in Borstals, reform of the law on abortion, and inflammable baby-clothes. He has heard in the Lobby that the Minister of Technology is to make a statement on the future of the Atomic Energy Authority's works at Bilslade, in a neighbouring constituency. The statement announces a new programme of work for the factory – which rumour had suggested was to be closed down – and Ember does not attempt to join in the questioning of the Minister which follows. After this, the Orders of the Day are reached. As it is a Supply Day the Opposition has the right to choose the subject for debate and they have selected the recently announced Government plans for the reorganisation and contraction of the Territorial Army. Ember does not intend to try to 'catch the Speaker's eye' and contribute to the debate, but as a 'three-line whip' has been circulated he will be required to vote at the end of the debate at 10 p.m.

As the leader of his party begins to deploy his case against the Government, Ember makes his way out of the Chamber as unobtrusively as he can, turning at the bar to bow towards the Speaker.

On his way to the cloakroom Ember glances at his watch: 3.45. He is due at a meeting of a committee of the British Timber Trades Federation at 4 o'clock. Parking will be difficult if he goes by car, so he walks through the subway to the Underground station and arrives at the meeting slightly breathless five minutes late. He is glad to find that cups of tea are being handed round.

The business before the committee is a draft report produced in conjunction with the Timber Development Association on the use of timber in industrialised housing. This is not, it has been decided, a suitable matter for Parliamentary Questions, still less for debate, and the report is intended for submission to the technical staff of the Ministry of Public Buildings and Works, with copies to the Minister of Housing, the Building Research Station, a number of other interested bodies and all the firms known to be involved in industrialised building. The Federation is worried lest the new techniques should involve a diminished use of wood in house construction and has produced designs for internal non-load-bearing wall units which could be fabricated in factories and easily erected on site. After the meeting Ember stays on to talk with a fellow-member of the Federation about the effects of the Forestry Commission's increasing supplies of mature timber on the importing trade. They agree that the Federation should organise a small delegation of importers and merchants to meet the Commission and urge the marketing of this timber through normal trade channels.

It is approaching 6 o'clock when Ember returns to the House and, after signing his letters, his next engagement is a meeting of the whole parliamentary party on Defence. This is largely devoted to our 'East of Suez' commitments, and a number of speakers attack a speech made in the House the week before by a member of the Shadow Cabinet. Ember speaks for a few minutes, urging that any appearance of disunity within the party on such an issue could have disastrous consequences. He suggests that the Shadow Cabinet should produce a statement which they can all accept and abide by.

On his way to the Smoking Room for a drink before dinner, Ember has a conversation with a Lobby correspondent who already seems to have a fairly good idea of what has been said at the meeting. Ember glances at the evening papers in the Smoking Room and then has dinner with two fellow backbenchers in the Members' Dining Room. One of them has been lucky in the ballot for Private Members' Bills and he manages to persuade Ember to attend the House on Friday to vote for the closure, which will probably be necessary as it is believed that the Government side will try to talk the Bill out.

After dinner, he makes his way to the Table Office and puts down his Question on children in hospital for the next day the Minister of Health is due to answer Questions. He goes along to the Library and looks up the point of landlord-and-tenant law his correspondent of this morning has raised, and jots down a request for the Library's Research Division to send him a note on Forestry Commission sales of various categories of timber over the last five years, and on the availability of any future projections.

As he is doing this he is approached by a backbencher on the Government side, asking him to sign a motion which will be printed on the Order Paper the next day. The motion already has sponsors from all three parties and reads as follows:

> ACCOMMODATION OF THE LEGISLATURE: That a Joint Committee of the Lords and Commons be set up to make a fundamental and comprehensive examination of the potential requirements in terms of accommodation of a modern legislature in the light of developments and changes which may occur over the course of the next half-century and of the capability of the Palace of Westminster, with such alterations and improvements as may be possible, of meeting those requirements, and to report.

Ember signs his name and then moves to an armchair and roughs out the weekly article he contributes to his local newspaper.

By this time it is 9.15; Ember returns to the Chamber to hear the two closing speeches in the debate on the Territorial Army, and afterwards records his vote with his party. The next business before the House is a Prayer to annul the Agricultural Lime Subsidy Regulations. Ember expects this will run for about an hour, and he returns to the Library to wait for the Adjournment Debate – the half-hour debate at the end of the parliamentary day. The debate is to be opened by a Government backbencher who sits for a constituency bordering Ember's. The subject is the improvement of a trunk road which ends at Seaport in Ember's constituency, and the Member initiating the debate has promised to allow Ember five minutes for a short speech.

At 11.15 Ember hears the tape machine, which records the progress of business in the House all over the Palace, begin the clatter which signals a new announcement and as soon as he sees the 'ADJ' of 'ADJOURNMENT' appear he hurries into the

Chamber. A few Members who have been discussing the previous motion are leaving, and soon the Chamber is deserted except for the Deputy Speaker in the Chair, a Clerk at the Table, the Serjeant-at-Arms, the Member speaking, Ember himself, a Government Whip and the Parliamentary Secretary to the Ministry of Transport who is to reply to the debate. Before going to his place, Ember whispers to the Deputy Speaker that the opener of the debate has agreed that he should have five minutes; he receives a nod in reply.

The Government backbencher develops his case for a high priority to be given to the improvement of the A346 and quotes a number of telling statistics of accidents, vehicle flow, population changes in the area, etc. When he sits down Ember gets to his feet and is called by the Chair. He compliments the hon. Member opposite for the skill with which he has developed his case, refers to the fact that it has the full backing of the local planning, highway and police authorities, briefly outlines its importance to Seaport – *not just a seaside resort, but also a manufacturing town and a port, making a small but important and growing contribution to our trade with Europe which will increase considerably should Britain join the Common Market* – and mentions finally the proposed expansion of Fettlebridge, which would also use the A346 as its main link with London.

When Ember sits down (he notes that he has spoken for precisely 4¾ minutes), the Parliamentary Secretary rises to reply. Ember thinks as he listens to the flow of words that this brief must be used several times a session, with just the placenames altered to suit the particular case. The Minister is saying *how glad he is to have an opportunity of discussing this important area – pays tribute to the persuasive case presented by his hon. Friend, and ably supported by the hon. Member opposite – the importance of the A346 is fully recognised by the Ministry and a number of minor improvements have been carried out since the war. However, the Ministry well recognise that more than this is needed and there is a plan for extensive stretches of dual carriageway* . . . here the Government backbencher interjects '*That plan was made 14 years ago*' . . . *but he is sorry to say that he can give no firm starting date for actual road works. It is unfortunately his duty to consider a large number of demands – all of them, no doubt, of the greatest local importance – and this particular scheme – valuable though it would be – has to take its place in the queue.*

H

The Parliamentary Secretary is a practised speaker in Adjournment debates and his rounded close comes almost on the dot 30 minutes after the debate began. Immediately he sits down, the Deputy Speaker rises, the Serjeant removes the mace and the House is adjourned for the day.

Ember walks across the floor to the bench on the Government side of the House where his fellow-fighter for the improvement of the A346 is gathering up his notes. They smile ruefully and walk out of the Chamber together towards the Smoking Room for a night-cap. They are joined in a few minutes by the Parliamentary Secretary.

'We shall have to get you people out', says Ember with a smile.

'You could have your road tomorrow if you'd vote for another shilling on the income tax', replies the Parliamentary Secretary. 'You should see the list of schemes all ready to go, bar the money. So long as you don't use it in evidence against me, I can tell you that your road is about six years away.'

'Never mind,' says the Government backbencher to Ember, 'you may be in his shoes before then.'

'You still wouldn't be able to fish it out of the queue,' says the Parliamentary Secretary with a grim smile.

*   *   *

At the end of the day we have described, Ember was in bed half an hour after midnight and fell asleep over the White Paper on the Adult Offender which had been issued that afternoon. As he dozed off he reminded himself to telephone his wife in the morning.

2. New MPs have kept their Zeal for Reform

From *The Times*

FOLLOWING the general election of March 1966, a 'new generation' of MPs was returned to the Commons. In this extract* the findings of a survey of the new MPs conducted by *The Times* is reported. The 'freshmen' MPs were asked about the House, and the proposals they had for changing it. While many of them were found to be critical of the facilities, procedures and customs, of the House, others thought that they were by and large satisfactory: differences in party were not, generally, responsible for differences that the Members had towards reforming Parliament.

Six weeks ago the new Parliament opened, and 83 brand new MPs took their seats. The word at the time was that this new intake was going to be a notable one, bursting with intellect and energy. In particular the new boys were said to take a dim view of the rusty machinery of Westminster. Mutterings about parliamentary reform were audible.

Their first short term is over. During their holiday *The Times* has been canvassing the new members to find out what they now think of the old place; and what proposals they have for changing it.

All 83 members were asked for their views. These were the newcomers; not recidivists like Mr Patrick Gordon Walker, returning to Parliament as 'new' members. Most of them were asked by word of mouth to give their opinions. The more elusive ones were invited by letter. In all, 37 replied.

This sample is not a representative cross-section of all MPs. There are 68 new Labour MPs, 11 Tories and four Liberals. And there are only three new women.

---

* Reprinted from *The Times*, 6 June 1966, with the permission of *The Times*.

Their replies show that some revolutionary zeal has survived. One fiery woman, asked for her opinion of Westminster, replied passionately: 'I suppose it's got to be printable if its going in *The Times*.' The more general view is that the new members think the House of Commons is an excellent place, worthy of almost unlimited improvement.

They were asked if they were able to make their presence adequately felt on matters of importance to the nation. Ten said Yes, 10 said No, and the rest were non-committal. 'I imagine so, but I have not yet discovered the technique,' sighed Mr Frank Hooley (Lab.). Almost as wistful in his reply was Mr Trevor Fortescue (Con.): 'Not yet; unless I can coin an immortal phrase.' 'My first feeling is of trying to make an impression on a vast and very absorbent sponge,' Mr David Watkins (Lab.) said.

The new members were happier about constituency matters in Parliament. Nineteen felt that they had opportunities to raise constituency points adequately; four felt they had not; and the remaining 13 hummed and hawed as inscrutably as veteran politicians.

They were asked if any of the ceremonies at Westminster were irrelevant. Nine replied that all the ceremonies were irrelevant and should be committed to the flames. 'All ceremony is, unless it also has a practical purpose.' Mr Benjamin Whitaker (Lab.) said as judiciously as Aristotle.

But six said that the ceremonies were all right, or that they preferred to keep them. And only one man in this school of thought was a Conservative.

Mr Michael Barnes (Lab.) said that the ceremony issue was a red herring: 'It is the day-to-day practice that is the important thing.'

The process of electing a Speaker was called 'ridiculous'. The State Opening was singled out with dislike by three. There were several proposals to dress the Serjeant-at-Arms and the Speaker in more sensible kit, such as grey flannels. 'Their clothes and headgear are farcical, and, I should imagine, uncomfortable.'

Calling each other 'The hon. member for Eatanswill' instead of say, Mr Fred Bloggs, displeases two down-to-earth members. Reading of long orders was picked out for disapproval. Two members particularly object to daily prayers – 'the majority are secularists, and I can therefore see no reason why the majority should be subject to the meaningless daily incantations: I am not suggesting that Christians should be deprived of opportunities for worship, but surely the chapel is the appropriate place.'

Members were asked for their suggestions for making the Palace of Westminster a better place, where they could do their jobs more effectively. Their replies fall into two broad categories. First there are the material comforts needed to improve 'the junior clerk's working conditions' of MPs. These suggestions are, rather touchingly, like the home-sick letters of a new boy: 'Dear Mum, yesterday we played a house match against the Blue House, and won by 361 votes to 249. Please could you send me some more jam, and a secretary, and an office; and could you pay for my telephone calls.'

Seven wanted a research department for MPs. 'I need to be able to get the information I want much more easily and much more quickly,' Mr Barnes said. Others wished for a filing cabinet, a telephone and their own typewriter. Some said the cost of telephone trunk calls should be met from public funds and it should be easier to get tickets to the Strangers' Gallery for constituents.

Mr Richard Wainwright (Lab.) complained of 'an absurd internal telephone plant, and the dreadful Gothicness of everything except the people'. Mr Hooley pleaded for some modern furnishing and décor – 'aesthetically the Palace of Westminster is ugly and depressing in the extreme; most of it is grisly Victorian. There is no sense of spaciousness or light, and the atmosphere is oppressive.'

There were several requests for better facilities for members' wives, such as a private sitting room where they could wait for their husbands, instead of sitting in the central lobby. Mr John Nott (Nat. L. & C.) wanted travel vouchers to take his wife with him to St Ives, his constituency. Her return fare to and from his constituency at present is £15, and 'crippling'. 'I could perform my constituency work much more usefully without destroying my family life if I had her support in Cornwall, and/or London, more often.'

Eight of those questioned supported the fashionable idea of

specialist backbench committees, on the American model, able to question Ministers about defence and finance, and to influence them before policy was evolved. Mr Wainwright observed that because there was not enough scope for backbenchers with specialist knowledge there were only three practising accountants besides himself in a House which spent most of its time debating company and commercial matters.

According to *The Times Guide to the House of Commons*, eight members are described as accountants.

There were 10 votes for shorter speeches, and various suggestions for rationing the time. For instance, a speech of one hour from the Government could be followed by four successive speeches of a quarter of an hour from the Opposition; 'there would then be considerable pressure from within the parties to keep speeches shorter'. Limit speeches to 10 minutes, said one laconic member.

The rigmarole of the voting system has annoyed several members. Some technological ones want to record their votes by pushing buttons instead of trooping in and out of lobbies. Others propose that voting should be by contracting out – all members would be presumed to have voted faithfully for their party line unless they registered with a clerk their wish to kick against the whips. The Liberal vote could be either recorded *en bloc* or identified individually.

'Abolish the House of Lords' was the time-honoured war-cry of only two new members. Five voted for starting and finishing their work earlier in the day, and for shorter recesses.

There were proposals that the Speaker should be less shackled to the rulings of his predecessors, particularly in the tendency to refuse to allow emergency debates under Standing Order No. 9. Standing Orders should be more clearly written out. Business should be arranged two weeks in advance. Recess dates should be announced earlier.

Mr Raymond Dobson (Lab.) said bitterly that it should be possible to book a speaking period in a debate, 'and so avoid hours spent on preparation of speeches that are not delivered'. There should be a more effective way of pursuing replies to parliamentary questions, especially written answers, which are 'downright evasive', Mr Walter Clegg (Con.) said.

The class of '66 are full of ideas and enthusiasm for reform.

A Conservative says that the reformers have their remedy in their own hands if they will only use it. Until Government back-benchers use their vote as a weapon against the executive, Ministers will ride roughshod over the rights of members, and the House of Commons will cease to have any real significance.

3. Sanctuary of Conservatism

By GEORGE CUNNINGHAM

GEORGE CUNNINGHAM, Labour MP for South-West Islington since 1970, considers that new MPs have a duty to the House to press their views on Parliament early in their careers. To this effect one of many reforms of Parliament that he suggests in this extract* is that maiden speeches should be used by new Members to speak 'not so much as Members of the House but as outsiders, expressing the views held by members of the public about the place'. His opinion of the rituals which characterise much of the business of the House is that they are not merely useless but positively harmful. Parliament has become 'the sanctuary of conservatism' – and is falling into decay.

It may seem odd that a new Member of Parliament with only a few weeks' experience in the House of Commons should offer his views on what should be done to change the place, particularly when his views are critical. But it is one of the erroneous assumptions of Parliament that its internal affairs are a mystique on which only the priests in the sanctuary can pronounce. There is in fact a growing number of people outside who have a deep knowledge of the affairs of the House and who are concerned not only about what it does but how it does it. Trade union officials, businessmen, Civil Servants, academics in the political sciences, lobbyists of all kinds – such people have to deal with Parliament and they are well placed to hold impartial as well as informed views on its methods. Their judgement – which is almost invariably critical – is at least as likely to be right as that of MPs themselves.

The House of Commons is a seductive place. I can't be the only new member who, after a few weeks, has felt a growing

---

* Reprinted from *Socialist Commentary*, December 1970, pp. 12–14, with the permission of the publisher and the author.

sense of cosiness in sitting on those warm green benches, a feeling that what matters in the country is what goes on there, who calls out the most effective interventions and who wins his debating points. The rules and procedure of the place are so complex that one quickly might feel that outsiders are unqualified to speak on the subject. And the cosiness is such that one quickly decides that the habits are not really so inefficient.

It is for this reason that I think new members *should* express their views on Parliament early in their careers. They will make some errors perhaps through lack of knowledge but this will be more than compensated by freshness of approach. I would have liked to make my maiden speech on this subject, but the opportunity did not occur. I wanted to suggest that the conventions attached to maiden speeches – that they should be uncontroversial, contain kind references to one's constituency, etc. – should be extended to encourage new members to speak for one last time not so much as members of the House but as outsiders, expressing the views held by members of the public about the place. For the House to put its indulgence to maiden speakers to this purpose would be a valuable innovation and not a useless ritual as are the traditions attaching to maiden speeches today.

Nor indeed would such speeches be based on total ignorance. I, for example, have had to do with the place for fourteen years. I have sat in one horse-box as a Civil Servant and in the other as a Transport House official. I have delivered only three five-minute speeches in the House but I have drafted quite a few for delivery from both sides. And I have drafted replies and tried to anticipate supplementary questions to far more parliamentary questions than I have so far been able to ask myself. Other new members have equally relevant experience.

If one is looking at the House with a fresh eye there is one feature which cannot be excluded however difficult it may be to deal with. There are too many of us. 630 representatives for a population of fifty-five million people is excessive. Even with improved procedures the existence of this number will always make it difficult for each member to play a full part. For a parliamentarian to recommend a reduction in numbers may be risky but somehow we are going to have to deal with this point and we might as well get used to it. The obvious way to deal with it is to lay down that the Boundary Commissioners in redrawing boundaries should do so in such a way that the number of constituencies is reduced. A reduction of ten each decade would get us down to about 530 in 100 years – hardly a revolutionary change.

At the beginning of a parliament the feature which impresses most strongly is the ritual. I am not opposed to ritual. I like a good show as much as the next man. But the British are so given to ritual that we really must prune it occasionally or we shall all suffocate. Ritual can be living or dead: most of that performed in the House of Commons died long ago. I feel sure that the reaction of most members of the public watching the Speaker's procession through the central lobby each day is not to admire the historic quaintness of it but to wonder how grown men can bring themselves to play such childish games. When some officer carrying a white billiard cue bows several times one is reminded of nothing so much as the Mikado's bodyless head going through its motions. When forms are observed and words uttered of which only the clerks know the significance it is time for the pruning knife. When the ritual is such that most people experience only embarrassment over it, the time is overdue.

Some people would argue that the ritual may be useless but is also harmless. I think it is positively harmful. It clutters up the procedure in the House, encouraging attachments to old ways, and to forms instead of substance. It creates a resistance to change. If we must have our charades, let us have charades which are relevant to the problems which Parliament faces at the present time. Are these problems so unimportant that we can afford to spend time celebrating victories over the threats of 300 years ago? When Black Rod has the door slammed in his face we celebrate the Commons' victory over the Stuarts. But the chances of the Queen arriving with a posse of policemen to chase members on to the terrace are remote. It is now over three centuries since that battle was decided. Are we to go on celebrating for another 300 years? Have we no current problems to have our stage shows about? Indeed we have. The problem now and for the rest of this century is the failure of Parliament adequately to control the executive. In so far as we have bad government it is often because Parliament has not permitted itself or equipped itself to do its job. The executive gets away with gross abuse of the legislature. So, instead of Black Rod, let us have the Prime Minister of the day knocking on the door asking for his salary three times and being refused twice. That would be no more nonsensical than the games we play now. It only seems so because it is not shrouded in the respectability of an established tradition.

It is this attachment to what was done last time which is making a mummy out of Parliament. If something has not been done before, then convention requires that it should not be done now. If it has been done before, convention requires that it should always be done. I get the impression that if I were to seize the mace, dash with it to the terrace and throw it in the river, then every year on the same day it would be incumbent on some member to do the same. The attachment to what was done last time also shows itself in the sheer perversity of some of the forms and procedures. Is it really necessary when a member wants to break off normal business and discuss an urgent matter, that he should have to move that the House should pack up and go home? There are, as everyone knows, members of the public in the gallery (most of them watching the performance with incredulous incomprehension); yet if a member mentions this fact the gallery has to be cleared. A member who had been a regular officer in the armed forces is called 'gallant' even if he never left Aldershot; a private with a VC is not. Would the pillars of the temple really fall down if we did as other people do and called each other by our names?

Along the carpet on the floor of the House there are two broad lines. As every tourist knows these mark the points beyond which members may not extend their swords. I may be disappointed but I doubt if sword fighting will break out in the House in my day. Could we not make use of those lines to depict lots of human figures so that we, with our eyes turned inwards to our own games, could read them to mean 'the public is watching you' and adapt our habits accordingly.

The intense conservatism of the House has meant that it has been slow to change its working habits. Surely it is obvious that members can only have an effect on the executive if they operate on particular subjects through committees. There is probably not a new member in the House who does not see this as a self-evident. Who would expect a body of 630 persons to do effective work? A committee system does not mean that the grand parliamentary occasion before the whole House is lost. The whole House is the right place for the most important business and the final stage of all business. The House from 2.30 to 4 p.m. on most days is the forum of the nation and performs an obviously necessary function. But the debates in the whole House when only half a dozen members are present are of less value. Members are not debating in any real sense of the term but only dictating passages for tomorrow's Hansard.

If the executive is going to be properly answerable to Parliament, subject committees with a fair degree of permanence and expertise must be allowed to go over Bills and scrutinize executive behaviour. There are difficulties and dangers in an elaborate committee system but the British Parliament, when real blood flowed in its veins, was not afraid of trying new methods. It was confident enough in its judgement to want to try them and to know that it could make later corrections if necessary. Surely it is better to make mistakes by doing something than by doing nothing. New methods introduced today may or may not be ideal for current needs; but the methods of the last century are *certain* not to be ideal. We have a choice between continuous adaptation or stagnation. Britain has become a country in which resistance to change is deeply ingrained. The pace at which the Victorians changed their habits and institutions was breathtaking compared with our own era. If there is an English sickness, this is it. The circumstances of life today require constant change and if we are not prepared to introduce reforms we shall not stay still, we shall fall behind – progressively less able to deal with our problems. The appetite for change must be fed or it will be lost.

If change is to take place there is no doubt where it ought to begin and where it is needed most – in the House of Commons. The Labour Government introduced some improvements – particularly by making more use of subject committees – but the changes were so few and so slow. Governments of both parties have been reluctant to see the nuisance value of Parliament increased. That attitude is not worthy of the Labour Party. Reform is needed not only to give Parliament its proper degree of power but also to ensure that we have good government. You will never get a good executive unless there is a good legislature breathing down its neck. To effect change in this direction needs no more than that parliamentarians should insist on it. It is not for the executive to introduce changes in parliamentary procedures but for Parliament itself. The Conservative Government's proposals continue the modest reforms of the Labour Government, but do not approach the radical changes advocated by the House's own Procedures Committee. Members on all sides of the House should combine to put through their necessary changes in defiance of the Executive. That this should sound revolutionary is itself only an illustration of the decay into which Parliament has fallen.

4. The Influence of the Backbencher: A Labour View*

By G. R. STRAUSS

THE authors of the next two extracts are experienced parliamentarians who have between them served in the House for over fifty years. The conclusions they draw from separate analyses of the influence of the backbencher within the Conservative and Labour parties are similar in two important respects. Firstly, the amount of influence the backbencher can exert over his party leadership is greater when his party is in opposition than it is in government. Secondly, the influence of the backbencher is greater behind the scenes of government than it is on the floor of the House. The authors also reveal notable differences between the influence of the backbencher in the Conservative and Labour parliamentary parties which, they suggest, rest on various structural, organisational, and leadership characteristics of the parties.

Outwardly Labour and Conservative backbenchers behave in much the same way. Left and Right wingers on both sides press their views with equal fervour, while the middle-of-the-roaders, who form the bulk of both parties, can normally be relied upon to support the policies of their leaders. The influence of backbenchers on parliamentary affairs takes place behind the scenes – in their subject groups, the gossip of the corridors, the conspiracies hatched in the Tea and Smoking Rooms of the House, and among the Tories no doubt in the clubs and private houses of the Establishment. It is there that discontents are first voiced and political pressures generated which the Front Bench ignores at its peril.

The main difference between the behaviour of the two backbenches stems from the contrasting attitude of the parties to public affairs. The Conservatives stand broadly for maintaining

---

* Reprinted from *Political Quarterly*, Vol. 36, 1965, pp. 277–85 with the permission of the publisher and the author.

the existing balances in society, making such adjustments in the economic field as are necessary to meet changing modern conditions, and in the social field such advances as are forced upon them by the pressure of public opinion. Labour stands for governmental action that will bring about a rapid change towards a more just and efficient society. At elections, Conservative candidates advocate the *status quo* with mild reforms while Labour candidates challenge the fundamentals of our social order and demand the application of drastic remedies. They are rebels, and exhilarated by victory enter Parliament as zealots, impatient to fulfil their pledges. They are determined not to betray the trust put in them by their keen party workers to whom they are largely indebted for their victory.

Moreover, they cover a far wider spectrum of political colour – from pink to scarlet. They range from radicals, intolerant of the nebulous policy of the Liberal Party, to near-Communists who consider that almost every major industry is a dominant height crying out for public ownership. And in foreign affairs, from those who consider the maintenance of the Atlantic Alliance to be the prime objective to those whose sympathies are with the Iron Curtain countries. There is an equally sharp division between the pro- and anti-Common Marketeers.

This variety in approach is paralleled by the widely different backgrounds from which the Labour Members are drawn. The Conservative Parliamentary Party is far more homogeneous. Its members mostly belong to the well-to-do middle class. The few who have sprung from the financially lower strata of society are treated with courteous disdain and are rarely integrated into the herd. Their voices do not ruffle the prevailing harmony of upper-class outlook.

The Parliamentary Labour Party today is far more broadly based. Its composition has changed greatly since the war. When I was first elected in 1929 most of my colleagues were men of working-class background who had become prominent in the Labour movement through years of trade union activity. Many had exhausted their vitality and were adopted as candidates by sympathetic selection committees, largely made up of union representatives, as a reward for their long service to their fellow-workers. The House of Commons was often regarded as a place of honourable retirement, an assumption readily accepted by the newly elected members when faced with the uncongenial and frightening atmosphere of the Chamber.

With the broadening of its appeal Labour has attracted more people from the professional classes and the earlier bias of the constituency parties against adopting them as candidates has almost disappeared; particularly outside the industrial and mining areas. It is interesting to recall that the most loudly applauded argument advanced by delegates at the Bournemouth Conference in 1938 in support of the Executive's decision to expel Sir Stafford Cripps was that he was an intellectual and therefore, by implication, unreliable.

In the present Parliament sixty-two out of the 310 Labour Members went to Oxford or Cambridge and eighty-eight to other Universities. The public schools educated fifty-seven, but significantly only two went to Eton as against eighty Conservatives. There are eighty-eight who went to grammar schools. Before entering Parliament thirty-two practised as barristers, fourteen as solicitors, forty-six as teachers and lecturers, and forty as journalists, writers and broadcasters. There are seven company directors and twenty-nine designate themselves as 'business men'. There are seven doctors and surgeons, nineteen engineers, nine economists, seven accountants and six stockbrokers. The only upper-class occupation in which the Parliamentary Labour Party is deficient is farming. There is only one farmer. The proportion directly associated with working-class activities, compared to the pre-war years, is small. Trade union officials number forty-three, industrial workers twenty-four, and the ex-miners, always well represented in the Parliamentary Party, twenty-one.

One effect of this diversification is that the interests of backbenchers are now less concentrated on matters directly affecting the welfare of the working class, such as insurance benefits and housing. And they are able to bring to bear a far wider range of technical knowledge on all aspects of public affairs.

It is mainly through the Party's eighteen subject groups that backbenchers exchange and formulate their views. On average two or three groups meet each afternoon. A Member can join as many as he likes, and non-members may attend any meeting, but not vote. The one exception is the influential Trade Union group which is only open to those sponsored by a union.

Attendance varies. Where there is a prospect of a dull meeting, or when, as often happens, two groups clash in time, there may not be more than half a dozen present. But at the foreign affairs groups, particularly when the Foreign Secretary is there to make a report or when there is likely to be a flare-up about some current event, 100 to 150 might attend. The groups invite distinguished people with specialised knowledge to address them, and receive deputations from representative bodies. For example, the Aviation Group recently listened to the views of the independent airline operators, and the Arts and Amenities Group invited the Director-General of the Arts Council to talk to them. The visitors' speeches are usually brief and most of the time is taken up by questions and answers.

By far the greater part of the Committees' activities are devoted to policy discussions with no outsider present. The Minister responsible for the subject-matter of each group, or his Under-Secretary, may attend on invitation, but does not do so by right. When he does he gives the group confidential background information. He outlines his objectives and explains the apparent defects in his administration or his alleged departure from Party policy. Criticisms which might otherwise be voiced on the floor of the House are discussed in a spirit of comradely understanding and usually a bond of sympathy is created between the Minister and the Members who specialise in the affairs of his department.

Sometimes the atmosphere is not so happy. The slightly petulant undertone of a backbencher's supplementary question in the Chamber may conceal a strongly held discontent that will express itself with explosive force in the privacy of a group meeting. Should the feeling there be strong and general the Minister knows that failure to pacify his critics opens up the unpleasant prospect of a rough time from his own side in the House. If such a conflict threatens to develop, the liaison committee, consisting of three backbenchers elected at the beginning of each session (Emmanuel Shinwell is the present Chairman) will be asked to intervene. On an important issue it may approach the Prime Minister and call his attention to the danger of a potential rupture between the Government and its backbench supporters. This happened on many occasions during the Attlee administration, but I am only aware of one in the present Parliament.

That was over the delay in raising pensions and allied social benefits. Then a special meeting of the full Party was called, where a senior Cabinet Minister explained the insurmountable difficulties that made an earlier starting date impossible. Some critics remained unconvinced but a major Party crisis was averted.

There are also nine geographical groups that consider social, economic or political problems of local interest. They function in the same way as the subject groups in that they crystallise opinion and are the channel through which discontents are made known to the Government, either directly or through the liaison committee. The Prime Minister visits them periodically with the purpose of maintaining personal contact with his supporters. He deploys on these occasions the unique expertise in giving disarming off-the-record talks and frank answers to questions that he customarily uses with Press correspondents. A good time is had by all.

A full Party meeting is held whenever the liaison committee considers it desirable – usually two or three times a month. When the Party is in opposition its leader takes the chair flanked by members of the Shadow Cabinet (more about this body later) and discussion will probably be on what attitude to adopt on Government legislation or what policy motions the Party should table. In short, on general tactics. When the Party is in Government the chairman of the liaison committee presides. The purpose of the meeting may then be to enable a Minister to explain his policy and answer questions on some matter that transcends any one of the smaller groups, possibly an important Bill he has just published. Or it may be that the Cabinet wants to dispel disquiet about some aspect of its policy. Or the Prime Minister wants to give a pep talk. On occasion the purpose may be to consider a breach of the Party's disciplinary code as set out in its Standing Orders. Members may raise any matter they like at the Party meeting, move resolutions and vote upon them.

In this lies the essential difference between a meeting of the Parliamentary Labour Party and its opposite number, the Conservative 1922 Committee. No votes are ever taken at the latter. What matters there is the 'feel' of the meeting, which presumably means the comparative vocal support given to the leaders and their critics. And the weight in the Party hierarchy of those who express the criticisms. The theory behind this procedure is not dissimilar from that hitherto accepted by the Conservatives in choosing their leader. It is the belief that gentlemanly behind-the-scenes consultations and pressure-gauging is less damaging to the Party's image than vote-taking which might provide evidence of a split. Pratically if the issue is an important one and the vote may be close. The prime objective is the appearance of Party unity.

That is not so in the Labour Party. There the emphasis lies in shaping policy, and never mind if this involves an acrimonious discussion at the Party meeting, reported next day with remarkable accuracy in all the newspapers. The publicity given to these private meetings has been the constant despair of the leaders, certainly during the thirty years of my experience. However much the chairman may exhort or threaten, however much indignation is expressed by the rank-and-filers, the happenings at the Party meetings, if newsworthy, appear the next day for the world to read. The leak is sometimes made deliberately to advance a point of view. But more often it is the fruit of the uncanny astuteness of the Lobby correspondents in picking up odds and ends of information and then, pretending they know all, worming the rest of the story out of some unsuspecting backbencher.

Meetings of the Parliamentary Labour Party are usually peaceful and harmonious. The number and intensity of the rows will depend on whether the Party is the Government or the Opposition and how soon the next election may be expected. They will reflect the current mood of unity or disunity in the movement outside the House. Little militancy will be displayed by minority elements when there is a risk that these might damage the Party's prospects of electoral victory. During the early years of the last Parliament clashes, partly on personal but mainly on policy matters, were fierce and frequent. They steadily diminished and gave way to an appearance, at least, of complete unanimity as the election approached. This was partly due to compromise on policy issues (Clause IV and unilateralism in particular) at the National Executive and Annual Conference levels, but also to the restraint members put on themselves. Their overriding obligation was to present a united front to the enemy in the coming battle. They would have been exceedingly unpopular in their constituencies and among their colleagues if they had done otherwise. And on a more selfish level, they would have jeopardised their chances of Ministerial appointment.

For the reasons outlined in the beginning of this article the number of clashes at Party meetings are probably more frequent and the heat they engender greater, than in the 1922 Committee. People who are rebels by nature are likely to be rebellious against their own leaders. Indeed in the political world often more so. Labour backbenchers cannot hope to influence the policy of the Conservative Party when it is the Government and there is no point in doing so when it is in Opposition. But they can influence the policy of their own Party. So when its leaders seem to them to be betraying its principles or not making the right response to the events of the day they joyously enter into battle against them. They feel angrier with their own leaders for not taking what they consider the right socialist line than they do with the Conservative leaders whose Tory attitude is only to be expected. The latter are a remote target. Their own leaders are easily get-at-able. They are part of the family and there is no row like a family row.

The running on these occasions normally comes from the Left – or rather that section of the Party which considers itself Left but is often regarded by the others to be doctrinaire and out of date. It possesses a common bond of outlook which enables its adherents more easily to take concerted action. They are helped too by the existence of the weekly *Tribune* which popularises their point of view among the faithful in their constituency parties. They know, moreover, that their views are likely to reflect those of most delegates to the annual conference, which always tends to be militant. This knowledge is shared by the Party leaders who therefore go as far as possible to be placatory. But the Left is a minority in the Parliamentary Party, rarely exceeding a third, and has little hope of voting down policy recommendations of the Party leaders.

Indeed the only time I can recall this happening was in March 1952 when I was personally involved. At the end of a defence debate in the House forty Labour backbenchers, including Aneurin Bevan and Michael Foot, abstained from voting to show their dissatisfaction with the Party's policy on nuclear arms as expressed in the Front Bench speeches, although that policy had previously been endorsed at a Party meeting. It was undeniably an overt and concerted revolt. The leaders, spurred on by angry right-wing trade union members, asked the Party meeting to endorse a motion to withdraw the Whip from the rebels. It was moved by Attlee from the chair. If carried it would have meant their expulsion from the Parliamentary Party. I moved, and John Strachey seconded, an alternative motion to reimpose for future application the Standing Orders disciplinary code, at that time in abeyance. After an exceptionally intemperate debate, our motion was carried. The Party was saved from a schism which would certainly have had a grave effect on its fortunes.

To appreciate the relationship between the back- and frontbenchers when the Party is in Opposition it is necessary to explain how its leaders are chosen and how they function. The Leader, his Deputy and the Chief Whip are elected annually, by ballot if there is a contest. They become *ex officio* members of the Parliamentary Committee, popularly but improperly called the Shadow Cabinet. This committee considers all policy matters and brings its recommendations to the Party meeting for decision. It also is elected annually and the competition to become one of its twelve members is keen. The number of votes each candidate receives is broadly the measure of his standing in the Party. If a candidate comes out third from the top one year and drops to tenth place the next, he feels he is slipping, and will probably intensify his parliamentary activities to restore his prestige among his colleagues. By no means all leading Members submit their names for nomination, but the ballot paper usually contains thirty to forty. Many deplore this annual popularity poll and dislike the procedure whereby the Parliamentary Committee is made up of those who represent particular currents of opinion, or geographical interests or have unusually agreeable personalities, rather than of the ablest men. A leftwing candidate has no chance of success because the centre and right will not vote for him. Aneurin Bevan was unsuccessful for years after he had shown himself to be an outstanding parliamentarian. At least one Scotsman will be elected as the Scottish members want representation on the Committee. So will a trade unionist. If there are two trade union candidates, their colleagues will agree among themselves which to plump for.

The Parliamentary Committee will be much influenced in its deliberations by its chairman, the Party leader. But it is by no means his creature. Decisions are reached by the normal democratic processes and each member of the committee becomes collectively responsible for them. He is not allowed to express a minority view when the Party meeting discusses the committee's recommendations. This rule is very occasionally broken when one of its members feels so strongly on some issue that he threatens to resign unless he is permitted to state his case to his colleagues. That occurred in the late 1930s when Hugh Dalton was granted the right to argue at a Party meeting for the reversal of the Party's opposition to rearmament.

In the Conservative Party there is no such democratically elected body vested with authority. Its Shadow Cabinet is the personal choice of the Party leader. He may, and probably does, take account of pressures inside his Party and the representative character of those he proposes to choose. In the end the result may be much the same.

The Labour Party leader does however decide himself, without reference to the Parliamentary Committee, which of its members, and which outside it, are to shadow the various Ministries. Here the word 'shadow' has a direct significance. It means studying the problems of the department and, on all parliamentary occasions, leading for the Party from the Front Bench. The potential Prime Minister is accorded this prerogative as he must have unrestricted freedom in choosing the individuals he may want as his Ministers and giving them the opportunity of mastering the affairs of the department to which he may appoint them. It does not follow that a Shadow Minister will be appointed to the department he was covering when in opposition – or to any other.

With Labour in Government the influence of the backbencher on policy is small. Decisions are made in the secrecy of the Cabinet. Prior consultation with backbenchers is impossible and subsequent rejection politically impracticable, particularly when the Government has a tiny majority. The possibility of an early election makes it essential to avoid the image of an indecisive government that can be diverted from its course by backbench pressures. Such pressures can sometimes be effectively brought to bear on administrative or minor policy matters. A recent example was the Minister of Transport's statement in the House on 31 March that all proposals for rail closures would in future be referred to the newly formed regional councils before he made his decision, and that legislation would be introduced to remove the embargo on railway workshops tendering for contracts outside the nationalised industries' field. This came about because backbench railwaymen and others had expressed their keen dissatisfaction with the inadequacy of the steps previously taken by the Minister on these two issues. But normally once Ministers have publicly committed themselves to a course of action, they are reluctant to reverse it. The weaker a Government is numerically, the stronger it must appear, and the more united its supporters. Behind the scenes advice may be given to the Prime Minister by the Liaison Committee about how the Party feels on some important issue, such as the nationalisation of the steel industry. And this may influence the Government's parliamentary tactics. Decorous criticism in the Chamber or in week-end speeches by individual MPs is permissible. But not a serious revolt.

The situation is entirely different when the Party is in opposition. Then the democratic machinery of consultation described above gives backbenchers a decisive influence. They act, of course, against the background of their electoral mandate and Conference decisions. These express the Party's attitude to current political issues, and lay down its broad social and economic objectives. The Parliamentary Party is however free to interpret them as it thinks best, to the extent even of ignoring them on fundamental issues, as it did when the Conference endorsed unilateral disarmament. Members cannot be bound by directives from outside bodies. They can and do take such directives into account, as they do the views of their constituency parties, the advice of their leaders, and their own predilections. And on a balance of these considerations, it is they, the backbenchers, who settle parliamentary policy.

5. The Influence of the Backbencher: a Tory View*

By RICHARD HORNBY

The counting of the ballot papers has been completed. The returning officer has announced the result, and the successful candidate, now the elected representative of his constituency, thanks the counting agents and promises the assembled company who have striven to achieve or prevent his election that he will endeavour to look after their interests regardless of their creed or political persuasion. A day or two later he packs his bags for Westminster, there to join 629 others, each of whom to a greater or lesser degree may be hoping to influence events in the House of Commons to the advantage of those whom he represents. To be more precise, if he is a Tory or Labour MP, he joins one of the great political coalitions, bent on attaining or retaining political power through their voting strength in the House of Commons. If he is sitting on the Government back benches, he will be voting in support of policies broadly outlined in his Party's election manifesto. If in opposition, his aim will be to probe and criticise the actions of the Government, drawing attention to those points at which they fall short of what the nation had been led to expect during the election campaign and indicating the better conditions that would ensue if his own party were in power. In the House of Commons there is no close season in the struggle for power. As soon as one election campaign has been completed, the next has begun; and the new Member, aware that a government's survival is dependent on its ability to hold the support of the House, is happy to think that he will be playing his part in the decisive area of the battlefield.

A year later, meeting the new Member on his way back to

---

* Reprinted from *Political Quarterly*, Vol. 36, 1965, pp. 286–94, with the permission of the publisher and the author.

Westminster after a weekend in his constituency, during which he had held his customary 'surgery', made a political speech at a village meeting, prepared a short statement of what he had said and despatched it to the local newspaper and opened a fête in support of a deserving charity, we may well find him in chastened mood. Conscientiously throughout the year, he has maintained his contacts with his constituents and his attendance at Westminster. Quickly he has discovered that it is less easy to influence events than he had imagined. True, he has been able – through correspondence with Ministers – to remedy a number of grievances on behalf of his constituents. But in the Chamber he has torn up more speeches than he has delivered and has come to realise that the backbench Member who gets one and a half hours of debating time for himself during a session has done better than average; and even at Question-time he has found that it may be many weeks before he can get a brief oral answer to a question he wishes to put. Inevitably also he has been confronted with a number of issues, on which the views expressed by the leaders of his Party have diverged from his own, and at the end of the day he has crowded into the lobbies alongside his colleagues, sadly aware that the difference of views within a party is sometimes quite as great as the differences between Government and Opposition front benches.

This chastened view of the influence and activities of backbenchers is shared by many members of the public today. Parliament recently has not had a good Press. It has been criticised on a number of counts. Sometimes it seems to be delaying unduly the passage of legislation; at other times it is said to be failing to provide a proper check on the executive or to scrutinise adequately public expenditure. Sometimes when there are only thirty or forty Members in the chamber, it gives an impression of idleness; at others when the benches are crowded and noisy, it seems guilty of rowdyism. To many the procedure seems archaic and the division records provide no guide to the many shades of opinion expressed in the course of debate. It is against this background of doubt about the effective performance of Parliament that the influence of the backbencher must be judged.

The most frequent and obvious opportunities for influence lie in the administrative field. Mr A writes to his Member about his pension which appears to be less than it ought to be. Mrs B says that her son is not getting from the local education authority a grant to which he is entitled. A parish council write, seeking support for the imposition of a speed-limit on the main road through their village. In none of these cases would action by the Member of Parliament be the only means of redress. If an administrative mistake had been made in the calculation of a pension, it would probably be revealed and corrected in due course. The decisions of an Education Authority are primarily for members of the Authority and not for Parliament. Nevertheless, the Member may well discover that his own Authority is acting in a different way from other Authorities and by drawing the attention of officers, or councillors, to this difference, he may well influence the subsequent decisions of the Authority. And by making known to the Minister the strength of local feeling when a traffic problem comes to Whitehall for decision, the Member can ensure that it is studied at a senior level and not dealt with automatically lower down in the department.

Cases of this kind are typical of much that emerges from a Member's 'surgery' or correspondence. The greater his activity in his constituency, the greater is likely to be the volume of this work. As to the results which the Member may achieve, there are perhaps three main reasons why he may have some success. First, the Member may well be able to help a constituent merely by the advice which he gives. To many of the public the machinery of local and national government is a complicated instrument. When faced with a problem, they turn to their Member of Parliament in the same way as some would turn to a Citizen's Advice Bureau or a family solicitor, and he may be able to help merely by advising them how to proceed, whom they should approach or in what way they should draft a letter. Secondly, Members have opportunities for influencing administrative decisions because of their right of access to Ministers. Letters from Members will go straight to the Minister's private office and will receive priority treatment in the department thereafter. This may well have some effect on the speed of decision and will give the Minister the opportunity of personally investigating the matter in question. Thirdly, there is the threat of publicity. If a Member is dissatisfied with a departmental decision or delay, he has opportunities at Question Time or through an Adjournment motion, with the probability of securing consequent publicity in the local, or even the national Press. No Minister likes adverse publicity or too many hostile questions in the House, which seem to reflect on his efficiency. The influence of Members in securing administrative action by these means should not therefore be lightly ignored. Nor should the criticism that assiduous constituency work turns the Member too readily into a glorified welfare officer be too easily accepted. Certainly, a Member is open to the temptation to take on, through his 'surgery', work which is properly the responsibility of someone else. Equally however – and quite apart from the immediate results that may be obtained for his constituents – a Member's correspondence and interviews enable him to see how the machinery of government is in fact working. They thereby provide him with material which may affect his thinking on policy as well as on administrative matters.

The extent to which backbenchers can influence policy is much more difficult to assess. There are some who say that their influence is virtually nil. Ministers, they say, decide the lines of policy and the contents of the Queen's Speech each year in Cabinet with the aid of their departmental briefs, and thereafter the lines of policy change little, whatever backbenchers may do. Too much face is lost if a Government changes direction sharply as a result of parliamentary criticism, and Ministers will usually be confident that Members of their Party who disagree with them will on nearly all occasions support them in the lobbies rather than overthrow the government which they were elected to sustain.

It is true that examples of policy decisions, which have been made and then substantially altered as a result of backbench pressure in the House of Commons, are hard to find. This does not mean, however, that decisions are taken without regard to the views of backbenchers. Policy decisions have generally been under discussion for a considerable time before a government publicly takes up its stand. During this time backbenchers have numerous opportunities of making their opinions known. Almost certainly the Ministers concerned will have come to the Party's parliamentary committee, which keeps a watching brief over the affairs of his department. There he will have explained the problems he is tackling and the measures he has in mind without committing himself to any precise detail. Afterward she will answer questions and listen to opinions of other Members. If the subject is a particularly confidential one, in the field of defence perhaps, or a taxation matter in the weeks preceding the Budget, the Minister may well have been severely restricted in what he would say. Even so, there will have been little difficulty in getting reactions from backbenchers to a number of possible courses of action. After this meeting the subject may well be discussed again by members of the committee, perhaps, but not necessarily, in the Minister's absence. If there is criticism of what he has said or seems likely to do, a number of things will then happen. First, individual Members may well write to the Minister urging him to consider their particular viewpoint. Secondly, views will be communicated to the Chief Whip. One of the Whips regularly attends each of the Party committees, and reports to the Chief Whip what has been said. The Chief Whip himself receives a steady flow of comment from backbenchers who write to him or walk into his office. In addition to expressing their views at the Party's departmental committee, Conservative Members may well seek wider discussion by raising the matter in the weekly meeting of the 1922 Committee, or wider publicity by placing a motion on the Order Paper of the House of Commons; or they may encourage others to write letters to the Minister or the Chief Whip. In all these events the Chief Whip will carefully collect and analyse the points made to him, assess the weight that should be attached to these representations, and report on them to the Prime Minister.

But how much notice will then be taken? Critics of Parliament will say that governments can afford to ride rough-shod over these backbench opinions, confident that Party discipline will prevail and that an adequate majority will be obtained in the lobbies. It would, however, be a mistake to minimise the attention paid by governments to backbench opinion. No government wishes to strain unduly its relations with its supporters because it needs from them much more than their votes. Any atmosphere of discontent in the Commons is quickly picked up by the lobby correspondents and finds its way into the Press and on to the television screen. Likewise the week-end speeches of Members in their constituencies will be less than enthusiastic if Members are doubtful about the wisdom of the policies their Ministers are pursuing. Thus the mood of Members will be communicated to the electorate, with consequences that will be reflected in the opinion polls and prospects for the next election. Some Members would declare that there is a close and definable affinity between changes of morale at Westminster and changes of electoral opinion in the country, and would even argue that there is a measurable time-lag between the two.

As to specific examples of government decisions which have been altered and influenced as a result of backbench pressure, it is impossible to give a full list because communications through the Whips' Office are of course confidential and it is difficult to assess how much weight was attached by individual Ministers or the Cabinet to doubts about Parliament's reactions. Even so, one or two examples immediately come to mind. In 1957 the Shops Bill was certainly dropped from the Government's programme as a result of backbench rebellion. The Macmillan Government's approach to the Common Market negotiations would almost certainly have been less cautious, had it not been for anxieties about the reactions of Members with special interests in agriculture and Commonwealth trade. Throughout the process of decolonisation in Africa the Tory Party had continually to be on guard against criticisms from Lord Salisbury and his friends in the Commons, and during the Suez crisis the Government could ignore neither the cries of 'those behind crying forward' nor 'those before crying back!'. The Rent Act and the abolition of resale price maintenance were other measures on which the Conservative Government had to work overtime to hold the loyalty of a number of Conservative Members.

A general point that seems to emerge from any study of the issues on which pressure from the backbenchers on the Government has been particularly strong is that the bigger the issue the more powerful the backbenchers become. It should not, for example, be forgotten that it was a vote in the Commons which brought about the fall of the Chamberlain Government in 1940. The reason is that 'big' issues are definable as those which arouse public opinion and capture attention in the constituencies and the Press. On these occasions Parliament, both behind the scenes in Party committees and on the floor of the House, becomes the sounding-board of public opinion and Members in their speeches are discussing matters about which their constituents themselves are likely to feel well-informed and concerned about their Member's opinion. A second point, especially emphasised by the Suez debates, is that where Members diverge in their views from their own front bench, they are much more vulnerable to criticism within their own Party if their divergence leads them towards the views of the Party opposite rather than to a more extreme position. Relations between those Conservative Members who opposed the Suez operation and their constituents became badly strained. The same was true of Mr Stanley Evans in the Labour Party, who supported the Government's case, whereas the eight Members on the right of the Conservative Party who resigned the Whip in 1957 appeared to have no difficulty in retaining the support of their constituencies. The moral seems to be that it is safe enough to differ from your leaders so long as you do not side with the enemy. One might also add that backbenchers feel it is safer to disagree with their own Government when their majority in the House is large. Backbenchers seldom want to destroy their own Government. In the early days of the 1959–64 Parliament however one used to hear Conservative Members mocking the divided ranks of the Opposition and considering how best to impose proper restraints on the executive from within their own ranks. One suspects that the job of a Chief Whip is not made easier by a majority of more than fifty.

Backbench Members also have opportunities of influencing legislation at the committee stage of Bills and through the use which they make of the ten Fridays in each session which are reserved for Private Members' Bills. At the committee stage the normal practice will be for relatively few speeches and amendments to be made from the Government back benches, whose general aim is to help their Party to get through its legislative programme with the best possible speed. Exceptions however occur and it is not uncommon to find a number of changes made in legislation as a result of pressure from Members in Committee. Private Members' Bills are usually concerned with limited and relatively uncontentious issues. The burden on an individual Member in drafting and carrying through a difficult

Bill is very great unless the Government offers its support. But it can be done. Mr Silverman's efforts in promoting the Murder (Abolition of Death Penalty) Bill is one example. Another was the achievement in the 1955–59 Parliament of Captain Corfield in carrying on Second Reading, against the advice of his own Minister of Housing and Local Government, a Bill to provide compensation at market values for compulsory purchases. Subsequently the main principles of Captain Corfield's Bill were accepted by the Government and included in a measure of their own.

The opportunities for influence on the Opposition back benches are rather different from those on the Government's side. The need for discipline is less, and activities are, therefore, more freelance in character. Some of these activities will be conducted in the background, and will be concerned, through the official Party committees and other small groups, with the formulation and discussion of policies, on which their Party will base its case at the next election. There the influence of individual backbenchers with specialised knowledge can often be considerable. Other Members will devote their energies to impeding the progress through the House of Government measures which they dislike and, by their criticisms on the floor of the House, to undermining the confidence of the Government. The quantity of backbench activity of this kind can seriously affect the speed with which the Government carries through its legislative programme. As an example of effective backbench action in Opposition, the tactics in 1961 of Mr Michael Foot and his colleagues on the left wing of the Labour Party deserve study. At a time when their Party was divided and dispirited, they frequently took it upon themselves to keep the House up late, regardless of the intentions of their own Whips, and succeeded by their example in injecting a new fighting spirit into their colleagues at a time when the Government was conveniently providing them with some ripe subjects for attack.

In general, however, the immediate opportunities for exercising influence are much less on the Opposition than on the Government side. Opposition Members can press an attack, they may even get a few lines of their speeches reported in the Press, but their attacks are in vain provided that the

Government retains the confidence of its own supporters and musters its strength. The views of Government backbenchers are much more important. Not only are they nearer to the sources of power and better able to influence decisions before they are taken; they also carry a greater threat to the Government's existence. The criticisms of Government backbenchers excite far more attention than the attacks of the Opposition because a government can only fall as a result of the defection of their own supporters. It is strange therefore how much pressure groups outside Parliament concentrate their fire and requests for help on the Opposition when it is in fact the Government backbenchers who could often do most to help them.

Thus far, examination of the influence of the backbencher has been confined to Parliament. It would be wrong to leave the subject without saying something of his influence elsewhere, notably in his constituency and through opportunities arising out of his work in Parliament for writing and broadcasting. The generally accepted view is that, in terms of votes cast at a General Election, the value of any particular personality is worth at most 500 votes to his Party. There seems to be no reason to doubt this assessment. In considering which way they will vote, the electors are asking themselves which Party they wish to see representing them in Parliament. To write off the influence of the individual Member on this account may well, however, be an over-simplification.

Throughout the life of a Parliament Members are regularly making speeches in their constituency and elsewhere, and a number of them are invited from time to time to broadcast or to write articles for the national and local Press. By what they say and write each week, they are contributing to the atmosphere of contentment or disillusion with the performance of the Government and thereby paving the way for the next election. What any one of them may say will not stand comparison in public attention with the views of the Party leaders. But the cumulative effect on the political atmosphere should not be ignored, bearing in mind also that the professional commentators in Press and broadcasting are drawing their impressions of the political scene from the views of backbenchers as well as from their interviews with Cabinet Ministers and their briefings in Whitehall.

Finally, it should not be forgotten that the backbenchers,

especially when one Party has been in power for a long time, are apt to include a number of senior ex-Ministers. The ability of the backbenchers to influence their Government is greatly increased if there is a potential leader in their midst. It was the absence of any such rallying point that enabled the Conservative Government to survive both the starting and winding-up of the Suez operation. And it was the presence on the back benches of a large number of influential Members with a bitter sense of grievance after Mr Macmillan's ministerial 'massacre' of July 1962 which made it unlikely that Mr Macmillan would thereafter be able to rekindle sufficient enthusiasm to win an election.

The record of recent years shows relatively few examples of the back benches exercising real power and altering the decisions of the Government, once they have been taken and publicly announced. But Governments are well aware of the damage that can be done to their prospects and reputation in the country, if their supporters in the Commons are apathetic or openly critical. Parliament is still the focal point of political discussion and comment. For that reason Governments probably pay more heed than is generally realised to the opinions of backbenchers, whose collective influence, especially when new policies and legislation are under consideration, can often be important. If the Cabinet is divided, it may well be decisive.

6. Returning to the House

By JULIAN CRITCHLEY

AFTER six years away from the House of Commons Julian Critchley was returned as Conservative MP for Aldershot in June 1970. In this article he compares today's Parliament with the one of the early 1960s. The two Parliaments are remarkably similar. Critchley finds that the main changes that have occurred throughout the period have come about in the social and ideological nature of the Conservative Party, and in the increasingly populist nature of the party in the constituency. 'The House', he writes, 'has changed least of all.'

I lost my seat at Rochester by a thousand votes in October 1964. I had won it five years previously by as many votes. I had been swept into Parliament, surprised but uncomplaining, on the coat-tails of Mr Harold Macmillan. 'Supermac' had spoken in Rochester in the election: he had admired the view of the castle, 'very fine' he had murmured, and had spoken inaudibly but elegantly to a crowd of shoppers. He spoke, I believe, of prosperity and progress, and then had hurried on to Faversham. Sir Alec came five years later, and although his message was much the same, the effect was not as great. I lost the seat on his coat-tails. Mr Heath's visit in 1966 served me no better, and it was not until June 1970 when totally unaided I was returned for Aldershot, that I sat again in the House of Commons. What after six years had changed?

Most of all perhaps, the Conservative Party has changed. Not out of recognition it is true, but it has altered none the less. My own circumstances are quite different: I have exchanged a working-class seat for a middle-class one. The House has changed least of all.

In 1959 one could tell a Conservative MP simply by looking at him. He was well suited. More often than not he wore a black jacket and striped pants. Nowadays only Mr Ronald Bell does so. The smoking room was an adjunct of the Carlton Club, and in the Members' Dining Room the Tory end was full, and the other, empty. Labour MPs – save for well known journalists like Dick Crossman and Woodrow Wyatt – clustered in the tea room; small, stocky men in boots with working-class haircuts whom one's colleagues would describe, after sharing with them some parliamentary visit abroad, as 'the salt of the earth'. They ate pie and chips, and the poorest of them eked out their £1,750 by taking a sleeping-car each night to their Northern constituencies, and returning to London the next morning. I think, too, the Tory Party was less aware then than it is now. Or is it simply that its leaders were more clever? I can remember elderly knights expressing a bewildered discomfort having listened to Rab Butler or to Harold Macmillan explain government policy to them at a meeting 'upstairs'. It was not that they had lost their trousers, but that they could not help glimpsing their knees. In 1960 the party was nearly pre-war in its social composition. The Prime Minister's kinsmen were in office as were the brighter of the middle class. An alliance of the Devonshires and the Research Department. The new members (described later by Butler as 'a pretty poor lot' sat uneasily in the 1922 Committee clutching their Bow Group pamphlets on rating reform while their elders spoke of foreign affairs and of agriculture. The humour was often unconscious (not least when one member, angry at the prospect of a rise in MPs' salaries, stated that he did not approve of professional politicians: Mr Butler, who had been at Westminster all his working life, was present at the time in his capacity as Leader of the House), and the '22' deserved its description, attributed, perhaps unfairly, to Humphry Berkeley as 'the longest running show on earth'.

The attitude to Members' salaries is an example of change. Whereas the majority of the party was once hostile there is now a sense of reform long overdue. The start of a debate upon this topic was invariably marked by the offer of refusal of the rumoured increase, invariably by someone to whom the extra would have gone straight to the Revenue. To be in Parliament was to fulfil one's social obligation: to receive money in return was for Labour members. The change is not only due to the *embourgeoisement* of the party, for our elder members are now in favour, but in part to Iain Macleod's will and widow. Macleod left little money; his widow received but a meagre pension. It is just a little ironic that the man who was 'too clever by half' should have scored so surprising a posthumous success.

The Conservative Party in the House today contains the party conference of ten years ago. Cheerful girls in hats who once moved conference motions on behalf of the Young Conservatives of some Midlands town are now its member. The Young Conservative National Advisory Committee has come in from the cold. Businessmen with provincial accents who pressed flatly for more competition; small town solicitors and surveyors, the politically active middle class who began by taking over the constituency parties, and are now taking over Parliament itself. The more traditional element is now either Bow Group or Monday Club. The Bow Group has since its inception been first-generation public school and Oxbridge, and can thus pass for white. Its better known members will probably make office, the less able serving to replace the knights-of-the-shires as the 'ballast' of the Tory Party. While I suspect we are more acute today, and certainly harder working, I know we are certainly sharper. The Member for the City of London wears shirts and ties of the same material, and the suits of the party are paler and off-the-peg. Some even wear suede shoes. It was reported recently that a former Member, who was asked at an extraordinary meeting of the Carlton Club, called to consider its finances, to admit to the club all the party's MPs, said 'I cannot; they are not all gentlemen'. He might not have said that ten years ago.

The constituency parties have changed in the last ten years. In a party which has, for its leader, swopped 'Disraeli' for 'Gladstone'; the activists are, in the safer seats, middle class but no longer deferential. After all to whom have they to defer? A party which elects its leader can dismiss him. The difference in my own case, between Rochester and Aldershot, is one of class and social occupation. Rochester and Chatham was a working-class seat from which the relatively small middle class had either moved or preferred to ignore local Conservative politics, which had been dominated for many years by the councils run by small shopkeepers and estate agents. The politics of the association had little intellectual, and no ideological content: only the abolition of resale price maintenance moved them to anger. There was little attempt at conference politics, and the towns were parochial in a way which, given their proximity to London, was quite surprising.

The Aldershot party is not only different socially; it reflects the change of attitude to which I referred earlier. The seat is safe (it has never elected anyone save a Conservative) but is no longer 'smart'. Before my selection as candidate, on the retirement of the then chairman, a baronet, the contest was between a Colonel from Fleet (a middle-class dormitory) and a solicitor from Farnborough. It was a battle between the old and the new; and the new, in the shape of the solicitor, won. The association became less upper-middle- and more middle-class, with the richer representing the villages, such as Hartley Wintney and Crondall, the commuter and the retired service officer representing Fleet, and the smaller business man with local interests, Farnborough and Aldershot. Although Aldershot might be thought of as a military seat, it is not. I believe the composition of its executive committee to be a little different from most Tory seats. Ten years ago it would have been more 'county': today it is predominantly middle-class.

What effect has the change had upon candidate and member? Selection committees are now looking for merit and achievement, however defined. They insist upon residence locally. They identify, but with people with whom they can identify. The member belongs to them, and the interests of both will tend to coincide. Their complaints are practical ones, about matters which concern themselves: taxation, enterprise, the wickedness of the unions. They hold views and do not hesitate to express them.

What of Parliament itself? To return after ten years is to find that more than half the House are strangers. From the vantage of early middle age, the Whips are now one's contemporaries. How easy it is to slip back quickly into a routine which it seems one has never left. The futility of Question Time (if it has a value it is for the Opposition), and the wisdom of raising constituents' questions privately with ministers. The need to relearn procedure and the discipline of preparing speeches which one is unlikely ever to be asked to deliver. How much more tempting the Bow Group 'occasional paper' or the Press release for a speech elsewhere, the publication of which can lead to publicity and to pounds. The tedium of long hours and the stimulation of many friendships; the two interwoven through long nights spent in defence of some contentious Bill.

It is curious how little the House itself has changed. The 'Crossman reforms' have come and gone. The morning sittings which were to change the composition of Parliament itself (by obliging MPs to abandon their outside interests) were done away with in 1969. I have not been invited to join a Select Committee, and I understand that the standing committees (on which new members are pressed to serve) now sit into the afternoons. Standing Order No. 9, whereby a short debate on matters of immediate concern may be held at the request of a member, is more easily invoked, and I am told that Orders may now be taken after 10 o'clock. I have yet to make use of the Ombudsman. But these are differences upon the margin. The Parliamentary Labour Party appears younger and less obviously working class. (A Tory Whip: 'Some of them are decent enough but when the chips are down you can't trust them.') The Liberals rest uneasily between the two great parties as before. The Labour 'left' is concerned less with neutrality and more with the defence of trade union interest. The Library has increased its staff and with them its facilities. There are girls recording the vote in the division lobbies. Postage is now free, trunk calls available, and the salary somewhat higher. There is even an allowance of £500 a year for half a secretary upon which the MP has to pay tax. Our cars are now worth 5p a mile. Our wives can join us four times a year free of charge. Some of us even have rooms.

How then should I sum up? The Conservative Parliamentary Party has changed. It is less socially cohesive, and more ideological in content. It is clearly less 'sound' than it once was. Ten years ago the rebuke of the Whips was exquisitely understated: it may no longer be understood. It is run still as a regiment, but one of the line. It is less whiggish, more Tory. In 1960, members spent their weekends in great houses, in 1970 they spend them in their constituencies. The '22' is less fun, more functional. At its best it is the forum for a punchy, brief debate to which the Government will listen: at its worst it resembles in its tedium the council chamber of a city suburb. In the '50s the party let down ladders of political opportunity. The YCs, the graduate and the businessman have climbed them into Parliament. By the election for the party leadership in 1965 the composition had already changed markedly. The contenders were all 'new' Conservatives; neither Christopher Soames nor Peter Thorneycroft was seriously considered.

In the constituencies the party is more populist. Conservative Associations in the towns have become the preserve of local interests; the 'gentleman', if he wishes to give public service, has exchanged the local for the county council. The views of the party conference are taken more seriously, while the Central Office plays a larger part in the formulation and control of party opinion. Party management is at a premium; the party may no longer defer to people, but it does to platforms.

In the House itself there is little difference. The procedures have barely altered. We exist to sustain the government. We continue the sham fight with wooden weapons, the clash of which acts as a substitute for real violence. After ten years, Parliament remains much the same as it ever did; the cockpit of the nation or the best club in London. Take your pick.

7. Parliament Now and a Hundred Years Ago

By JOHN P. MACKINTOSH

IN this extract* John P. Mackintosh, Labour MP for Berwick and East Lothian and former Professor of Politics at Strathclyde University, compares the influence of backbenchers in the 1850s and the 1960s. The 1857–59 sessions were chosen by Mackintosh as representative of a so-called 'Golden Age' when backbenchers' power was at a maximum 'in that they were able to change a government without suffering a dissolution or any other penalty'. In the 1967–69 sessions backbenchers' power was also at a high level – two major government Bills were withdrawn and attempts were made to unseat the Prime Minister. Mackintosh uses the experience of the 1850s to examine the following questions: why were there so many rebellions between 1967–69? Did containing them have any influence on the government's thinking, morale or conduct? In what ways other than abstaining and occasionally voting with the Opposition did Labour MPs affect the government? And, does the House of Commons have any effect on the executive?

Comparisons in politics are inherently difficult. If an attempt is made to compare the power or position of the House of Commons with that of the Bundestag, the French National Assembly or Congress, it can always be retorted that the countries and the political systems are different and so attempts to draw any conclusions are bound to be invalid. The other possible comparison, and one which is inherently more acceptable, given British pride in 'the Westminster Model', is to compare the influence of the House of Commons with what it used to be in other eras. Here again, the situations have changed, but at least they

---

* Extracted from a paper entitled, 'The Influence of the Backbencher, Now and a Hundred Years Ago', read to The Manchester Statistical Society, 11 March 1970. Reprinted with the permission of the Society and the author.

constitute variations on a pattern which has clear connections. The difficulty in this case lies with the views of the commentator. Some historians and political scientists who liked the balance between the executive and the legislature struck in the mid-Victorian period have called it 'the Golden Age of the Private MP' and have praised the concept of a House of Commons prepared to install and remove governments and to reject or alter legislation. For them, in contrast, the present is a position where the balance has altered decisively in favour of the executive, MPs no longer have this degree of independence and they conclude that many of the virtues of the old Westminster Model have disappeared.

The other approach, commoner peculiarly enough among Conservatives, is to argue that since on crucial occasions British governments can be persuaded to listen to public criticism, this is all that is needed. A greater degree of subservience to a legislature is undesirable; it could not be reintroduced today and parliamentary reform with this in mind is bound to fail. From this point of view, looking back into the nineteenth century, some commentators have noticed the complaints of certain mid-Victorian politicians that it was very hard to run a stable executive when the House of Commons did enjoy such powers and they have argued that the situation between 1832 and 1867 (or 1884) was abnormal. Others, such as Mr Ronald Butt, have sketched the argument further and tried to make a case that in reality the mid-Victorian House of Commons did not exercise more influence than parliaments have done since the Second World War.

This paper does not seek to show that either the present or the past situations are to be preferred. What it sets out to do is to estimate just how much power backbenchers did deploy and by what methods in the two sessions 1857–59 compared with the two sessions 1967–69. The reason for choosing the first period is that a parliament was wanted in the so-called 'Golden Age' between 1832 and 1867 and this particular parliament began with a general election which 'was partly a vote of personal confidence in Lord Palmerston, and partly an endorsement of the Crimean War' after which 'Lord Palmerston proceeded to act on the assumption that he could do precisely what he pleased. He had for the first time a real majority in Parliament, and a majority elected for the express purpose of supporting not his measures, nor his colleagues, but himself.' Yet despite this unusual strength, Palmerston was defeated by this same House of Commons in February 1858 and these MPs maintained a Conservative Government under Lord Derby and Disraeli in office till June 1859. Thus this seemed to be a case of the maximum power of backbenchers in that they were able to change a government without suffering a dissolution or any other penalty.

To be fair, it is necessary to compare these two sessions with two that revealed the most extreme instances of backbench influence in recent times. Though possible candidates were the sessions of 1962–63 and 1963–64 when the Conservative Government was unpopular and only just pushed through the Resale Price Maintenance Bill, it seemed better to take the sessions of 1967–68 and 1968–69 because some commentators have claimed that Labour backbenchers are inherently more rebellious, because there were attempts to unseat the Prime Minister and because two major measures, the Parliament (No. 2) Bill and the proposed Industrial Relations Bill had to be withdrawn. Such abandonments of entire projects to which a government had set its hand are unprecedented in post-war years and therefore suggest that backbench influence reached a peak of success. So these parliaments were chosen as offering examples of the most that backbench power could do in each respective period.

After analysing the voting behaviour of MPs and studying the earlier period, it is difficult to evaluate the power of the House of Commons as against that of the executive. The Government could keep the House sitting, as it did in the summer of 1857, but it could not control the time debates would take or the motions and amendments that would come up. Thus ministers had to attend the House every night and react to the atmosphere they encountered. In terms of legislation, Bills could be pushed through, as Palmerston pushed the Divorce Bill, but he had to accept amendments. On the other hand, the House forced Disraeli to give up his first India Bill. But when he framed a Bill with Lord John Russell's aid, based upon the sentiments of the House, he was able to carry it. The Commons could and did sack individual ministers who had erred, as they got rid of

Ellenborough and would almost certainly have forced Palmerston to remove Clanricarde. The House was also able to appoint Committees and Commissions of investigation, though only if this made sense – Disraeli's attempt to get a Commission on the causes of the Indian Mutiny was regarded by the House as ill-timed and therefore rejected even by his own supporters. A further power was the capacity to extract information from the executive, the Foreign Secretaries being forced to lay Blue Books publishing all their despatches on aspects of their policies.

In the most extreme example of their power, which was the sanction making all the rest possible, the House could and did dismiss a government. However, the division list figures show that it is wrong to suppose that governments were subjected to continual defeats on specific issues. Governments were normally given the benefit of the doubt, their supporters felt obliged to attend a little more regularly and the opposition did not hesitate to cross-vote to keep a reasonably competent government in power. To remove a government required an important issue which epitomised the outlook and conduct of the Prime Minister or the Cabinet as a whole. The debate, in such a case, would be lengthy. MPs would realise what was at stake, the numbers swelling, members coming up from the country so that the discussion would last as long as anyone wanted to speak and could hold the attention of the House. Each night, the Whips would try and estimate feeling and the Prime Minister's letters to the Queen showed that the estimates rose and fell, depending on the force of particular speeches, the release of fresh evidence and so on.

Thus this was a time when the House did have very considerable power and the government of Britain did turn on the relations between the Cabinet and the House. Though the 'separation of powers' did not exist, these were two fairly independent forces, each with the power to destroy the other and realising that on the accommodation they reached depended the government of the country. There was little thought of or appeal to the electorate. Though the voters did respond to Palmerston in 1857, this was an exception and its value in terms of power as against the House of Commons was revealed when that House, deliberately and after careful thought, turned Palmerston out twelve months later, there being no suggestion that, only a year into a new parliament, he could go back to the voters and appeal to them over the heads of his opponents in the House. Thus the relationship was complex and subtle, but this was a period when there was a balance of power between the House and the executive and this was the central and determining factor in shaping the character and direction of British government.

Turning to the two recent sessions, 1967–68 and 1968–69, so much has altered that it is difficult to make comparisons, the process of understanding being hampered by the use, with different nuances, of so many of the same words and phrases to describe the institutions and situations. The major change that can be registered statistically is the growth of the electorate from about 800,000 in the 1850s to 36 million in the 1960s. The advent of a mass electorate has altered almost out of recognition, the relations between the private MP and his constituents, and the attitudes and demands of these constituents on the government; it has created the need for organisations or parties to simplify the choices for a mass electorate and has set up a new direct relationship between the voters and the party leaders which largely bypasses the House of Commons.

The first change, the increase in the numbers of the electorate, took place by stages, as the Reform Bills of 1867 and 1884 expanded the right to vote. The concurrent and partly consequential increase in party conflict inside the House of Commons was measured by A. L. Lowell.

TABLE 1

Party Votes in the House of Commons, 1883–1903
'Whip' Divisions only

Year	No. of Divisions	Conservatives (per cent)	Liberals (per cent)
1883	194	68	58
1890	208	97	65
1894	214	94	89
1899	318	97	77
1903	225	91	90

Since the turn of the century, 'party votes' as defined by Lowell, that is occasions where nine-tenths of the major parties vote together, have risen to be the habitual situation in all whipped divisions. Cross-voting in the sense of joining the opposition (or the government) to vote against the MP's own party when a two- or three-line whip is in force is so serious a breach of discipline and political practice that in the Labour Party the MP is considered for 'withdrawal of the Whip', that is expulsion from the parliamentary party and among the Conservatives strong action is usually taken by the member's constituency party. A member who does so is taking his political life in his hands.

Because of this, other less offensive methods of registering disagreement have arisen, all carefully geared to the problem of public expression of disagreement which does not in any way endanger the existence of the government. (This applies but with a little less force to opposition MPs.) For instance, the practice of positive abstention unknown in the nineteenth century, has developed. Abstention means that the government's majority is reduced by one, not by two, as would happen if there was cross-voting and this action evades the charge by party loyalists that the culprit 'voted with the Tories'. Also such abstentions can be carefully calculated by the groups of MPs who wish to register dissent, the total being kept down to a level where there is no risk to the government, but a level which will, it is hoped, worry the government or at least permit the abstainers to claim some credit among the sections of the public that agree with them. Similarly cross-voting is not an offence of the same magnitude if the opposition does not vote, because again the exercise carries no element of threat to the government's majority. The difficulty is that once actions such as these lose their sanction in that they are used only if they have no hope of success: if there is no chance of a Bill being rejected, a minister being censured or the government defeated, so long as aberrant voting behaviour has to be conducted within the framework that the government must never be seriously threatened, it greatly diminishes its effect.

Table 2 sets out all major revolts against the government in the two sessions 1967–68 and 1968–69. To these division lists, it is necessary to add a comment on the Kenyan Asians Bill Committee Stage and the same stage of the House of Lords Reform Bill. In the Kenyan Asians Bill (properly named the Commonwealth Immigrants Bill) the Committee stage included eight divisions in which the official Conservative policy was to

TABLE 2

All Major Labour Revolts in 1967–68 and 1968–69 Session 1967–68

Date	Issue	Votes For	Abstentions	Votes Against	Opposition's Action
5.12.67	Motion against IMF 'letter of intent'	233	16–32	19 (18 Lab. + 1 Nat.)	Abstained
18.1.67	Devaluation cuts in expenditure	306	26	11 (10 Lib. + 1 Nat.)	Abstained
20.2.68	Expenditure cuts – Stamp and School Milk, 2nd reading	218	46–54	10 Lib.	Abstained
26.2.68	Expenditure cuts – Stamp Committee Stage	207	up to 20	31 (22 Lab., 8 Lib., 1 Con.)	Abstained
26.2.68	Expenditure cuts – School milk committee stage	152	up to 50	39 (30 Lab., 8 Lib., 1 Con.)	Abstained
27.2.68	Kenyan Asians Bill, 2nd Reading	374	31–40	64 (35 Lab., 15 Con., 12 Lib., 2 Nat.)	Free vote (160 voted for)
28.2.68	Kenyan Asians Committee Stage	(8 votes, see separate discussion below)			
21.5.68	Prices and Incomes Bill, 2nd Reading	292	32	257 (245 Con., 8 Lib., 2 Nat., 2 Ind., 1 Lab.)	Voted against
30.5.68	Prescription Charges	131	25–50	52 (49 Lab., 2 Lib., 1 Nat.)	Abstained
25.6.68	Prices and Incomes, Report Stage	283	20	265 (240 Con., 23 Lab., 2 Nat.)	Join Labour left in Division
27.6.68	Prices and Incomes, 3rd Reading	282	29–32	240 (235 Con., 3 Lib., 2 Ind.)	Voted against
22.9.68	Rhodesia, Fearless terms	179	up to 75	58 (51 Lab., 6 Lib., 1 Nat.)	Abstained
23.9.68	Justices of the Peace Bill, Lord's Amendments	197	up to 19	84 (76 Lab., 7 Lib., 1 Nat.)	Voted with Gov. (117 voted)

PARLIAMENT NOW AND A HUNDRED YEARS AGO

Date	Issue	Votes For	Abstentions	Votes Against	Opposition's Action
20.11.68	Lord's Reform White Paper	272	up to 49	161 (104 Con., 47 Lab., 7 Lib., 2 Ind., 1 Nat.)	Free Vote (40 voted for the Gov.)
26.11.68	Votes at 18 (Amdnd to Votes at 20)	277	up to 25	123 (111 Con., 12 Lab.)	Free Vote (34 Voted for the Gov.)
28.11.68	Purchase Tax Increases	284	23	244 (238 Con., 4 Lib., 2 Ind.)	Voted against
12.12.68	Foreign Affairs (Falklands, Biafra)	295	12–20	236 (all Con.)	Voted against
3.2.69	Lords' Reform (Parl. No. 2) Bill, 2nd reading	287	10–50	137 (105 Con., 27 Lab., 2 Nat., 3 Lib.)	Free Vote (59 Con., 3 Lib. voted for the Gov.)
12.2.69	Lords' Reform (Parl. No. 2 Bill Committee stage, see separate discussion below)				
11.2.69	Nat. Industries Committee and the Bank of England	103	up to 40	63 (39 Lab., 15 Con., 8 Lib., 1 Nat.)	Abstained (1 voted against)
3.3.69	In Place of Strife, White Paper	226	about 42	64 (55 Lab., 9 Lib.)	Abstained
5.3.69	Defence White Paper	281	32	234 (232 Con., 2 Ind.)	Voted against
13.3.69	Nigeria (Foreign Affairs debate)	234	up to 41	64 (35 Lab., 20 Con., 7 Lib., 1 Nat., 1 Ind.)	Abstained (20 voted against)
21.4.69	Budget (Selective Employment Tax)	285	39	257 (241 Con., 11 Lib., 2 Ind., 2 Nat., 1 Lab.)	Voted against
20.4.69	Post Office Bill, Report Stage	208	up to 47*	203 (173 Con., 16 Lab., 11 Lib., 2 Nat., 1 Ind.)	Join Labour left in Division
7.5.69	Education (Scotland) Bill	84	85*	72 (all Con.)	Voted against
20.6.69	Finance Bill, Committee Stage	265	18–23	236 (226 Con., 8 Lib., 2 Nat.)	Voted against
10.7.69	Nigeria	164	up to 70	45 (20 Lab., 16 Con., 6 Lib., 2 Nat., 1 Ind.)	Abstained (16 voted against)
21.7.69	Charges for Teeth and Spectacles	201	20–45	61 (55 Lab., 6 Lib.)	Abstained

* These were not deliberate abstentions – they failed to attend owing to general disgruntlement.

leave members a free vote. During the debate, which lasted all through the night and closed at 7.20 the next morning, government support began at 220, slipped slowly to 124 and finished at 147. The opponents started at 28, rose to a peak of 78 and then declined to 28, picking up a little to 33 in the last division on the Third Reading. The lowest majority the government had was 77, its opponents then consisting of 34 Labour, 18 Conservatives and 11 Liberals. Among the government total on that occasion of 140 votes, there were 12 Conservatives and 128 Labour MPs (of whom 50 were ministers) so that even if the dozen Conservatives had not supported the Bill, there would still have been an adequate ministerial majority. It has to be remembered that the Government has over 80 ministers in the House and is therefore seldom likely to be in difficulties if the Conservative members mainly abstain or do not oppose. Moreover if the Opposition opposes, all the forces of party loyalty come into play to reduce or prevent abstention and cross-voting.

As with the Commonwealth Immigrants Bill, the Committee stage of the Parliament (No. 2) Bill (on House of Lords Reform) was taken on the floor of the House. In the first case, this was done because the government was in a great hurry, in the second because, being a Bill affecting the constitution, it was felt proper to have it in Committee of the Whole House. Starting on 12 February 1969, the House spent 9 days on the Parliament (No. 2) Bill, there were 55 divisions and by then only 5 out of the 20 clauses had been passed and the Bill was abandoned. During the nine days, the government usually had some 130 voting in favour with about 40 Conservatives taking advantage of a free vote to oppose the Bill. The number of Labour rebels once reached 30 but usually averaged 14 so that government majorities were normally of the order of 75. The problem for the government was that if it proposed either a guillotine or sending the Bill to a Committee, the Conservatives would have opposed this as improper on such a measure and it would have required some effort to get these motions carried, given the apathy of many Labour members and the active hostility of a small group.

In this discussion of voting during these two sessions, the emphasis has been on the government and its supporters because opposition cross-voting is both less likely and less important. As was the case in Palmerston's time, the Conservatives are more disciplined and less likely to fly off at tangents on particular issues. Apart from the free votes or abstentions listed above when a few Conservatives voted for or against the government (twice on Nigeria against the advice of the Shadow Cabinet), the only rebellion was on the Second Reading of the Race Relations Bill when 24 or 25 abstained as they, the left wing of the Party, favoured the Bill and did not wish to support the Shadow Cabinet's critical amendment.

Examining these 26 divisions (the only ones in two years when there was a rebellion of over 10 Labour MPs against the government), in only 10 were the Conservatives voting against the government, 8 on their own amendments and 2 by joining left-wing Labour rebels. In the 8 where the opposition's intention to oppose the government was known, no Labour MPs cross-voted apart from two cases, one on the Selective Employment Tax and one on Prices and Incomes. The average number of abstentions was 27 at a time when the government's normal majority was a little over 50 so that the government was never in serious danger of defeat. The one occasion when, had the Conservatives not voted with the government, its majority on the existing figures would have disappeared, was the relatively minor question of Justices of the Peace in the City of London. In fact this was an exceedingly unusual case. Lord Gardiner had accepted an amendment to the Bill for the government in the Lords on his own initiative. It was known that had he not publicly committed the government in this way, the whip would have instructed Labour members to vote the other way, so that members felt little compunction in voting as they wanted against the clause.

The problem in assessing the situation that has been described is quite different from that of assessing the voting records for 1857–59. Then MPs were willing to defeat the government, they were much less easily controlled and with this power behind them, they could exercise a pervasive and often decisive influence. In 1967–69, as it is clear that the Labour rebels, who usually kept their abstention level down to about 27, had no intention of defeating the government and would have behaved very differently (as they did between 1964 and 1966 when the government's majority was between 3 and 6) if there had been any such danger. As a result the government was much freer to carry on as it liked. With this accepted, other questions arise. Why did the rebels engage in these demonstrations and did the effort (or was it an effort?) of containing them exercise any influence on the government's thinking, morale or conduct? Have MPs influenced the government in any other ways and how far, putting all this together, has the House of Commons any effect on the executive? Finally, can the present-day situation be compared with the situation described in the 1850s?

In the first instance, the reason for the abstentions and occasional cross-votes (apart from strongly held convictions which are often shared by many who do not rebel) is largely to be found in terms of the effect outside the House of Commons. Unlike the objectives in the 1850s when voting was directed at certain results inside the House, these demonstrations, which receive considerable press publicity, are done because MPs want to show those outside Parliament that their point of view is represented in the Commons and that a gesture has been made. In the Labour Party, there is the peculiar fact that the Left are supposed to be nearer the 'soul' of the Party than other sections, and rebellions of this kind are often acclaimed in the constituencies, making those involved well known and, for instance, improving their chance of election to the National Executive of the Party. The object here is not to suggest base motives but to point out that the aim of the activity is not primarily to alter the government's policy, though if this did happen, it would be welcomed by the critics. The aim, as with so much that goes on in the present House of Commons, is to signal to certain groups outside.

But it is also clear that the government does all it can both to reduce the number and the extent of these rebellions. The publicity that they receive is considered damaging to the government's image; the party is revealed as divided and it appears to the electorate that even the government's own MPs do not support its policies. There are ministers, including the Prime Minister [Harold Wilson], who say they take no notice whatever of this kind of gesture politics, of these rebellions that are never expected to succeed. On the other hand, ministers are conscious of their popularity rating in the Party, they like applause and dislike being barracked and, other things being equal, would prefer to avoid all such episodes. They know that control of the parliamentary timetable plus the block support founded on the payroll vote and the party loyalty of the majority of government backbenchers, will see them through. But they would prefer an enthusiastic and willing backing.

To consider this degree of influence, it is worth examining three episodes – the Commonwealth Immigrants Bill, the Parliament (No. 2) Bill and the proposed Industrial Relations Bill. The Commonwealth Immigrants Bill was a hastily devised measure introduced in early 1968 to stem the flow of British citizens of Asian origin coming in from East Africa. It aroused deep feelings among many sections of the Labour Party. The Opposition supported the Bill but left their members a free vote. Apart from one small handful of Conservatives who were eager to back a further limitation on coloured immigrants and who supported the government, and another small group who regarded the Bill as a betrayal of pledges made to the East African Asians at the time when these countries became independent, the Conservatives kept out of the argument and left it to the Labour backbenchers. The latter were helped by the speed with which the government had to push the measure through (two sitting days) and maintained an attack throughout the Committee stage. For a time during the middle of the night, the House bore some resemblance to its mid-Victorian predecessors in that the press gallery was empty yet the House was relatively full. Members were making their speeches not to their constituents or to impress their leaders but to each other. Short debating speeches followed in rapid succession with the ministers rising frequently to explain points and defend themselves. As a result of the speeches, some waverers changed their minds and went into a different (i.e. anti-government) lobby. But by the end of the debate, the 50-plus ministers and a core of loyalist MPs behind them, the government were able to carry the Bill without making any substantial concessions.

The Parliament (No. 2) Bill was peculiar in that the substance was agreed between the two front benches but when the inner-party talks broke down, the Shadow Cabinet gave their members a free vote and a block of them steadily resisted the measure. The problem in this case for the government was that the normal forces of party loyalty could not operate on their behalf precisely because there was no official opposition and the main points of the Bill were the result of bi-partisan front-bench agreement. Moreover the government was unable to force through a guillotine or to send the Bill to Committee because they feared the opposition would then join with the Labour rebels to defeat it. Thus each amendment which was accepted by the Speaker had to be debated as long as he refused to grant the closure. Also, the government could not force members to stay up all through the night (one of their normal sanctions) because the uninterested majority of supporters simply did believe that either the fate or the prestige of the government hung on their vote and they drifted home to bed, forcing the Whips to give up work at a reasonable time. Thus, though the government never lost and never looked like losing a division, it made slow progress, progress that would have appeared perfectly satisfactory in the 1850s when Whips were used to proceeding at a pace dictated by the House of Commons, but one which caused much irritation to modern ministers who were used to fixing a timetable and finishing with a matter. A combination of the need to free the House's timetable for more important business, and the disinterest or even distaste felt by many ministers for the Bill, led to its abandonment.

The abandonment only a few months later of the proposed Industrial Relations Bill, has been cited by some commentators as a real sign that the same power still remains with the House of Commons while others attribute the government's retreat to the strength of the TUC. In fact neither of these explanations can stand on its own. The Minister of Employment and Productivity, Mrs Castle, had decided that unofficial strikes were a menace to the economy and could be reduced by introducing ballots on strikes and imposing penalties on unofficial strikers. This was taken as a terrible threat by many trade unionists and their MPs, and was considered unworkable and ineffective by other backbenchers. Since 55 Labour MPs voted against the White Paper *In Place of Strife* and about 42 abstained, there was a potentially serious situation if the Conservatives (who had abstained on the White Paper) opposed the Bill and the same number rebelled on the government side. No one however expected that this would happen. Nevertheless this issue came closer to the bone for many Labour MPs than almost anything else; for some, loyalty to union came before party loyalty. At the same time support for the government was at a catastrophically low ebb in the country and morale in the Parliamentary Party was severely shaken. Mr Wilson felt that to be tough with the unions would bring electoral dividends and he was determined to persist despite the oppostion of the TUC. Few in the House doubted that if there was a straight vote on the Bill with the Conservatives on one side and the government on the other, it would be passed. But the recent experience with the Parliament (No. 2) Bill showed that the great problem for the government would be procedural. Labour rebels might decide to vote against motions to send the Bill upstairs to a committee or to provide a guillotine on the floor of the House, on the grounds that the government could not say it was seriously damaged by such procedural defeats. If the committee stage was taken on the floor of the House the debates could be dragged out and concessions wrung from the government.

At the last Cabinet on this subject, the Chief Whip told the Prime Minister that he could not guarantee to carry these two procedural motions. At the same meeting, most of the Cabinet advised the Prime Minister to settle with the TUC either because of what the Chief Whip said or more generally because they felt that the dispute was breaking up the Party. The Prime Minister may have felt that he could defy both these elements – that if he insisted on the Bill, MPs would never desert the party in sufficient numbers on a crucial division. As a result, he may have thought that, if he told the Cabinet he could not reach an honourable settlement with the TUC and must therefore proceed with the Bill, there would not be more resignations than he could fill without serious political embarrassment. But according to one account, before he and Mrs Castle went to the last meeting with the TUC, senior ministers such as Mr Crossman and Mr Jenkins contacted him to stress the importance of a compromise. With this kind of pressure on him and realising that Mr Callaghan, his chief critic, could thus expect a wider backing than before, Mr Wilson met the TUC and settled. The precise weight to attach to the threats by Labour backbenchers in achieving this result is hard to estimate but it clearly had some importance in building up the atmosphere of crisis, in convincing the Chief Whip and helping to convince the Cabinet that the situation was dangerous and in leading senior Cabinet ministers to take their stand.

The most extreme power exercised by the Commons between 1857 and 1859 was the removal of the Prime Minister by the defeat of his government. This cannot be done today. Nor is it possible, unless under wartime crisis conditions, for MPs to remove their Prime Minister without leading to the fall of their government, something which they will not contemplate. In the spring of 1969, after abandoning the Parliament (No. 2) Bill, in the middle of the crisis over the Industrial Relations Bill and trailing far behind the Conservatives in the opinion polls, Mr Wilson was at his weakest. A determined attempt was made to remove him as Prime Minister by a mixed selection of backbenchers, but they found they could do nothing. There was no machinery except a vote of confidence at a party meeting. The Parliamentary Party Chairman said he would not accept such a motion unless there were 120 signatures – that is (given 100 ministers) unless the vote was a foregone conclusion. Not enough MPs could be persuaded to stand up and be counted on such an issue – the forces of party loyalty and party patronage were too great. Yet the fact that these moves were going on did contribute to the pressure on the Prime Minister over the Industrial Relations Bill and formed the background to the reminder by senior ministers that they were not prepared to support Mr Wilson on this issue, a threat which would clearly have strengthened the hand of Mr Wilson's chief critic and opponent, Mr Callaghan.

In conclusion, voting behaviour is not of great help in assessing the influence of the modern House of Commons. Indeed the task of reaching any conclusions in much harder because the Commons cannot remove a government, nor can it be seen to reject a Bill in the clear-cut way possible in the 1850s. It has control over its own timetable only on quite exceptional occasions, and normally the executive looks over its head directly to the electorate. What the House can affect and what the level of abstention and cross voting can help indicate is the morale in the party, it can form part of the background of pressures and responses which the government has to take into consideration in reaching its decisions.

Bibliography

THE following bibliography provides a guide to the most recent books and articles about the backbencher and Parliament. Excluded from the bibliography are works concerned with Parliament which place little or no emphasis on the backbencher. If the reader is interested in such works he is referred to the comprehensive bibliography in R. M. Punnett, *British Government and Politics* (Heinemann, 1968) pp. 423–65, especially pp. 435–6 and 458–61. It has not been possible to provide a collection of articles written by backbenchers themselves: these are numerous and can be frequently found in the daily and Sunday press, and in periodicals such as *The New Statesman*, *The Spectator*, *Crossbow*, and *Socialist Commentary*.

Alderman, R. K., 'Discipline in The Parliamentary Labour Party, 1945–51', *Parliamentary Affairs*, Vol. 18, 1964–65, pp. 293–306.
Alderman, R. K., 'The Conscience Clause of the Parliamentary Labour Party', *Parliamentary Affairs*, Vol. 19, 1965–66, pp. 224–33.
Alderman, R. K., 'Parliamentary Party Discipline in Opposition: The Parliamentary Labour Party, 1951–64', *Parliamentary Affairs*, Vol. 21, 1967–68, pp. 124–37.
Barker, A., 'Party and Supply', *Parliamentary Affairs*, Vol. 17, 1963–64, pp. 207–18.
Barker, A., 'Parliamentary Studies 1961–65: A Bibliography and Comment', *Political Quarterly*, Vol. 36, 1965, pp. 347–59.
Barnett, M. J., 'Backbench Behaviour in The House of Commons', *Parliamentary Affairs*, Vol. 22, 1968–69, pp. 38–62.
Barr, J., 'The Hustings Wives', *New Society*, 17 March 1966, pp. 5–6.
Berrington, H. D., 'The Conservative Party: Revolts and Pressures', *Political Quarterly*, Vol. 32, 1961, pp. 363–73.
Bromhead, P. A., *Private Members' Bills in the British Parliament* (Routledge, 1956).
Brookes, P., *Women at Westminster* (Davies, 1967).
Buck, W. P., *Amateurs and Professionals in British Politics 1918–59* (Chicago U.P., 1963).
Butt, R., *The Power of Parliament* (Constable, 1967).

Campion, Lord, *Parliament: A Survey* (Allen & Unwin, 1963).
Chester, D. N., and N. Bowring, *Questions in Parliament* (Oxford U.P., 1962).
Coombes, D., *The Member of Parliament and The Administration* (Allen & Unwin, 1966).
Crick, B., *The Reform of Parliament* (Weidenfeld & Nicolson, 2nd ed. 1968).
Crocket, D. G., 'The MP and His Constituents', *Parliamentary Affairs*, Vol. 20, 1966–67, pp. 181–4.
Dowse, R. E., and T. Smith, 'Party Discipline in The House of Commons – A Comment', *Parliamentary Affairs*, Vol. 16, 1962–63, pp. 159–65.
Epstein, L. D., 'British MPs and Their Parties: The Suez Crisis', *American Political Science Review*, Vol. 54, 1960, pp. 374–91.
Epstein, L. D., 'New MPs and The Politics of the PLP', *Political Studies*, Vol. 10, 1962, pp. 121–30.
Epstein, L. D., *British Politics in The Suez Crisis* (Pall Mall, 1964).
Fellowes, Sir E., 'Changes in Parliamentary Life, 1918–61', *Political Quarterly*, Vol. 36, 1965, pp. 256–65.
Finer, S. E., H. B. Berrington and D. J. Bartholomew, *Backbench Opinion in The House of Commons, 1955–59* (Pergamon, 1961).
Frasure, R. E., 'Constituency Racial Composition and the Attitudes of British MPs', *Comparative Politics*, Vol. 3, 1971, pp. 201–10.
Fulford, R., *The Member and His Constituency* (Ramsay Muir Trust, 1967).
Goldsworthy, D., 'Parliamentary Questions on Colonial Affairs: A Retrospective Analysis', *Parliamentary Affairs*, Vol. 23, 1969–70, pp. 141–54.
Hale, L., 'The Backbencher', *The Parliamentarian*, 1966, pp. 191–8.
Hanson, A. H., and H. V. Wiseman, *Parliament at Work* (Stevens, 1962).
Hanson, A. H., and B. Crick, eds., *The Commons in Transition* (Fontana, 1970).
Hanson, A. H., and M. Walles, *Governing Britain* (Fontana, 1970).
Hill, A., and A. Whichelow, *What's Wrong With Parliament?* (Penguin, 1964).
Holt, R. T., and J. E. Turner, 'Parliamentary Party Discipline in Government: The PLP 1964–68', in W. G. Andrews, ed., *European Politics*, Vol. 2 (Van Nostrand, New York, 1969).
Hornby, R., 'Parties and Parliament 1959–63: The Labour Party', *Political Quarterly*, Vol. 34, 1963, pp. 240–8.
Houghton, D., 'The Labour Backbencher', *Political Quarterly*, Vol. 40, 1969, pp. 454–63.
Hughes, E., *Parliament and Mumbo Jumbo* (Allen & Unwin, 1966).

BIBLIOGRAPHY

Jackson, R. J., *Rebels and Whips* (Macmillan, 1968).
Jennings, I., *Parliament* (Oxford U.P., 2nd ed. 1957).
Johnson, D., *On Being an Independent M.P.* (Johnson, 1964).
Johnson, N., 'Parliamentary Questions and The Conduct of Administration', *Public Administration*, Vol. 39, 1961, pp. 131–48.
Johnson, N., *Parliament and Administration* (Allen & Unwin, 1966).
Kavanagh, D., 'The Orientations of Community Leaders to Parliamentary Candidates', *Political Studies*, Vol. 15, 1967, pp. 351–6.
Kavanagh, D., *Constituency Electioneering in Britain* (Longmans, 1970).
Kimber, R., and J. J. Richardson, 'Specialisation and Parliamentary Standing Committees', *Political Studies*, Vol. 16, 1968, pp. 97–101.
Lynskey, J. J., 'The Role of British Backbenchers in The Modification of Government Policy', *Western Political Quarterly*, Vol. 23, 1970, pp. 333–48.
Mackintosh, J., 'Failure of a Reform: MPs' Specialist Committees', *New Society*, 28 November 1968, pp. 791–2.
Mackintosh, J., *The Government and Politics of Britain* (Hutchinson, 1970).
Marquand, D., 'Backbench Power', *New Society*, 24 April 1969, p. 640.
Martin, C., 'Out of The Way', *New Society*, 23 January 1964, p. 25.
Morrison, Lord, *Government and Parliament* (Oxford U.P., 3rd ed. 1964).
Muller, W. D., 'Trade Union Sponsored Members of Parliament in The Defence Dispute of 1960–61', *Parliamentary Affairs*, Vol. 23, 1969–70, pp. 258–77.
Nicolson, N., *People and Parliament* (Weidenfeld & Nicolson, 1958).
Ranney, A., 'Inter-Constituency Movement of British Parliamentary Candidates, 1951–59', *American Political Science Review*, Vol. 58, 1964, pp. 36–46.
Ranney, A., *Pathways to Parliament* (Macmillan, 1965).
Richards, P. G., *Honourable Members: A Study of The British Backbencher* (Faber, 2nd ed. 1964).
Richards, P. G., *Parliament and Foreign Affairs* (Allen & Unwin, 1967).
Richards, P. G., *Parliament and Conscience* (Allen & Unwin, 1970).
Rush, M., *The Selection of Parliamentary Candidates* (Nelson, 1969).
Ryle, M., 'Private Members' Bills', *Political Quarterly*, Vol. 37, 1966, pp. 385–93.
Seymour-Ure, C., 'The Misuse of The Question of Privilege in The 1964–5 Session of Parliament', *Parliamentary Affairs*, Vol. 18, 1964–65, pp. 380–9.
Thompson, G., 'Parties and Parliaments 1959–63: The Conservatives', *Political Quarterly*, Vol. 34, 1963, pp. 249–55.

Vig, N. J., and S. A. Walkland, 'Science Policy, Science Administration, and Parliamentary Reform', *Parliamentary Affairs*, Vol. 19, 1965–66, pp. 281–95.

Walkland, S. A., *The Legislative Process in Britain* (Allen & Unwin, 1968).

Wiseman, H. V., ed., *Parliament and The Executive* (Routledge, 1968).

Index

Abortion Act, 37. *See also* Private Members' Bills
Abrams, Mark, 52n
Abse, Leo, 126, 130
Abstentions, 249, 254
Adjournment debates, 108–25, 143, 153, 200, 231
   and the backbencher, 110–18, 124
   geographical context, 113–15, 124–5
   subject matter and the Government, 113–25
Almond and Verba, 29
Attlee, Earl, 57, 59, 221, 225

Balfour reforms, 91
Barber, James David, xiv
Barker, Anthony, 29–46
Barnes, Michael, 208, 209
Bartholomew, D. J., 172n
Benn, Anthony Wedgwood, 166–7
Berkeley, Humphry, 130, 239
Berrington, H. B., 172n
Bevan, Aneurin, 224–5
Black Rod, 214–15
Blenkinsop, A., 111
Boeing Airplane Company, 82
Boundary Commissioners, 214
Bow Group, 239–40, 242
Bowring, Nora, 109
Boyle, Anthony, 128
Bradshaw, K. A., 89n
Brewis, J., 115
British Steel Corporation, 189
Brittan, Samuel, 136
Bromhead, P. A., 127
Brown, Clifton, 105
Buck, P. W., xv
Butler, David, xiv, 17n

Butler, R. A., 239
Butt, Ronald, xiii, 172n, 245

Cabinet, the
   and policy, 222, 226
   policy committee of, 142
   relation with backbenchers, 83, 233, 237, 247, 257–8
Callaghan, James, 257–8
Castle, Barbara, 256–7
Chamberlain, Neville, 79
Chester, D. N., 90, 100, 109
Civil Service, 62, 69, 158, 172, 184
   Civil Servants, 64, 70, 73, 90, 94, 150, 170, 212
   Civil Service Examinations, 98
   Civil Service Department, 106
Clark, H., 118
Class of M.P.s, *see* Member of Parliament: social background
Clegg, Walter, 210
Clerks, *see* House of Commons Clerks
Committee of the Whole House, 141, 143, 144–7, 149–50, 154–5
Common Market, 104, 233
Commonwealth Immigrants Bill, 252, 255
Communist Party, Parliamentary candidates of, 18
Congress, *see* United States Congress
Conservative Party
   Central Office, 14, 17, 19, 346
   Conservative 1922 Committee, 222, 232, 239, 242
   constituency association, 3, 4, 5, 12, 15, 19, 20
   Constituency Party Executive Committee, 18

Conservative Party—*continued*
  Executive Council, 45, 185
  National Union, 4
  selection committee, 3, 4, 5
  selection conference, 10–14
  standing advisory committee (on candidates), 4
Constituency associations, 3, 24, 19, 49; *and see under individual parties*
Crane, W., 48, 53 n
Crick, Bernard, xvi, 47 n, 59
Cripps, Sir Stafford, 220
Critchley, Julien, 244
Crossman, Richard, 80, 109, 160, 257
Cross-voting, 248, 249, 254
Cunningham, George, 212–18

Dalton, Hugh, 226
Davies, Ednyfed Hudson, 115
Davies, S. O., 83
Defence White Paper, 81
Derby, Lord, 246
Disraeli, 246, 247
Division lobbies, 150, 154
Division of the House, 147, 148
Dobson, Raymond, 210
Donnelly, Desmond, 184
Douglas-Home, Sir Alec, 238
Dowse, Robert E., 46–61
Du Cann, Edward, 15

Eckstein, H., 172 n
Eden, Sir J., 122
Egypt, 16
Electorate, growth in, 248
  working-class votes, 52
Epstein, L. D., 19 n
European Economic Community, 101
Evans, Stanley, 234

Fabian Journal, 57 n, 59 n
Finer, S. E., 172 n
Foot, Michael, 85, 224, 235
Fortescue, Trevor, 208
Freidman, Karl A., 111 n

Gallup Poll, 14
Gardiner, Lord, 253
General Election: (1964), 21, (1966), 22
Gerth, H. H., xv
Glasgow, 13
Goodhart, Philip, 47 n
Gordon Walker, Patrick, 207
Government Departments
  Agriculture, Fisheries and Food, 106, 119
  Attorney-General, 106
  Aviation, 106
  Colonies, 106
  Commonwealth Relations, 106, 119
  Defence, 106, 119, 169
  Duchy of Lancaster, 106
  Economics Affairs, 106, 119
  Education and Science, 106, 119
  Environment, 94
  Foreign Office, 65, 104, 119
  Health, 106, 119
  Home Office, 57, 65, 119
  Housing (and Local Government) 106, 119
  Labour (*later* Employment and Productivity), 107, 119
  Land and Natural Resources, 107
  Lord President of the Council, 107
  Overseas Development, 107, 119
  Paymaster-General, 107
  Pensions, 107
  Minister without Portfolio, 107
  Post, 107, 119
  Power, 107
  Public Building and Works, 107, 119
  Scotland, 107, 119
  Social Services, 107, 119
  Technology, 107, 119, 165
  Trade, 94, 107, 119
  Transport, 107, 119
  Treasury, 107, 119
  Wales, 107, 119
Government Chief Whip, *see* Whips' Office

INDEX

Hanson, H., 59, 108
Harrison, W., 47
Hastings Agreement, 8
Healey, Denis, 168
Heath, Edward, 25, 137, 238
Heffer, E., 112
Herbert, Sir Alan, 126
Herman, Valentine, 108–26, 141–56
Hogg, Quintin, 128
Hooley, Frank, 208–9
Hornby, Richard, 228–38
House of Commons Clerks, 98
House Purchase (Temporary Provisions) Bill, 198
Housing, 53, 55, 59, 60
Howarth, R., 122
Howie, Will, 80
Hughes, Emrys, 83
Hughes, Robert, 139
Hunt, Norman, 74–80

Immigration and Nationality Department, 70
Industrial Relations Bill, 86, 246, 255–6, 258
Interest groups, 112. *See also* Pressure groups

Jackson, Senator Henry, 82
Jenkins, Roy, 140, 257
Jennings, Sir Ivor, 49n, 51, 108, 126, 127n, 131
Johnson, Neville, 109n
Joseph, Sir Keith, 128

Kavanagh, Dennis, 21–9
Kenya Asians Bill, 249–50
Kilmuir, Lord, 5
King, Anthony, 17, 61–74, 80–9, 134
King, Dr Horace, 90, 92–93, 102–3
Kitchen Committee, 106
Klaus, Boehm, 175n
Klein, Rudolf, xv

Labour Party
 Annual Conference, 223
 composition, 219–20
 constituency party, 6, 9, 12, 19–20
 executive committee of constituency party, 6–9, 18
 General Management Committee 78
 National Executive Committee, 8, 84, 185, 223, 254
 Parliamentary Labour Party, 84–5; Arts and Amenities Group, 221; Aviation Group, 221; Foreign Affairs Group, 221; Trade Union Group, 220
Laski, H. J., 172
Lasswell, Harold, xiv
Leader of the House of Commons, 80, 102, 107, 137, 160
Legge-Bourke, Sir Harry, 165–6
Leonard, Dick, 3–21, 126–140
Liaison Committee, 227
Liberal Party
 Liberal Association, 9
 Smith Square, 24
Lloyd, Selwyn, 14
Lobby, 92
Lowell, A. L., 248

Mackintosh, John P., 244–59
McNamara, Kevin, 139
Marquand, D., 113
Maxwell, Robert, 131
Mayhew, Christopher, 136
Menhennet, David, 195–207
Mikardo, Ian, 189
Milne, E., 111
Mitchell, B. R., 175n
Mitchell, D., 113
Monday Club, 240
Morris, Alfred, 156
Member of Parliament
 and constituency parties, 19–20, 24, 27, 84, 227
 relationship with party leaders, 25, 28
 and local council, 60, 111
 social background, 16–17, 134, 139, 160–1, 179, 181–3, 219–20, 242–3

INDEX

National Environmental Research Council, 156, 165–7
National Party Executives, 185. *See also individual party executives*
Nettl, P., 172n
Nicolson, Nigel, 10, 33, 59n
Nott, John, 209

Office of the Speaker, *see* Speaker; Speaker's Office
O'Malley, B. K., 189
Opinion polls, 21, 23, 25, 27
Oppenheim, Sally, 139
Opposition, the
  Leader of the Opposition, 103
  Opposition Chief Whip, 103
  Opposition front bench, 102
  Opposition spokesman, 110
  Opposition Whips, 110
Order Paper, 98, 103, 232
Ovenden, Keith, 171–95
Owen, David, 113

Palmer, Arthur, 156–71
Palmer, John, 195–207
Palmerston, Lord, 245–7, 253
Parker, John, 139
Parliament (No. 2) Bill, 255–8
Parliamentary Committees, 110, 123, 186, 222, 225–6, 253
Parliamentary Labour Party, *see* Labour Party
Parliamentary questions, *see* Questions
Parliamentary and Scientific Committee, 156, 159–60
Parliamentary Private Secretaries, 131
Pensions, 53, 65
Pinto-Duschinsky, Michael, xiv
Plaid Cymru, 110
Platt Committee of the Central Health Services Council, 196
Pressure groups, 48
Prices and Incomes Bill, 81
Prime Minister, 74–6, 79, 83, 93, 100–1, 107, 221–2, 227, 232, 247, 258

Principal Clerk, *see* House of Commons Clerks
Private Members' Bills
  Abortion Reform Bill, 132
  Administration of Estates Act, 139
  Anti-Blood Sports Bills, 128
  Civic Amenities Act, 130
  Clean Air Act, 131
  Divorce Reform Bill, 132
  Divorce (Scotland) Bill, 137
  Family Law Reform Act, 1969 (Amendment) Bill, 139
  Hare Coursing (Abolition) Bill, 139
  House of Commons (Conditions of Service) Bill, 139
  Interest on Damages (Scotland) Act, 139
  Law Commission Bills, 139
  Murder (Abolition of Death Penalty) Bill, 235
  Protection of Human Rights Bill, 139
  Sexual Offences Bill, 130
  Shops (Weekday Trading) Bill, 139
  Sunday Entertainments Bill, 139
Private notice questions, *see* Questions
Privy Councillors, 47
Procedure Committee, 217

Quennell, Joan, 58n, 122
Questions, 143, 153, 200, 230, 241
  Business questions, 102
  general rules of admissibility, 96
  future of Question Time, 104–5
  Length of Question Time, 91–2
  Limitation on number of Questions, 92–3
  numbers of Questions, 90–1
  oral Questions, 90–6, 98–102, 107
  Opposition and Government, 102–5
  periods of notice, 95–6
  Prime Minister's Questions, 92, 94, 100–1, 103
  private notice Questions, 92, 101–3

INDEX

Questions—*continued*
  Question hour, 100
  Questions on overseas aid, 94
  restrictions on Members' freedom to ask Questions, 91
  rota of answering Ministers, 93–4
  supplementary Questions, 99–100
  use of questions by backbenchers, 102–5
  written Questions, 90, 92, 98, 101
Queen's Speech, 231

Race Relations Bill, 253
Randall, H., 112
Ranney, Austin, 18n
Redmayne, Martin, 74–80
Rees-Davies, W., 112
Rent Act, the, 81, 233
Report stage (of legislation), 141, 143–7, 149–50, 154–5
Reports from Select Committee: on Procedure, *see* Select Committees on Procedure
Resale Price Maintenance Bill, 246
Richards, Peter G., xiii, 48n, 57n, 58, 109, 127, 136, 172n
Robinson, Kenneth, 85
Roman Catholics, 13
Rose, John, 89–107
Rose, Richard, xiv, 21–9, 172n
Rush, Michael, 18n, 29–46

Salisbury, Lord, 233
Sandys, Duncan, 38, 130
Scotland, 13, 22, 134, 137–8
Second Readings of Bills, 141, 170
Select Committees, 195
  Select Committee on Estimates, 197
  Select Committee on Science and Technology, 156, 158, 160, 166–7, 169
  Reports of Select Committee on Procedure, House of Commons Papers (1959), 100n; (1961), 95n; (1964), 63n; (1965), 100n; (1967), 96–7, 100n; (1970), 90, 92, 95–6, 98–102, 103n
Selective Employment Tax, 110, 253
Sessional Orders, 95, 137
Shils, Edward, 59n
Shinwell, Emmanuel, 221
Shops Bill, 233
Silkin, John, 80–5
Silverman, Sydney, 126, 235
Smith, Ian, 33
Smith, Trevor, 48n, 60n
Soames, Christopher, 243
Speaker, 90–2, 97, 99–100, 102, 105–7, 144, 214, 256
  Speaker's Office, 102
  Speaker's Chair, 97
Standing Committee A, 198
Standing Committee, 144, 150, 174, 195
Standing Order No. 9, 242
Standing Orders, 222, 225
Steel, David, 126
Steel, Renationalisation of Steel Bill, 171, 174–5, 181, 186–9
Stout, H. M., 47n
Strachey, John, 225
Strauss, George, 218–28
Suez
  and Member's constituency support, 19–20, 33
  rebellion over, by Conservative Members of Parliament, 81, 233–4
  survival of the Government, 237

Table Office, 91, 96–7, 99, 103, 197, 203
Television, 25, 46, 106, 232
Thorneycroft, Peter, 243
Times, The, 207–12
Torrey Canyon, 165
Trade unions, 6–8, 14, 16
  trade union officials, 212
  Trades Union Congress, 256
  loyalty of Members of Parliament to their unions, 257

Transport House, *see* Labour Party
Treasury, 164
Tribune, 224
Turton, Sir Robin, 92

United States Congress, 81–2, 157
USDAW, 139

Vietnam, 81

Wainwright, Richard, 209
Wales, 13, 22
Walkland, S. A., 142, 172n
Watkins, D., 208
Weber, Max, xv
Wheare, K. C., 57n
Whips' Office, 75, 77, 233
  Conservative Whips, 132, 138
Government Chief Whip, 74–5, 80–6, 232, 234, 257–8
Labour Whips, 132
resignation of the whip, 234
Shadow Chief Whip, 225
Whips, 74–5, 93–4, 131, 170, 184, 225, 235, 247, 253, 256
withdrawal of the whip, 84, 249
Wilson, Harold, 25, 80, 84–5, 137, 254, 257–8
Windlesham, Lord, 172
Winstanley, Dr M. P., 124
Whitaker, Benjamin, 208
Whitelaw, William, 137–8
Women parliamentary candidates, 13–14
Woolrige-Gordon, Peter, 115
Wyatt, Woodrow, 184